The Battle of Stone's River, 1862-3

The Battle of Stone's River, 1862-3

Seven accounts of the Stone's River/
Murfreesboro' conflict during the
American Civil War

Henry Kendall

Milo S. Hascall

Wilson J. Vance

Gilbert Kniffin

Frederick Phisterer

Alexander F. Stevenson

LEONAUR

The Battle of Stone's River, 1862-3
Seven accounts of the Stone's River/Murfreesboro' conflict during
the American Civil War
Henry Kendall
Milo S. Hascall
Wilson J. Vance
Gilbert Kniffin
Frederick Phisterer
Alexander F. Stevenson

First published under the titles
The Battle of Stone River
Personal Recollections and Experiences Concerning the Battle of Stone River
Stone's River,
The Third Day at Stone's River
Army of the Cumberland and the Battle of Stone Riverl
The Regular Brigade of the Fourteenth Army Corps,
in the Battle of Stone River, or Murfreesboro', Tennessee,.
and
The Battle of Stone's River Near Murfeeesboro', Tenn.

FIRST EDITION

Leonaur is an imprint of Oakpast Ltd
Copyright in this form © 2010 Oakpast Ltd

ISBN: 978-0-85706-228-4 (hardcover)
ISBN: 978-0-85706-227-7 (softcover)

http://www.leonaur.com

Contents

TOPOGRAPHICAL SKETCH
of the
BATTLE FIELD
of
STONE'S RIVER
NEAR MURFREESBOROUGH, TENN.
December 31st 1862 to January 3rd 1863
between the Forces of the United States
MAJ GEN W.S. ROSECRANS
Commanding and the Forces of the Confederate
BRAXTON BRAGG
Commanding the Confederate Forces

The Battle of Stone River

By Henry Kendall

After the battle of Perryville, October 8, 1862, a rather leisurely pursuit of Bragg's retreating forces was made on the roads to Cumberland Gap, but no engagement was brought on. It soon appeared that Bragg did not intend to again give battle in Kentucky, but would withdraw into Tennessee and join the force under Breckenridge which had been left to watch Nashville during the invasion of Kentucky. Buell concluded that Bragg would concentrate his entire force near Nashville and endeavour to capture that place and somewhere in its vicinity fight a decisive battle which would determine the fate of West Tennessee and Kentucky. Buell therefore discontinued his pursuit and turned his forces toward Nashville, placing them mainly at Bowling Green, Glasgow, and other points on the Louisville and Nashville Railroad.

A great deal of pressure had been brought to bear upon the Administration to make a campaign in East Tennessee, a mountainous region whose people were mostly loyal. General Halleck in Washington planned a campaign in that region and called upon Buell to carry it out. But Buell declined. His reasons were that such a campaign would place him at a long distance from Louisville, his base, dependent upon wagon transportation alone over almost impassable roads, in a country devoid of supplies and especially suitable to defensive operations. Again, he would be forced to make great detachments to guard Nashville and his lines of communications, since these would be especially open to the attack of the enemy, who was well known to be superior in cavalry.

Buell considered Nashville the vital point of the theatre, and was satisfied that it would be the main point of Bragg's attack. He therefore ignored Halleck's elaborate plan and set about repairing the railway to Nashville and moving his troops in that direction. His previous slowness and indecision had brought him greatly into disfavour, and on the 30th of October he was relieved by Major-General William S. Rosecrans. The district was called thereafter the Department of the Cumberland and the army in the field was designated as the Fourteenth Army Corps. Halleck's plans were urged upon Rosecrans, but he was of the same opinion as Buelll, and it had by that time become plain that Bragg was doing just what Buelll thought he would do. Rosecrans concluded to go on in the same direction as had Buelll, and the events showed clearly that Halleck's bureau-made plans, based upon theory alone and without an intimate knowledge of the real conditions, were the veriest nonsense, and that Buelll and Rosecrans were quite right in ignoring them.

Rosecrans organized the army into right wing, centre, and left wing. The right wing, under McCook, consisted of Johnson's, Davis's, and Sheridan's divisions. Thomas commanded the centre, which consisted of five divisions under Rousseau, Negley, Fry, Mitchell, and Reynolds. The left wing was commanded by Crittenden, and comprised Wood's, Palmer's, and Van Cleve's divisions. The total available strength of the army formed not more than 60 *per cent.* of its paper strength, owing to absenteeism. Every endeavour was made to remedy this state of affairs, a condition not peculiar to this army alone, but affecting all the armies almost equally, and constituting a serious evil, for the correction of which severe measures were an absolute necessity.

The army was very deficient in cavalry, and a large portion of its meagre force was very poorly armed. In this condition the army was at a great disadvantage opposed to Bragg, whose cavalry, under Forrest, Morgan, and Wheeler was much greater in numbers and better mounted and equipped.

Rosecrans made strenuous efforts to improve the condition of his cavalry, and succeeded in increasing it to about 4,000 and in obtaining Stanley to command it. But at its greatest strength it was less than half the opposing cavalry force.

Rosecrans' future base of operations was Nashville, but he would be dependent for supplies upon the maintenance of the railroad to Louisville. He hastened to increase the garrison of Nashville, but could not for some time concentrate there owing to the destruction of a railway tunnel near Mitchellsville, which limited him to wagon transportation over bad roads for thirty-five miles. The railway was opened

November 26th, and the army was then concentrated near Nashville, with the exception of Reynolds' division and all but one brigade of Fry's, which were assigned the duty of protecting the railway.

Before advancing it was absolutely essential to place in Nashville a large supply of rations, ammunition, etc., sufficient to support the army during the longest probable break in the railway, as a result of the forays of the rebel cavalry. This required an entire month, and the administration was greatly dissatisfied at the long delay. Rosecrans went through an experience very similar to that suffered by Thomas at the same place later in the war. But to the threats to relieve him he made the blunt reply that if confidence did not exist he was perfectly ready to turn over the command and abide by the issue. Halleck then explained that it was not intended to threaten him, but that there was great anxiety in Washington over the slow course of events in Tennessee. He explained that this arose from diplomatic reasons. It had been greatly desired that a decided advantage be gained over the rebels before the opening of the British Parliament, otherwise the advocates of intervention in favour of the Confederacy would be able to point to the possession of Tennessee as a proof that the South was gaining on the North. It would seem, however, that this was only one of the long series of attempts by Halleck to run the war from an office in Washington—a course that never did and never could result in any good.

Rosecrans continued his preparations carefully, and Bragg concluded that he was going into winter quarters at Nashville. Bragg therefore placed his army in winter quarters at Murfreesboro' and vicinity, and detached his cavalry for operations in West Tennessee and against the railway in Kentucky. This was just what Rosecrans wanted. He wanted Bragg to draw near to Nashville so that his own line of communications might be short and a reverse less disastrous. Rosecrans was also anxious that the rebel cavalry should be distant when he advanced, as his army was very deficient in cavalry.

Morgan's cavalry made a raid upon Hartsville, Tennessee, and on the 7th of December captured a brigade of infantry placed there by Thomas to guard the crossing of the Cumberland. The capture of this brigade was due to neglect of the simplest precautions. No outposts or sentinels of any kind seem to have been used, and the rebel cavalry was in line only 400 yards away before it was discovered. The infantry turned out in great disorder and was badly managed, so that it was forced to surrender. No word was sent to a supporting brigade but a few miles away, and Morgan was allowed to get away without any loss. He then started for Kentucky and on the 27th of December captured Elizabethtown and destroyed a large section of railway. He kept on to Muldraugh's Hills and destroyed two trestles, each about 500 feet long and 90 feet high. The railway communication was thus effectually broken, and if Rosecrans had remained in Nashville the condition of his army would have been critical. But having completed his preparations and finding the conditions favourable, owing to the absence of Bragg's cavalry, Rosecrans advanced from Nashville on the 26th of December.

Mitchell's division was left to garrison Nashville so that Thomas's command was reduced to Negley's and Rousseau's divisions and Walker's brigade of Fry's. McCook's and Crittenden's wings were on the pikes south and southeast of Nashville. The main body of Bragg's force, consisting of Polk's corps and part of Breckenridge's division of Hardee's corps, was at Murfreesboro'. The remainder of Hardee's corps was near Eaglesville, about twenty miles west of Murfreesboro', McCown's division of Hardee's corps, with a division under Stevenson, formed a separate corps under Kirby Smith at Readyville, twelve miles east of Murfreesboro'.

Rosecrans' plan was to advance in three columns, refusing his right. McCook's corps was to use the Nolensville pike, Thomas the Franklin Pike, and Crittenden the main Murfreesboro' pike. McCook was to attack Hardee and if the enemy held his ground and was reinforced Thomas was to support McCook. If, however, Hardee retreated, McCook was to detach a division to pursue or observe him and move with the remainder of his corps so as to come in on the left rear of the main rebel force. Crittenden was to attack supported by Thomas, whose force was to be directed against the enemy's left.

McCook advanced and after skirmishing all day, followed by a brisk fight towards evening, took possession of Nolensville and the heights about one and one-half miles in front. Thomas followed on the right, closing Negley's division on Nolensville and leaving Rousseau's division on the right flank. Crittenden advanced to LaVergne, with heavy skirmishing, through a rough country, intersected by forests and cedar brakes.

On the 27th, McCook advanced on Triune, but his movements were retarded by a dense fog, which made it impossible to tell friend from foe. Stanley, with the greater part of the cavalry, had joined McCook, and in the fog the cavalry was fired upon by the infantry. The march was stopped until the fog lifted, and Triune was therefore not reached until late in the day, although it was only seven miles from Nolensville.

Thomas moved eastward to Crittenden's right. Crittenden moved forward slowly, delaying his movements until the action of McCook's corps should determine the real state of affairs. Thomas was now in position to support either McCook or Crittenden, as the case might require.

On the 28th, McCook made sure by a strong reconnaissance that Hardee was retreating, and Thomas closed on Crittenden, who remained in position, bringing up his trains and making ready for battle.

On the 29th, McCook left one brigade of Johnson's division at Triune to cover the right and rear, and advanced to within about six miles of Murfreesboro'. The corps was encamped in line of battle with Sheridan's division on the left, Davis in the centre, and Johnson on the right. Negley's division of Thomas's corps advanced in support of Crittenden's corps, the head and flank of which reached a point about two miles from Murfreesboro'; Rousseau's division remained at Stewartsboro'. It was now plain that the enemy would give battle near Murfreesboro'. During the afternoon a report reached Rosecrans from Palmer that he was in sight of Murfreesboro' and the enemy was running. He therefore ordered Crittenden to occupy Murfreesboro' with a division. Crittenden sent a brigade across Stone's river and surprised a regiment of Breckenridge's division and pushed it back on the main line. It was found that the rebels were occupying a strong position in force, and, it being then dark, the brigade was withdrawn across the river. Fords were prepared by the pioneer brigade. Negley's, Palmer's and Wood's divisions were in line with Van Cleve's division in reserve.

On the 30th, Rousseau moved up and took position in reserve in rear of Palmer's right. Negley advanced slightly as did McCook's corps. The line generally faced east, but part of McCook's right division was retired so that it faced to the south.

Rosecrans now decided to give battle on the 31st, and made the following plan: McCook was to hold strong ground, refusing his right, and make strong dispositions to resist the attack of the enemy. If, however, the enemy did not attack, McCook was to attack sufficient to hold all the force on his front and prevent the enemy from detaching any troops to the right, the real point of attack. Thomas' corps and Palmer's division were to open with skirmishing and engage the enemy's centre and left as far as Stone River. Van Cleve's division was to cross the river and advance on Breckenridge, followed by Wood's division by brigades on its right, and carry everything before them into Murfreesboro'. In front of Crittenden's corps across the river was high ground, the occupation of which would enable an enfilade fire to be brought on the remainder of Polk's corps. Palmer and Thomas were to follow the movement, advancing in its support.

After taking Murfreesboro', Crittenden was to move westward and getting in on the flank and rear of the enemy drive them off their line of communications. The success of the whole plan of course depended upon McCook's being able to hold on without support, and Rosecrans criticised his line, saying it was an error for it to face so much to the east. He thought it should rather face to the south and impressed the fact on McCook that he must be careful and make a strong disposition. McCook was ordered also to build fires to his right prolonging the general line and simulating the camps of a large force. It was hoped in this way to draw off a large part of the rebel force from the real point of attack.

Bragg formed an exactly similar plan of attack. Hardee with two divisions was to advance on the left and force back the Union right. Then Polk was to push the centre. By a steady wheel to the right on the right of Polk's corps as a pivot the Union force was to be thrown back on Stone river, off its line to Nashville, the objective of his campaign. The plans being identical a good deal depended on which army began the movement first. Rosecrans' orders were for the attack to begin at seven o'clock, while Bragg ordered the attack to begin at daylight.

Rosecrans' movement began on time and for a time was going very successfully. But about 6.30 a. m. the enemy in force attacked McCook's right and found that the two brigades were weakly posted, without support, the remaining brigade of Johnson's division being nearly a mile and a half to the rear at Johnson's headquarters. The command was not in any way ready for battle. The horses of some of the batteries were being watered at the stream and the men of one brigade were cooking breakfast. Kirk's brigade, the first attacked, tried to make some resistance and called for help upon Willich's brigade, but Willich was absent at headquarters and his brigade was without a commander and made no effort to support Kirk. Both brigades were quickly rolled up. Baldwin's brigade, in reserve, was moved up, but was too far distant, and the rout of the other two brigades was complete before assistance could be rendered. The weight of the attack then fell upon Baldwin, whose brigade, with Simonson's Fifth Indiana Battery, succeeded in checking the assailants and inflicting heavy loss, but was soon forced to retire to avoid being surrounded.

Meanwhile a severe attack had been made all along McCook's front, and after the rout of Johnson's division the flank of Davis's division was exposed. The enemy's attack was repulsed, but he soon reformed, brought up his reserves and renewed the attack. The attack was again repulsed. Davis's division now formed almost a right angle with Sheridan's, and the rebels directed the next attack on the vertex of the angle. Davis's division was driven out of its position, being greatly overlapped, and Sheridan had to withdraw his right, gaining time to do so by charging with Robert's brigade. His new line was at right angles to his first position. Here he held on desperately, trying to reform the broken division to his right. After repulsing several attacks, his ammunition was exhausted and he was forced to fall back, as was also Negley, whose division had been heavily engaged in front and afterward on the right flank.

Word had been sent to Rosecrans soon after seven o'clock that McCook's corps was heavily pressed and needed assistance. But he did not realize the extent of the disaster, and it was not until informed by a second messenger that the right wing was being driven that he realized the true state of affairs. He found then that he must abandon his plan and take every means to prevent the terrible disaster that seemed imminent. He directed the movement on the left to be suspended and placed Rousseau's division in the cedar brakes to the right and rear of Sheridan. As soon as it became plain, from the great amount of fugitives, that McCook's wing was routed, Van Cleve's division was placed on the right of Rousseau's, and a brigade of Wood's division to its right. Negley's and Sheridan's divisions fell back upon this new line. Upon this line the rebels made four distinct attacks, but were repulsed with very heavy losses. The fighting was almost hand to hand, and the losses on both sides were heavy. That of the regular brigade was especially severe, being 637 out of a total of 1,566. The new line succeeded in holding its ground and driving back the enemy from its front.

The left had also had severe fighting, becoming gradually engaged as Bragg's turning movement went on. As the change of front went on the left became more important until when the final line was formed, close to the Nashville turnpike, the left became the vital point, since a disaster there would have permitted the line to be enfiladed and the stragglers would have carried any resulting disorder along the whole line. During the afternoon Breckenridge made several heavy assaults on Palmer's division, but was repulsed.

Rosecrans succeeded in placing his troops in rather a strong line near the road, and the subsequent assaults of the enemy were repelled. The army slept in the position, spare ammunition was issued and found to be sufficient for another battle. The left was withdrawn slightly to more advantageous ground, and Rosecrans determined to await the attack of the enemy in his new lines, but if Bragg did not attack to do so himself.

During the morning of the 1st of January the rebels made repeated attempts to advance on Thomas's front, but were repulsed. During the afternoon the enemy massed a large number of troops in front of the right but did not attack. Bragg's object was evidently to feel the Union lines and find out if Rosecrans was retreating. Satisfied that he was not, he felt himself unable to attack in view of the heavy hammering his army had received the day before. Rosecrans passed Van Cleve's division across the stream and occupied some hills which threatened Polk's lines in enfilade. Next day Bragg tried to drive back Van Cleve's division, which was commanded by Colonel Beatty. The movement failed after severe fighting. During the night Bragg massed his force on his former right and Rosecrans greatly strengthened his left.

On the 3rd Bragg caused a constant picket firing to be kept up to determine if Rosecrans was still holding on. Finding that such was the case he concluded, after consultation with his generals, to retreat. He retreated in good order, his cavalry holding Murfreesboro' until the 5th. On the 5th Thomas's entire command, preceded by Stanley's cavalry, marched into Murfreesboro'. The object of the campaign had been accomplished. Up to the 31st everything had gone favourably for the Union Army; the fighting of the morning of the 31st had been all in Bragg's favour, and had almost resulted in the total defeat of Rosecrans; but from that time on, everything had again been in[Pg 13] Rosecrans' favour. His losses were on the whole greater than those of Bragg, but the latter's retreat gave the victory to Rosecrans.

Rosecrans' force on the battlefield was 43,400; his losses were 13,249, more than thirty per cent. Bragg's total force on the field was 44,750, and his loss 12,334, about 28 *per cent*. Rosecrans lost 28 pieces of artillery and a large portion of his wagon train, but Bragg lost only three pieces of artillery.

While the result of the campaign was attained the army had nevertheless been very severely handled, and for a time was on the verge of utter ruin. Rosecrans' plan was not at all carried out. The reason for this was the faulty posting and handling of McCook's wing and the fact that Bragg started in earlier in the execution of his attack. Rosecrans knew on the night before the battle that McCook's wing was not correctly placed and ordered changes in it. These were not carried out and Rosecrans made no apparent effort to see that they were.

There has been a great deal of controversy about this matter. One of McCook's division commanders, Johnson, stated in his report that McCook told him that his left was opposite the rebel centre, and he expected to be attacked in great force next day. This was, in fact, true, yet McCook certainly did not make such dispositions as to resist any such attack even for a short time, and was compelled to call for such assistance as to wreck the whole plan of battle. If he had placed his corps in a strong defensive position and entrenched it he might have resisted for such a length of time that the main attack could make such progress as to compel Bragg to give up his plan and conform to Rosecrans' movements; just as, in fact, Rosecrans was forced to comply with those of Bragg. The battle is singular in that the opposing plans were identical. It has been called Stone's River by the Union forces and Murfreesboro' by the Confederates.

For the next six months little was done—the Union Army occupying Murfreesboro' and the Rebel army a position near Tullahoma.

Then followed the campaign which terminated in the battle of Chickamauga.

Personal Recollections and Experiences Concerning the Battle of Stone River

By Milo S. Hascall

A Paper Read by Request before the Illinois Commandery of the Military Order of the Loyal Legion of the U.S., at Chicago, Ill., Feb. 14, 1889.

As will be perceived by the above caption to this paper, it is proposed to relate what happened to me, and what I observed during the battle alluded to, and might not inappropriately be styled "What I know about the battle of Stone River."

In doing so I shall not undertake to give a general account of the battle, but shall confine myself to that portion which came under my own observation, and to necessary inferences as to what happened elsewhere. In setting out it will be well to give a brief account of the history of the Army of the Cumberland, and its commanders, so far as I know, up to the time of the memorable battle which is the subject of this paper. My having been a cadet at West Point from June, 1848, to June, 1852, when I graduated in the same class with Sheridan, Stanly, Slocum, Crook, Bonaparte and others, whose names have since become so distinguished, and my service in the regular army subsequently till the fall of 1853, threw me in contact with, and was the means of my knowing personally, or by reputation, most, if not all the prominent characters on both sides, that were brought to the knowledge of the public by the War of the Rebellion.

This knowledge of the men in the army of those times served me

18

well all through the war, as it was seldom I came in contact with an officer on the other side, but what I knew all his peculiar characteristics, and idiosyncrasies. For illustration of this idea, as we were approaching Atlanta, my division had the advance of the Army of the Ohio the morning we came in sight of the city. My advance guard captured a rebel picket post, and one of the men captured, had a morning paper from Atlanta, in which was Johnston's farewell order to his troops, and Hood's order assuming command. I had been three years at West Point with Hood, he having graduated in 1853, in Schofield's class. I knew Hood to be a great, large hearted, large sized man, noted a great deal more for his fine social and fighting qualities, than for any particular scholastic acquirements, and inferred, (correctly as the result showed) that Johnston had been removed because Davis, and his admirers, had had enough of the Fabian policy, and wanted a man that would take the offensive.

I immediately sent word to Gen. Sherman, who, with his staff, was not far off, and when he came to the front, informed him of the news I had, and the construction I put upon it, and in consequence, an immediate concentration to resist an attack was made in the vicinity, where we were. It was none too soon, as Hood, upon taking command immediately moved out to Decatur with nearly his entire army, fell upon McPherson's corps, with the besom of destruction, killing the gallant McPherson early in the engagement, and with his vastly superior force, beating back the Army of the Tennessee so fast, that there is no telling what might have happened, had we not made the concentration we did, and been prepared to give them a tremendous enfilading fire as soon as they came opposite the flanks of the Army of the Ohio.

It was my fortune to be stationed at Ft. Adams, Newport, Rhode Island, as soon as my furlough expired after graduating at the Military Academy, and there found Lieut. W.S. Rosecrans, (afterward the commanding general at Stone River), and from being stationed some ten months at the same post, became somewhat familiarly acquainted with him and his peculiarities. I had never met Gen. Don Carlos Buell, and knew but little of him, although he was a regular army man, until the fall of '61, upon my return from service in West Virginia, during the first summer of the war. I was then Colonel of the 17th Indiana, and was assigned to the command of a brigade in Nelson's Division of Buell's Army, which was then in and around Louisville, Ky., and whose purpose was a forward move against Nashville.

While Buell's Army, the Army of the Cumberland, was concentrating in and about Louisville, preparing for the forward movement, Gov. Morton, of Indiana, was frequently in Louisville, consulting with Gen. Buell, and offering suggestions as to army movements etc., and these, after a time, came to be regarded by Gen. Buell as meddlesome, and uncalled for, so much so, that he finally intimated to Gov. Morton that it would be as well for him to attend to his duties as Governor of Indiana, while he would attend to his as Commanding General of the forces in the field.

It is important to mention this circumstance here, as it will be seen further on, that this matter had an important bearing upon Gen. Buell's subsequent career. It will not be necessary, nor appropriate in this paper, to enter into a detailed account of the operations of the Army of the Cumberland in its march upon, and capture of Nashville—in its subsequent march to Shiloh, and the part it took in that most unfortunate, not to say (in many respects) disgraceful battle to our army—in its subsequent advance upon Corinth, and its operations there—in its subsequent march into northern Alabama and the vicinity of Chattanooga, and the forced march back to Louisville, made necessary by Bragg's advance upon that city through the Sequatchie Valley, from Chattanooga.

All this is known to the public, and the public has arrived at its own conclusions as to the merits or demerits of these various operations. It is not too much to say, however, that those of us who accompanied Gen. Buell in this remarkable march and counter-march, and particularly those who had important commands during the same, had ample opportunity to arrive at intelligent conclusions as to the merits and demerits of the man. It may be inferred from what has already been said that, Gen. Buell was not particularly popular with political soldiers, newspaper correspondents, and others who were carrying on the war from safe distances in the rear. He was eminently and emphatically a soldier, with no ambition or expectations outside the line of his duty, and with honour and integrity so entirely above suspicion, that the camp follower and money getter did not presume to even enter into his presence.

Notwithstanding all this, by the time of the return of the Army of the Cumberland to Louisville, though that army had then performed services that justly entitled it to the lasting gratitude of the country, and notwithstanding its eminent commander enjoyed, so far as I knew, the entire confidence of the officers and men in regard to his loyalty, patriotism and ability, yet there had sprung up a fire in the rear party that was constantly impugning his loyalty, his ability, and his fitness to command, and demanding his removal. In the light of what has already been said, it can now be seen whence, and from what source this hue and cry proceeded.

On account of a contemporaneous popularity that Gen. Rosecrans had achieved about that time, at the battle of Iuka, there arose a demand in the press that Gen. Buell be superseded in the command of the Army of the Cumberland by that officer. As I have said, my acquaintance with Gen. Rosecrans previous to his assuming command of the Army of the Cumberland, had been confined to the ten months I had been stationed with him at Newport, R.I., in '52-3.

My recollections of him were not such as to inspire me with confidence in him as the proper person to be placed in command of an army. At that time he seemed to be a great enthusiast in regard to the Catholic Church; seemed to want to think of nothing else, talk of nothing else, and in fact do nothing else, except to proselyte for it and attend upon its ministrations. No night was ever so dark and tempestuous, that he would not brave the boisterous seas of Newport Harbor to attend mass, and no occasion, however inappropriate, was ever lost sight of to advocate its cause; in fact, he was what would nowadays be called most emphatically a crank on that subject, and might not inappropriately be considered a one-ideaed man lacking in the breadth and poise, so necessary to success in the commander of an army in the field.

While Buell's Army was in Louisville getting reinforcements and preparing to renew operations against Bragg, I obtained a few days leave of absence and had no end of inquiries on my way home and after arriving there, as to what I thought of the propriety and necessity of relieving Buell. I uniformly replied that as far as the Army was concerned there was not that I knew of, any want of confidence in Buell, but on the other hand, nothing but the most sincere confidence and respect. That the only reason that could be assigned was the want of confidence that the fire in the rear might have caused in the country at large, and that even if this was thought to be necessary, it would be very bad policy to substitute Rosecrans in his stead. How near correct I was in this estimate the public is now prepared to judge.

Of course the possibility of Buell's removal dispirited him, and perhaps inspired some of the officers under him, that might by possibility be selected to succeed him, with a desire that such might be the case. At all events, shortly after the army again took the offensive, the notorious and disastrous affair at Perryville took place, in regard to which it was charged at the time by Gen. Buell, and believed by others, that it was brought on by Gen. A. McD. McCook separating himself more from the body of the army than his orders justified, and beyond supporting distance, in order that an engagement might be brought on, in which, if successful, he might claim the sole credit, and thereby supersede Buell in command. However this may be, this engagement was the culminating affair in Buell's career. The blame was (as I think) unjustly attached to him, and he was relieved of his command, and Gen. W.S. Rosecrans appointed in his place.

After this battle, the Army resumed offensive operations against Bragg and in due time arrived in Nashville, when offensive operations were for a time suspended, in order to get supplies forward, and put the army in shape for active, and if possible, decisive operations. During the weeks that we thus lay encamped about Nashville I had frequent opportunities to see Gen. Rosecrans and observe his manner, characteristics and surroundings and had hoped to be enabled to form a more favourable opinion of the man and his fitness for the high position to which he had been called than I had theretofore entertained. I was sorry, however, to be forced to the conclusion that my estimate of the man had been even more favourable than the facts would justify. His head seemed to have been completely turned by the greatness of his promotion. Instead of the quiet dignity, orderly and business methods that had formerly obtained at the headquarters of the Army, the very reverse seemed to be the rule.

Having by this time surrounded himself, in addition to the usual staff and appliances ordinarily to be found at the headquarters of an army in the field, with a numerous coterie of newspaper correspondents, and Catholic priests, who seemed in his estimation to be vastly more important than anyone else about him, and laid in a good supply of crucifixes, holy water, *spiritus frumenti*, Chinese gongs, *flambeaux*, jobbing presses, printers' devils, javelins, white elephants, and other cabalistic emblems and evidences that a holy crusade was about to be entered upon, and having daily announced through his various newspaper correspondents, jobbing presses, and other means of reaching the public and the Confederate Army lying immediately in our front, exactly what was going on, one could but wonder at the sublime indifference of Bragg, and his Army remaining in the State of Tennessee, in the midst of preparations for their destruction such as these.

As this magnificent and resplendent cavalcade of Holy, Oriental, and gorgeous splendour moved about from camp to camp during the weeks that we lay at Nashville making these gigantic and awe-inspiring preparations for the advance, every knee was bowed, and every tongue confessed, that Allah was great, and thrice illustriously great was this Saviour that had been sent to us. All things though, however grand and glorious, must have an end, and it was finally announced during the last days of December, 1862, that the army was ready for a forward move. You will not be surprised to be informed after what has preceded, that it was my opinion that the Catholic officers having command in that army would fare well when the honours of the campaign came to be distributed.

Accordingly, I made a prediction in writing that every one of these, consisting of Brig.-Gen. Philip H. Sheridan, Brig.-Gen. D.S. Stanly, Brig.-Gen. James S. Negley, and Capt. James St. Claire Morton, would all be promoted entirely regardless of what the fortunes of war might have in store for them. This I did without the slightest feeling of unkindness or jealousy towards these officers, but simply on account of my belief that the Commanding General was such a narrow-minded bigot in regard to Catholicism, that it was impossible for him not to allow considerations of this kind to control his estimate of men. We shall see how nearly correct I was in this estimate further on. At the time this campaign was entered upon the National Forces had not been divided into Army Corps and numbered. Each Army commander divided his army as to him seemed best. Rosecrans divided his into three grand divisions called the Right, Centre, and Left, and each of these into three ordinary divisions of four brigades each, the Right, Centre and Left commanded respectively by Generals A. McD. McCook, George H. Thomas and Thos. L. Crittenden.

At the time of this advance and for a long time previous thereto, I was commanding a brigade in Gen. Thos. J. Wood's division of the left wing. The advance movement all along the line finally commenced about the 26th day of December, 1862. The first day Palmer's division of the left wing had the advance and on the evening of that day, had reached the vicinity of Lavergne, having had some pretty sharp skirmishing in so doing. The next day by rotation Wood's division had the advance.

It was not the place of my brigade to lead the division that day, but I was specially requested to take the advance, however, as the progress made the day before had not been satisfactory. I consented

23

to do so upon condition that the cavalry, which had been in advance the day before should be retired to the rear of my brigade ready to be brought into use should we succeed in routing the enemy, and should the topography of the country admit of the successful use of cavalry. I had seen so many disastrous results ensue from the use of squadrons of cavalry in advance of an army under such circumstances as we were advancing, that I did not want to run any such risks in addition to the ordinary and inevitable risks of such advances against an army in the field. The cavalry necessarily has to retire before any effective work can be done, and usually comes back pell-mell with a lot of riderless horses, and creates infinitely more confusion, consternation, and even danger to the advancing army, than anything the enemy would be likely to do at that stage of the operations.

Having thus arrived at the front and got the cavalry out of the way to the rear, I found the enemy securely lodged in the town of Lavergne, and masked from our view by the buildings, shrubbery and fences. My orders contemplated an immediate advance along the main pike toward Murfreesboro. Thus no opportunity was given for flanking them, and so compelling them to abandon the town. The country was open between my command and the town, and afforded no shelter whatever for the troops. I formed the brigade in two lines about 200 yards apart, with a strong line of skirmishers about the same distance in advance of the first line, with a section of artillery in the interval between the infantry lines.

As these dispositions were about completed preparatory to ordering an advance of the line a heavy infantry fire was opened upon us from the buildings and cover the town afforded to the enemy, and their fire was taking effect even upon the first line of infantry back of the skirmish line. At this juncture I ordered the infantry to lie down, the artillery to open with shot and shell upon the town, and the heavy line of skirmishers to fix bayonets and on double quick to make the distance between them and the town; to be immediately followed by the main lines of infantry as soon as the skirmishers had reached the town. This movement was entirely successful; we soon had routed the enemy from the town, but had left some forty or fifty dead comrades behind us to be cared for by those in our rear.

As soon as we had driven the enemy beyond the town, we continued the same order with two regiments in line of battle about 200 yards apart to the left of the main pike, and two to the right in like manner, all preceded by a heavy line of skirmishers, and pushed forward with all possible dispatch. A heavy rain set in about the time we commenced the advance beyond the town, which continued all day, so the cornfields and other ploughed fields soon became ankle deep with mud. Nevertheless we pressed forward continuously. If we encountered the enemy in any considerable force, the skirmish line gradually slackened their progress until the main line came up with them. Artillery was brought forward and fired advancing along the road. In this manner we kept up an almost continuous advance, our dead and wounded being cared for by those in our rear.

By nightfall we had made an advance of nearly eight miles, to Stewart's Creek. As we approached Stewart's Creek we discovered that the enemy had set the bridge over the same on fire. I immediately concentrated four pieces of artillery on a little eminence to the right of the road, and commenced shelling the enemy beyond the creek. Under the cover of this fire the infantry was ordered forward at double quick, and succeeded in subduing the flames before sufficient damage had been done to prevent the use of the bridge by our army. So rapid had been our advance that three companies of rebel cavalry that had been hovering on our left flank during the advance, were cut off before they reached the bridge, and were captured by us with all their horses and accoutrements. In the evening we were congratulated by all our superior officers for having accomplished a very satisfactory day's work.

This brought us up to the evening of the 27th of December. During the time between this and the afternoon of the 30th of the same month, all portions of our army had pressed forward along the different lines of march laid out for them, encountering the usual incidents of driving in the enemy's cavalry and outposts, until finally at that time our entire army had arrived along the left bank of Stone River, opposite the city of Murfreesboro, some two or three miles further on. Here we encountered the enemy in force and their fortifications were plainly visible all along opposite us on the right bank of the river, between it and the city of Murfreesboro, and here it was very evident Bragg intended to make his stand and accept the gauge of battle.

There was desultory firing all along the line during that memorable afternoon, but during that time our army was finally concentrated, McCook, with his three divisions on the right, Thomas, with his three in the centre, and Crittenden, with his three on the left. The whole line, with the intervals for artillery and cavalry, occupying a distance of two or three miles, more or less. Crittenden's three divisions were formed, two divisions in line of battle, and one in reserve, as follows: Palmer's division on the right, Wood's on the left, and Van Cleve in reserve opposite the interval between Palmer's and Wood's, and each division consisting likewise of three brigades, were formed in like manner, two in line and one in reserve.

In Wood's division Wagner's brigade was on the right, my own on the left, and Harker in reserve. This arrangement brought my brigade on the extreme left of the entire army. During that evening we were made acquainted with the plan of the attack which was to be made by our army under cover of the gray of the morning the following day, the memorable 31st day of December, 1862. This was for the left wing (Crittenden's) to cross Stone River—which was at that time fordable at all points for all arms of the service—and deliver a furious attack on the enemy's extreme right, this to be followed up by a wheel to the right by other portions of our army in case Crittenden was successful in his attack, until all portions of our army should become engaged and the battle become general all along the line.

This plan was well conceived, and might have worked well enough perhaps, if the enemy had waited for us. The same mistake (or a similar one rather) was made here that was made by Grant at Shiloh, only the latter was much more faulty. In that case Grant was moving his army up the Tennessee River to Savannah, the object being to attack Beauregard, then at Corinth, some twenty miles from Savannah, as soon as he should have made a junction with Buell's army, then at Nashville, Tenn., and which was to march from that place to Savannah. Grant's army proceeding by boats, arrived at Savannah by detachments first, and should have all been landed on the side of the river toward Grant's reinforcements, instead of on the side toward the enemy—unless he considered from the time he landed, anything more than a picket force of cavalry to keep him advised of the enemy's movements on the side toward them—that he had enough to successfully cope with him. If he thought the latter, he should have been with his troops on the side of the river toward the enemy instead of eight miles below on the other side.

Thus the most elementary principles of grand tactics and military science, that, in case two armies are endeavouring to concentrate with a view of delivering an attack on a superior force of the enemy, the inferior force nearest the enemy, should be careful to oppose all natural obstructions, such as rivers, mountains, heavy forests, impassable marshes, between it and the enemy until a junction can be made. In this case the detachments of Grant's army were allowed to land on the side toward the enemy, select their locations as best they could without instructions or concert of action of any kind, and this within fifteen to eighteen miles of the enemy in force, in the enemy's country, where it was known to all that he had daily and hourly opportunity from the citizens who fell back before our forces, to find out all the time the exact locations and strength of Grant's and Buell's armies, respectively.

Under circumstances like these, the merest tyro in military knowledge ought to have known that an experienced, able officer, such as Beauregard was known to be, would not wait for the concentration, before anticipating the attack. So it was no surprise to anyone except the troops on that side the river towards Corinth, and possibly to Grant, then at Savannah, that on that fatal Sunday morning in April, 1862, when Grant had got sufficient troops on that side of the river to make it an object for Beauregard to destroy or capture them, and when Buell's advance had approached within twenty to twenty-five miles of Savannah, that Beauregard determined upon an attack, and declared he would crush or capture the troops on that side, and water his horse in the Tennessee River that night, and that but for the timely arrival by forced marches of Buell's advance of two divisions on the field about four o'clock that afternoon, he would undoubtedly have executed his purpose.

If Buell had been guilty of such blundering (not to call it by any worse name than this) it would have been impossible to make the country at the North believe that he did not meditate its destruction. For this blunder Grant was promptly relieved of his command, by the proper authorities, and it was many years afterwards, before anyone was found, who did not think this was very moderate punishment, under such circumstances. The fault in the case under consideration differs in kind, but not in its disastrous effects upon our cause and our army.

The right of our army at Murfreesboro, judging from what happened (and as I said at the outset, when I don't know personally what happened, I speak from necessary inference) seemed to think that inasmuch as our plan of battle contemplated an attack by the extreme left, to be followed up by them subsequently during the day, that they had nothing to do at that early hour in the morning, but to keep a picket force out, send their artillery horses to a distant point for water, stack their arms, and get breakfast. They did not seem to think possibly Bragg might have plans of his own, and that our attack might be anticipated, and that our right might receive a desperate attack while our left was preparing to deliver one. This, as you all know, was what happened, and you all know its disastrous results.

Current reports at the time were to the effect that the right was found when the attack came upon them in the condition already described, and the prompt manner in which they were hurled from the field, corroborates this view of the case. This, of course, caused the troops to their left to be immediately out-flanked, and no resistance, to amount to anything, from that portion of our line could be expected under such circumstances. How much Gen. Rosecrans and his staff are properly to blame for the state of things existing on the right at the time of the attack, I have no means of knowing, and do not undertake to say but that it was the prime cause of the very serious disaster to our arms, and to the prestige of our army that happened at that battle, there can be no doubt or chance for two opinions. How the battle raged, and what happened, so far as I then knew, I cannot better describe than by extracting from my official report of that day's proceedings, made on the 6th of January, following, and which I do as follows:

Headquarters 1st Brigade, 1st Div'n, Left Wing,
near Murfreesboro', Tenn., Jan. 6, 1863.

Capt. M.P. Bestow, A.A.A.G.:

Sir: I have the honour to submit the following report of the operations of my brigade, (formerly the 15th Brigade, 6th Division, but under the new nomenclature, 1st Brigade, 1st Division, left wing) on the eventful 31st of December, 1862.—During the night of the 30th I had received notice through Gen. Wood, our division commander, that the left wing, Crittenden's corps, would cross Stone river and attack the enemy on their right. My brigade was posted on the extreme left of our entire line of battle and was guarding and overlooking the ford over which we were to cross.

On the morning of the 31st heavy firing was heard on the extreme right of our line, (McCook's corps) but as they had been fighting their way all the distance from Nolensville as we had from Lavergne, no particular importance was attached to this, and I was getting my brigade into position, ready to cross as soon as Gen. Van Cleve's division, which was then crossing, was over. All this time the firing on the right became heavier, and apparently nearer to us, and our fears began to be aroused that the right wing was being rapidly driven back upon us. At this juncture Gen. Van Cleve halted his division and the most terrible state of suspense pervaded the entire line, as it became more and more evident that the right was being driven rapidly back upon us.

On and on they came till the heaviest fire was getting nearly around to the pike leading to Nashville, when General Rosecrans appeared in person, and ordered me to go with my brigade at once to the support of the right, pointing toward our rear, where the heaviest fire was raging. Gen. Van Cleve's division and Col. Harker's brigade of our division received the same order. I at once changed the front of my brigade to the rear, preparatory to starting in the same direction, but had not proceeded more than 200 yards in the new direction before the fugitives from the right became so numerous, and the fleeing mule-teams and horsemen so thick, that it was impossible for me to go forward with my command without its becoming a confused mass.

I therefore halted, and awaited developments. Gen. Van Cleve and Col. Harker not meeting with so much opposition pressed forward and got into position beyond the railroad, ready to open on the enemy as soon as our fugitives were out of the way. They soon opened fire, joined by some batteries and troops belonging to the centre (Gen. Thomas' corps) and Estep's battery of my brigade, and after about an hours' fighting along this new line, during which time I was moving my command from point to point, ready to support any troops that most needed it. The onslaught of the enemy seemed to be in a great measure checked, and we had reasonable probability of maintaining this line.

During all this time my men were exposed to a severe fire of shot and shell from a battery on the other side of the river, and several men were killed. About this time an aid of Gen. Palmer's came galloping up to me, and said that unless he could be supported his division would give way. Palmer's division formed the right of Gen. Crittenden's line of battle on the morning of the 31st. After consulting with Gen. Wood he ordered me to send a regiment to support Gen. Palmer. Accordingly I sent the 3rd Kentucky regiment, commanded by Lieut. Col. Sam'l

McKee. Before the regiment had been ten minutes in its new position, Capt. Kerstetter, my Adjutant General, reported to me that Col. McKee had been killed and the regiment badly cut up. I therefore moved with the other three regiments of my command to their relief.

The line they were trying to hold was that port of our original line of battle lying immediately to the right of the railroad, and forming an acute angle with the same. This portion of our original line, about two regimental fronts, together with two fronts to the left held by Colonel Wagner's brigade, was all of our original line of battle but what our troops had been driven from; and if they succeeded in carrying this they would have turned our left, and a total route of our forces could not then have been avoided. Seeing the importance of the position, I told my men that it must be held even if it cost the last man we had.

I immediately sent in the 26th Ohio, commanded by the gallant Major Wm. H. Squires, to take position on the right of the 3rd Kentucky, and support it, and dispatched an aid for the 18th Indiana battery to come to this point and open on the enemy. No sooner had the 26th Ohio got in position than they became hotly engaged, and the numerous dead and wounded that were immediately brought to the rear told how desperate was the contest. The gallant Lieut. McClellan of that regiment was brought to the rear mortally wounded, and expired by my side in less than five minutes from the time the regiment took position. Still the fight went on, and still brave men went down. The 3rd Kentucky, now reduced to less than one-half its original number, with ten officers out of its fourteen remaining ones, badly wounded, was still bravely at work.

In less than ten minutes after the fall of Lieut. Col. McKee, the gallant Major Daniel R. Collier, of that regiment, received two severe wounds, one in the leg and one in the breast. Adjutant Bullitt had his horse shot from under him, but nothing could induce either of them to leave the field. Equally conspicuous and meritorious was the conduct of Major Squires and Adjutant Franklin, of the 26th Ohio. Major Squires' horse was three times shot through the neck; nevertheless, he and all his officers stood by throughout and most gallantly sustained and encouraged their men.

Estep's battery came up in due time, and taking a position on a little rise of ground in the rear of the 26th Ohio, and 3rd Kentucky, opened a terrific fire of shot and shell over the heads of our infantry. About one hour after the 26th Ohio got into position, this terrible attack of the enemy was repulsed, and they drew back into the woods, and under cover of an intervening hill, to reform their shattered columns and renew the attack. I now took a survey of the situation, and found that along the entire line to the right and left of the railroad, which had not yet been carried by the enemy, I was the only general officer present, and was therefore in command, and responsible for the conduct of affairs.

Col. Hazen, commanding a brigade in Gen. Palmer's division, was present with his brigade to the left of the railroad. Col. Gross, commanding another brigade in the same division, was also present with what there was left of his brigade, and most nobly did he co-operate with me, with the 6th and 25th Ohio to the right of the railroad, while Col. Wagner, commanding the 2nd brigade, 1st division, (left wing) nobly sustained his front, assisted by Col. Hazen to the left of the railroad. I now relieved the 3rd Kentucky regiment, who were nearly annihilated, and out of ammunition, with the 58th Indiana regiment of my brigade, commanded by Col. Geo. P. Buelll; and this being a much larger regiment than the 3rd Kentucky, filled up the entire space from where the right of the 3rd Kentucky rested, to the railroad.

I then threw forward the right of the 6th Ohio regiment of Col. Gross' brigade, which was on the right of the 26th Ohio, so that its line of battle was more nearly perpendicular to the railroad, and so its fire would sweep the front of the 26th Ohio, and 58th Indiana, and supported the 6th Ohio with Estep's battery on a little eminence to its right, and brought the 97th Ohio, Col. Lane, from Wagner's brigade, to still further strengthen the right. These dispositions being made, I galloped a little to the rear, and found Gen. Rosecrans, and called his attention to the importance of the position I was holding, and the necessity of keeping it well supported.

He rode to the front with me, approved of the dispositions I had made, spoke a few words of encouragement to the men, cautioning them to hold their fire until the enemy had got well up, and had no sooner retired than the enemy emerged from the woods over the hill, and were moving upon us again in splendid style, and in great force.—As soon as they came in sight, the 6th and 26th Ohio, and Estep's battery opened on them, and did splendid execution; but on they came, until within 100 yards of our line, when Col. Buelll, of the 58th Indiana, who had lost three men, but had not fired a gun, ordered his men to fire. The effect was indescribable; the enemy fell in winrows, and went staggering back from the effects of this unexpected volley. Soon, however, they came up again and assaulted us furiously for about one and a half hours, but the men all stood their ground nobly, and at the end of that time compelled the enemy to retire as before.

During the heat of this attack a heavy cross fire was brought to bear on the position I occupied, and Corporal Frank Mayer, of the 3rd Ohio Volunteer Cavalry, in command of my escort, was shot through the leg, and my Adjt. General, Capt. Ed. R. Kerstetter, was shot through his coat, grazing his back. The regiments all behaved splendidly again, and the 58th Indiana won immortal honours. Lieut. Blackford, of that regiment, was shot dead, and several of the officers, including Capts. Downey and Alexander, badly wounded. Estep's battery was compelled to retire from the position assigned to it after firing a half dozen rounds, but it did terrible execution while there.

The 6th and 26th Ohio did noble service, as did the 97th, but their own immediate commanders will no doubt allude to them more particularly. Thus ended the third assault upon our position. I should have remarked that the 100th Illinois, the other regiment composing my brigade, which was in reserve during the first engagement described above, had, under instruction of Col. Hazen, moved to the front on the left of the railroad, and taken up a position at right angles with the railroad, where they fought splendidly in all the actions that took place on the left of the road. There was no formidable attack made upon them, though they were almost constantly under fire of greater or less severity, particularly from shot and shell, and suffered quite severely in killed and wounded.

Lieut. Morrison Worthington, of that regiment, was killed while gallantly sustaining his men, and six other commissioned officers, including Major Hammond, were wounded. Their operations being to the left of the railroad, in a wood, did not come so immediately under my personal observation, but their conduct, from Col. Bartleson down, was such as leaves nothing to be desired. The 58th Indiana having now been over three hours in action, and the 26th Ohio about four hours, were exhausted and very near out of ammunition. I therefore relieved the 58th Indiana with the 40th Indiana from Col. Wagner's brigade, and the 26th Ohio was relieved by the 23rd Kentucky.

There was now not more than an hour of the day left, and though the enemy was constantly manoeuvring in our front, no formidable attack was made upon us, except with artillery. The enemy having been three several times repulsed in their attack on that position, seemed satisfied to keep at a respectful distance, and the sun set upon us, masters of the situation. We had sustained ourselves *and held the only portion of the original line of battle that was held throughout by any portion of our army.* To have lost this position would have been to lose everything, as our left would then have been turned also, and utter rout or capture inevitable.

During the evening of the 31st, I was officially notified that in consequence of the indisposition of Gen. Wood, and a wound received by him during the forenoon of that day, he was relieved of the command of the division, and that the same would devolve upon myself. I therefore turned over the command of the brigade to Col. Geo. P. Buelll, of the 58th Indiana, and assumed command of the division. All of which is respectfully submitted.

Milo S. Hascall, Brig. Gen. Vols., Com's Brigade.
Ed. R. Kerstetter, Capt. & A.A.G. (Official.)

After the battle was over, during the evening, Colonel Harker's brigade that had gone to the assistance of the right, returned to where we had been in action during the day, and thus the division was once more together, and on this ground we did the best we could towards getting something to eat, and prepared to bivouac on the same ground for the night. About eleven o'clock that night, I was visited by Capt. John Mendenhall, Chief of Artillery on Gen. Crittenden's staff, and who belonged to the Regular Army of the United States, and a gentleman of first-class intelligence, and purity of character, and informed that since the cessation of hostilities for the night, a council of war had been held at Gen. Rosecrans' headquarters, by himself and his Grand

Division Commanders, and that a general retreat to Nashville had been decided upon, and that all except Gen. Crittenden concurred in the advisability of such movement, and he was overruled by the others, and that in pursuance of such determination, I was forthwith to send all the transportation of my division, except one wagon for each brigade, to the rear, and when the transportation was all under way, this was to be followed by a general retreat of our army to Nashville.

Mendenhall said that Crittenden was very much incensed at the proposition for retreat; said his army was in position and on hand, and that if he were overruled and if a retreat was decided upon, that he would cross the river and retreat by way of Gallatin to Nashville. However, the retreat was decided upon, and the baggage had been sent to the rear as above directed, and we were laying on our arms awaiting the further order to retreat, when a very singular circumstance caused Rosecrans to change his mind, and conclude to fight it out where we were. A large number of our straggling, demoralized detachments in the rear of our army, being hungry and thirsty, had concluded to disobey orders, and make fire and try and get something to eat. One party would make a fire, another would go there to get a fire brand to start another, and when this became general along our rear, Rosecrans concluded the enemy had got in our rear, and were forming line of battle by torch lights, and hence withdrew the order for a general retreat.

After this, about one o'clock, I was informed also by Capt. Mendenhall, that the retreat had been given up, and that I was ordered to fall back with my division about half a mile, and take up a position that would there be assigned me. Accordingly I did so, and in the morning found myself occupying a position with no advantages for offensive or defensive operations, and very much exposed to the enemy's fire, with no chance for returning it with any effect. The enemy were occupying the position I had fallen back from, and at that point concentrated a large number of pieces of artillery, with which, about nine o'clock in the morning, they opened upon us a tremendous artillery fire, under the cover of which I supposed their infantry would charge upon us, but for some strange reason or other, they did not do so.

Desultory firing afterwards, was kept up during the day, until about three o'clock in the afternoon. In the meantime we had sent a division across the river to the left, which was occupying the high ground near where the enemy's right was resting originally. About three o'clock Breckenridge's troops, of the rebel army, fell furiously upon this division, and drove them rapidly from their position, on account of their superior numbers. At this juncture Crittenden ordered Mendenhall to concentrate his artillery on the bank of the river to our front and left, which he promptly did, and ordered me, with my division, to promptly cross the river in support of the division already there in retreat. Upon our arrival on the other side of the river, the furious fire from Mendenhall's artillery had checked the rebel advance, and the division over there turned upon their assailants, and with the assistance of my division, drove Breckenridge back to the position he had occupied before making the assault.

The latter part of these operations were carried on in the darkness, and we slept upon our arms, amidst the dead and wounded. It had been raining hard all the night, and the river was rising very rapidly, so much so that if we had remained there until morning, there would have been danger that the river would become impassable, and the divisions been left there by themselves in the presence of the whole rebel army. Accordingly, about two o'clock at night, we were ordered to recross the river, and take up positions where we had been during the previous day. We arrived back there between that time and morning, thoroughly wet through, and completely jaded out, having had no sleep, and but little to eat during the previous forty-eight hours.

Both armies continued after this during the third day, to occupy the positions they had on that morning. It was cold, wet, and very disagreeable weather; both armies were completely tired out, and seemed content to do nothing more than to engage in some desultory firing, and watch each other closely. On the morning of the fourth day, January 3, or rather, during the forenoon of that day, the stragglers from the right, during the first day's battle, who had not stopped in their flight until they reached Nashville, began to return in large numbers, in companies, and even regiments, and Bragg, observing this, concluded we were receiving large bodies of reinforcements from the north, and therefore concluded to fall back and give up the contest. He accordingly did so, and on the fourth day, January 4, he took possession of Murfreesboro without the firing of a gun.

Thus ended the great battle of Stone River. We had not made a single attack during the whole time; were badly beaten and well nigh driven from the field the first day, and only saved from an ignominious retreat upon Nashville by the ridiculous misconception on the part of Rosecrans, already alluded to on the first night after the battle commenced. As it was, we lost all our transportation, by sending it to the rear, that night, preparatory for the retreat, the whole having been burned by the rebels at Lavergne, notwithstanding we were supposed to have some cavalry in our rear, under Gen. Stanley. Where it was at the time our transportation was being burned by the rebel cavalry, I have never heard.

Finally our fugitives from the first day's battle began to return, thereupon Bragg became very much frightened and beat a retreat, and we thus gained Murfreesboro. After this reports were written up to praise the men it had been determined upon in advance to promote, and these identical men that I had predicted would be favoured, were promoted; one of them, St. Claire Morton, from Captain to Brigadier-General, while others, upon whom rested the heat and burden of the day, and who saved the army from utter annihilation, were not only not promoted, but in many instances not even mentioned. It was, for instance, Sheridan's fate to be early driven from the field, whether from his fault or not, it is not necessary to inquire. Enough for this occasion that it was so, and the facts of his subsequent career no more justify what was done for him on this occasion, than would the subsequent illustrious career of Gen. Grant justify his promotion for the terrible blunders committed by him concerning the most unfortunate battle of Shiloh.

In what I have said in this paper in regard to the Catholic Church, I do not wish to be understood as having any desire to say anything against that church, but simply to condemn the idea of making membership in that, or any other particular church, a necessary concomitant to advancement, either in a military or civil capacity, under our government. Farther, in all that I have said nothing has been said in malice towards any officer or person, but simply that that criticism so necessary to the establishment of right and justice in regard to the late war may be freely indulged in, whether it affect the highest officer, or the lowest private that offered his life in defence of his country. It will be seen that my estimate of the fitness of Gen. Rosecrans to command an army was not enhanced by his career during and preceding the battle of Stone River.

When disaster came to the right, he should have given his attention personally to that, and lent the magic of his personal presence to rallying the fleeing troops from that division, in place of going to the extreme left himself—instead of by a staff officer—for ordering the movement of troops in that direction. When the whole affair was over, and quiet restored, I made an application to be transferred to another army on account of want of confidence in him as the commander of an army in the field. This I supposed would cause my arrest, and give an opportunity for me to demonstrate the great cause that existed for my apprehensions, but instead of doing this, he returned my application endorsed that he could not spare the services of so useful an officer as myself, and that there would be no forward movement of the army for six months, and detailed me to proceed to Indianapolis, Ind., to superintend the work of returning deserters from Ohio, Indiana, and Illinois. Just before my leaving Murfreesboro for Indianapolis we saw Bragg's telegraphic account to Richmond, of the first day's proceedings. It was as follows:

> This morning, under cover of the darkness, we attacked the enemy on his extreme right, and have routed him from every portion of his line except upon his extreme left, where he has successfully resisted us.

As I left there was a proposition started in Crittenden's command to raise money to present Bragg a sword for making the above truthful statement of the first days operations. While at Indianapolis, I was, at the request of Gen. Burnside, transferred by the War Department, to the army of the Ohio and given the command of a division in that army. The next that we heard of Gen. Rosecrans was at the battle of Chickamauga, and that was the last we heard of him in a military way, and all can now see how much cause there was for the apprehensions I entertained. This was not the first instance that great unfitness achieved high rank in our armies and it was quite common for great merit to be entirely unrewarded, and indeed entirely unknown. But time is a great healer, and let us hope that honest merit will in the end get its recognition, trusting in the truthfulness of the idea that

Ever the world goes round and round,
And ever the truth comes uppermost,
And justice shall be done.

Stone's River

By Wilson J. Vance

To My Wife

PREFACE

While many authorities were consulted in the preparation of this work, particular acknowledgment is due John Formby's *The American Civil War*, wherein was suggested the proposition that is here laid down and expanded; to Van Horne's *History of the Army of the Cumberland*, which gives the campaigns of that organization in minute detail; to several of the papers and books of Charles Francis Adams,—documents that deal principally with the diplomacy of the Civil War, and to the published and spoken words of the author's father,—the late Wilson Vance,—orderly to the brigade commander whose charge against orders turned defeat into victory in the battle here described. The book grows out of a short article published in the Newark *Sunday Call*, December 29, 1912,—an article that attracted considerable attention, rather because of the novelty of the theory advanced than because of other merit.

It may be permissible to add that few persons,—comparatively,—conceive the bearing on the outcome of the Civil War, of the campaigns and battles that took place beyond the Alleghanies. There is more than one pretentious history, which would lead a reader to suppose that all of the events of importance took place upon the Atlantic seaboard. It does not diminish in the least either the merit or the renown of the armies that measured their strength in that confined arena to suggest that the movements that resulted in the transfer of the control over hundreds of thousands of square miles of territory,—

territory that teemed with the fruits of the earth,—was, taken in connection with the naval blockade, a very considerable factor in the wearing down and final collapse of the Southern Confederacy.

Newark, N. J., July 14, 1914   Wilson J. Vance

INTRODUCTION

On the banks of a shallow winding stream, traversing the region known as Middle Tennessee, on the last day of December, 1862, and on the first and second days of January, 1863, a great battle was fought,—a battle that marked the turning point of the Civil War. Stone's River, as the North designated it, or Murfreesboro,—to give it the Southern name,—has hitherto not been estimated at its true importance. To the people of the two sections it seemed at the time but another Shiloh,—horrifying, saddening, and bitterly disappointing. Its significance, likewise, has escaped almost all historians and military critics. But now the perspective of half a century gives it its proper place in the panorama of the great conflict.

Gettysburg, indeed, may have been the wound mortal of the Confederacy. But Gettysburg was, in very truth, a counsel of desperation, undertaken when the South was bleeding from many a vein. When Lee turned the faces of his veterans toward the fruitful fields of Pennsylvania, a wall of steel and fire encompassed his whole country. Warworn Virginia cried out for relief from the marchings of armies, that her people might raise the crops that would save them from starvation. Grant had at last established his lines around the fortress that dominated the Mississippi, and only by such a diversion, was there hope that his death-grip would be shaken. The day after Pickett's shattered columns had drifted back to Seminary Ridge Vicksburg was surrendered, and the control of the mighty river passed to the forces of the North.

But it was at Stone's River that the South was at the very pinnacle of confidence and warlike power; and it was here that she was halted and beaten back,—never again to exhibit such strength and menace. It was here that the tide of the Confederacy passed its flood, henceforth to recede; here that its sun crossed the meridian and began its journey to the twilight and the dark. Southern valour was manifested in splendid lustre on many a field thereafter, but the capacity for sustained aggression was gone. After Stone's River, the Southern soldier fought to repel rather than to drive his foe.

Yet Stone's River was almost a tale of triumph for the Confed-

39

eracy.

"God has granted us a happy New Year!" was the message flashed to Richmond at the close of the first day's fighting by General Braxton Bragg, Commander of the Army of the Tennessee. Two-thirds of the Army of the Cumberland had been hurled out of line, and now lay clinging with desperation to the only road from which it could secure supplies, or by which it could retreat, and to lose which meant destruction. There was reason, therefore, in the Southern general's exultation, as he waited for the morrow to give him complete success. He could not know that the army upon which had been inflicted so terrific a blow was to gather new strength out of the very magnitude of its disaster and to return such a counter-stroke as would give it the field and the victory. Neither could he see that his failure here meant failure for his cause; that because at Stone's River success had not crowned his efforts, his own magnificent army was to be pressed further and further from the territory it claimed as its own; that Fate had here entered the decree,—against which all appeals would fail,—for the preservation of the Federal Union and the death of the Confederate States of America.

Wilson J. Vance.

Chapter 1
North and South in 1862

Confederate enterprise, energy, and expectation were at the zenith in 1862. No other year saw the South with so promising prospects, with plans of campaign so bold, with such resources, both latent and developed. Her armies were at their fullest strength, for the flower of her youth had not yet been destroyed in battle. Want and hunger had not yet begun to chill the hearts of her people. Her political machinery, under the direction of able leaders, had been skilfully adjusted to the needs of the new nation and was now working smoothly and effectually. There had, indeed, come a change of sentiment in the Southland. That boastful and flatulent spirit,—the spirit that contemptuously slurred the strength and courage of the foe and counted upon an easy victory,—was gone. In its place was a temper far more formidable. The South realized now that before it was a task of greatest magnitude, but her people rose to it in a spirit of splendid sacrifice and with high, stern resolution.

The early part of the year, indeed, brought a series of reverses, particularly in the West,—reverses that would have seemed fatal to a cause, less resolutely supported. In January was fought the battle of Mill Springs, where Thomas, in routing the Confederate forces, achieved the first considerable Union success of the war. In February came Grant's capture of Forts Henry and Donelson, which not only yielded thousands of prisoners but left Middle Tennessee open to the invaders. The same month witnessed the opening of operations in North Carolina by Burnside, which resulted in the capture of Roanoke Island and (in March) of New Berne. Pea Ridge, fought in March, dashed Confederate hopes of Missouri,—for a season,—and the capture of New Madrid proved another heavy loss to the South, in men, guns, and munitions.

Early in April Fort Pulaski yielded to Gillmore, and McClellan's great army began its progress up the Peninsula, with Richmond as its announced goal. The siege-artillery of the Army of the Potomac was still thundering at Williamsburg, when, on May 6 and 7, was fought the bloody battle of Shiloh, in which the Confederates,—after a striking initial success,—were driven from the field by Grant and Buelll, with the death of their loved commander, Albert Sidney Johnston, to make more bitter their defeat. The echoes of Shiloh's guns had scarcely ceased, before Island No. 10, with many prisoners and supplies, fell to Pope, and the crowning Confederate disaster came on May 28, when Farragut received the surrender of New Orleans,—the commercial metropolis, the largest and wealthiest city, and the greatest seaport of the South.

But Confederate prestige, which had suffered sadly in these events, was speedily restored in fullest measure. While McClellan was toiling slowly up the Peninsula, Jackson was electrifying the whole South by his campaign in the Shenandoah Valley, where, with a small force, he neutralized armies aggregating 70,000 men, and terrorized the Federal capital. Kernstown, Front Royal, Winchester, Cross Keys, and Port Republic, are names that serve to recall some of the most brilliant exploits of the war.

His work in the valley accomplished, Jackson then slipped away in June to aid Lee in the battles around Richmond,—battles that were to culminate early in July in the retreat to Harrison's Landing and the reluctant and humiliating withdrawal from the Peninsula of the Army of the Potomac. While the withdrawal was still in progress, Lee fell upon the luckless Pope, and in the second Battle of Bull Run all but crushed his newly-constituted Army of Virginia. Then Lee gave the Northward road to his victorious legions, and early in September began the invasion of Maryland.

After the battle of Shiloh, the Confederate forces of the Middle West,—under Beauregard,—had retired to Corinth, Miss., which Halleck, at the head of more than 100,000 men,—having gathered together Grant's army, Buell's and all the other forces under his command,—approached with ridiculous caution. After a somewhat farcical siege, in which Beauregard played successfully for time, Corinth was suddenly and expeditiously evacuated, and the Confederate Army reappeared in a strong position at Tupelo, when, Beauregard having fallen ill, Bragg assumed command.

Halleck now divided his forces again, Buell,—at the head of what was now known as the Army of the Cumberland,—being sent into Middle Tennessee to begin a campaign long urged by President Lincoln for the relief of the Unionists in the eastern part of that State, and Grant being left in Mississippi, with somewhat widely-separated detachments, which ultimately he was to concentrate in the campaign for Vicksburg. The taking of Memphis (June 6) had already given the Union forces a foothold on the great river and domination over Western Tennessee. Halleck was summoned to Washington in July, to take command of all the armies in the field.

The dispersion of the Union forces in his front did not pass unnoticed by Bragg, who soon conceived and put into execution one of the boldest plans of campaign of the war. Early in June he began the shifting of his Army of the Tennessee to Chattanooga, where, in conjunction with Kirby Smith,—commanding a Confederate Army in East Tennessee,—he perfected his scheme of operation. The prelude of his campaign was exhibited in the form of extensive raids by Forrest's Cavalry and Morgan's, in which the Federal lines of communication were repeatedly cut, huge stores of supplies taken or destroyed, and several important posts captured. Early in August the heavy columns of Confederate infantry and artillery began pouring through the mountain passes into the coveted territory of Kentucky.

Bragg's invasion of Kentucky was thus practically simultaneous with Lee's invasion of Maryland; and the two movements caused the direst foreboding and dismay in the North. The war was coming very close to the people of that section when Confederate detachments appeared in the rear of Covington, in sight of Cincinnati, and when the chief Confederate Army crossed the Potomac into the Maryland that the Southern poets had already immortalized in song. Not the least of the objects of these two campaigns was the winning to the Confederate cause of the States invaded.

Nelson, with a small Union force, was badly beaten by Kirby Smith at Richmond, Ky., August 23, and Louisville experienced the agonies of a panic, for it was practically defenceless. Buelll had been so mystified by Bragg's movements that he did not start in pursuit until September 7, and even then might not have reached Louisville in time, had not the Confederate forces lost precious hours in taking Munfordville. But having reached that city, Buelll held the key to the situation, and Bragg was forced to retire,—which he did slowly and carefully. At Perryville a portion of Buelll's army and some of Bragg's troops met on October 8 in a fierce battle,—an engagement that will always be a source of mystery to students, in that neither side took advantage of obvious opportunities.

Bragg, in this campaign, failed of a major object, which was to rouse Kentucky for the Confederacy, though he went through the form of inaugurating a Provisional Governor at the State capital, Frankfort; but he did return South with long trains of fine horses and beeves, with wagons richly laden with food and clothing, and with almost enough recruits to offset the human wastage of his army on march and in battle. Moreover, at the close of the campaign he was in the possession of some territory heretofore held by Federal forces,—territory that was not yielded up until almost a year later.

The disorganization in and near Washington,—consequent upon Pope's defeat,—gave Lee an advantage which he improved by celerity of movement; and he was well into Maryland before a Union army was got together to oppose him. The command of this army was entrusted to McClellan, who exercised his customary super-caution, one result of which was that Harper's Ferry, with thousands of prisoners and great stores of military supplies, fell,—with scarce a struggle,—into Lee's hands. This very success might have been fatal to Lee,—for he had scattered his army to accomplish this and other objects,—but McClellan, though fully aware of the situation, moved too slowly, and the Southern general had time to concentrate on the banks of Antietam Creek. Here, on September 17, was fought one of the bloodiest battles of the war,—a battle in which the Confederate Army stood off a foe twice as strong in numbers, and at length retired at leisure, without further molestation. Like Bragg, Lee had failed to win the State that he had invaded, but though he had suffered tremendous losses, he had accomplished some important results.

The people of the North, it may be remarked without disparagement, were better informed as to the events of the war than were the people of the South. Their more thickly settled territory was abundantly supplied with telegraph lines and railways, and their numerous populous cities boasted many strong newspapers. Of these, not a few were hostile to the administration, which also had to contend with a well-organized opposing political party. To many persons in the North the campaigns of Lee and Bragg seemed conclusive proof that the Confederacy, after almost two years of fighting, was not only not weaker, but could at will practically carry the war into Northern territory.

Lincoln, accepting the check at Antietam as a victory, had (September 22) issued his preliminary Emancipation Proclamation, but the first effect of this was probably adverse, for the fall elections went almost uniformly against the President's party. The Nation's credit fell to a low ebb, and offerings of Government bonds found few takers, only $25,000,000 worth being sold during the year. Gold mounted to high and higher premiums, and general business,—despite the artificial stimulus incident to the production of war materials,—was dishearteningly poor.

Buelll, because of his failure to do more against Bragg, was relieved of the command of the Army of the Cumberland, which fell to Rosecrans, who had achieved success at Corinth, during the fall. McClellan, because of his failure to follow Lee after Antietam, was ordered to turn over the Command of the Army of the Potomac to Burnside. As the end of the year drew nigh, Rosecrans was established with his army at Nashville, and Bragg was at Murfreesboro, 30 miles south. The events of that season were well calculated to enthuse the Confederate and to depress the Federal force. On December 13 was fought the Battle of Fredericksburg, where the Army of the Potomac was repulsed, with frightful slaughter, by the Army of Northern Virginia, under Lee. A week later, the immense depot of supplies at Holly Springs,—supplies that Grant had gathered to aid him in his campaign against Vicksburg,—was captured. On December 29, Sherman, in a preliminary movement of this campaign, was hurled back, stunned and bleeding, from an assault upon Chickasaw Bluffs.

Two days later was to open the pivotal battle in Middle Tennessee.

CHAPTER 2
FOREIGN RELATIONS IN 1862

The outbreak of hostilities between the North and the South was greeted with obvious delight by the majority of public journals, and with thinly veiled satisfaction by many of the public officials of the more important nations of Europe. Russia, indeed, showed a substantial and potent friendship for the United States, and Italy,—where the movement for liberal institutions had already won important victories,—evinced a sympathy both general and genuine. But these were the exceptions. In Austria and the German States the hostile feeling for the American Republic had little effect at the time. The attitude of France and Great Britain was vastly more hurtful.

Napoleon III was then at the very height of his power, and his bizarre performances and dreams of conquest had dazzled the imagination of his countrymen to an extent that it is difficult to realize at this day. Nay, more,—he had cast such a spell over the minds of Her Britannic Majesty's ministers as to have led to a practical alliance upon certain important subjects. The French Emperor saw in the disruption of the United States a vindication of his own usurpation and an opportunity to plant an Imperial Government under his own guidance in Mexico. In addition, the shortage of cotton, due to the blockade of Southern ports, was causing very serious distress in the textile districts of France; so there was perhaps one real reason for the Emperor to show some concern in trans-Atlantic affairs, and repeatedly to proffer his unfriendly "friendly offices." However that may be, his suggestion of mediation and intervention did not fall upon deaf ears across the Channel, though, with characteristic caution, the British Government deferred action until its opportunity had passed.

French ill-opinion could have been borne,—even if it had taken the form of countenancing contracts for Confederate ships-of-war and winking at aid and comfort given to the cruisers of that unrecognized power. But British unfriendliness took a form that, short of actual war, could scarcely have done more to harm and exasperate the government and people of the United States. The recognition of the belligerency of the Confederates,—which (candour compels the statement) had much in logic and reason to justify it, however it may have savoured of technical irregularity—was but the least of the offendings.

In plain defiance of international law, splendid vessels were built in British yards for the purpose of sweeping the commerce of the United States from the seas; Confederate rifles and cannon were readily procured from British dealers; Confederate loans were floated by British bankers, and over-subscribed by the British public; the sale of shares in British blockade-runners to Confederate ports was an easy matter, as it appealed not only to the cupidity but to the prejudice of the purchaser. All grades of publications,—from the newspapers to the stately reviews,—teemed with abuse of Americans,—abuse written in almost inconceivable ferocity and malice. The humorous organ, *Punch*, did not check its "scurrile jester" in the drawing of most offensive cartoons of the President of the United States; practically the whole of the aristocracy was hostile; in all Parliament but one voice was raised for the North, and that was the voice of John Bright.

While the rancour and venom were expended upon the North, and while that section suffered solely from the violations of international law, it must not be supposed that the British press, patricians, and politicians were actuated by any genuine motives of good will to the South. Their hope and prayer were for the disruption and destruction of the Republic, in which the nobility recognized their most powerful,—however passive,—enemy; and the trading classes thought they saw the ruin of their commercial rival. There was, however, one great element in England that was stanchly on the side of the North throughout the whole conflict; and though it did not possess the franchise, this element was not without its influence.

The working classes of the kingdom were able to penetrate the mists that blinded their superiors in station, and they saw from the beginning that, whatever the ostensible purpose, the actual result of Northern triumph would be the end of slavery. It is at once a pathetic and magnificent fact, that no amount of specious argument, such as was frequently addressed to him, that no reflection upon his own sufferings, could win the Lancashire cottonspinner,—starving, because of the shortage in the great staple of his industry,—from the cause of human freedom.

It is, perhaps, too much to say that the British Ministry had always inclined to a recognition of the Confederacy. But as the war progressed and its desperate and extensive character began to be revealed, the project of some action tending to this end was frequently discussed in Downing Street. The British premier at this time was Lord Palmerston, and next in rank to him in the Cabinet was Lord John Russell, Secretary of State for Foreign Affairs. Practised and polished politicians both, they had been able to adjust their ambitions and predilections in this instance to mutual satisfaction. But a third member of the Ministry, the Chancellor of the Exchequer gave them both great concern. William Ewart Gladstone,—whose genius was then being revealed in full proportion to the English public,—was too able, too popular, and, above all, too formidable to be left out of the Coalition Cabinet. But it is well established that he was regarded with personal dislike and with professional jealousy by his veteran colleagues. This feeling of animosity was to lead to a most singular consequence,—one that had a grave bearing on American affairs.

The stopping by a United States warship of the Royal Mail Steamer *Trent* in November, 1861, and the removal therefrom of the Confederate envoys, Mason and Slidell, brought the two countries to the brink of war. Only the prompt, complete, and skilful disavowal of the American Government served to avert hostilities, preparations for which had already begun on the part of Great Britain. The temper and disposition of Her Majesty's Ministry were plainly shown in the truculent tone of the demand framed by Russell,—a paper that was adopted by the Cabinet, though Gladstone suggested some modifications. However, it would have been sent as written, had not the Queen, acting on the advice of the Prince Consort, insisted upon a modification of some of the more offensive phrases. Had it not been for this kindly and sagacious interposition of Queen Victoria, the situation might have gone beyond the power of the Lincoln Government to control.

The smothering of the *Trent* incident in the honey of diplomacy left the Ministry without an immediate and direct pretext for unfriendly action, but there remained a feeling of irritation and a tacit determination to do something when a proper opportunity should occur.

The Confederate successes in the summer of 1862 were convincing proofs to the British mind that the independence of the South was only a matter of time, and discussions of the subject were frequent at the Cabinet meetings. Those were anxious times for the American Minister, Charles Francis Adams, whose personal luggage was kept packed in anticipation of a sudden breach of diplomatic relations which would necessitate his departure from the Court of St. James.

Near the close of the summer, Gladstone wrote to his wife: "Lord Palmerston has come exactly to my mind about some early representations of a friendly kind to America, if we can get France and Russia to join." At about the same time he wrote to another correspondent: "My opinion is that it is vain, and wholly unsustained by precedent, to say that nothing shall be done until parties are desirous of it," and went on to repeat the former suggestion.

About two months later Palmerston wrote to Gladstone saying that he and Russell were agreed that an offer of mediation should be made by Britain, France, and Russia, and that the Ambassador at Paris was to be instructed to communicate with the French Government on the subject. "Of course," he added, "no actual step would be taken without the sanction of the Cabinet."

Lord Russell had but a few days previously written a letter to Palmerston, which had been shown to Gladstone, in which he said: "I agree with you that the time is come for offering mediation to the United States government with a view to the recognition of the independence of the Confederates. I agree further that, in case of failure, we ought ourselves to recognize the Confederate States as an independent State."

With the words of these two letters singing in his mind and mingling with the mental harmonies he himself had conceived, Mr. Gladstone went to Newcastle to partake of a banquet prepared for him by party admirers, and to utter on October 7, 1862, in the course of a general speech, a comment upon American affairs that was to vex him to the end of his life. Said he:

> We know quite well that the people of the North have not yet drunk of the cup,—they are still trying to hold it far from their lips,—which, all the rest of the world see, they, nevertheless, must drink of. We may have our own opinions about slavery; we may be for or against the South; but there is no doubt that Jefferson Davis and other leaders of the South have made an army; they are making, it appears, a navy; and they have made,—what is more than either,—they have made a nation. We may anticipate with certainty the success of the Southern States, so far as their separation from the North is concerned.

It is difficult to exaggerate the profound sensation that this passage in Gladstone's speech made in the United Kingdom, on the Continent, and in the United States. There was no escaping its significance. It meant that the British Government was on the point of recognizing the independence of the South, and such an act must have led to war between Great Britain and the United States. Aware of the sentiment that pervaded the Cabinet, Minister Adams had sought explicit instructions from the United States State Department, which instructions had come in unequivocal terms in a letter from Secretary Seward. Mr. Seward wrote:

If contrary to our expectations, the British Government, either alone or in combination with any other Government, should acknowledge the insurgents, while you are remaining without further instructions from this Government concerning that event, you will immediately suspend the exercise of your functions.... I have now, in behalf of the United States, and by the authority of their Chief Executive Magistrate, performed an important duty. Its possible consequences have been weighed and its solemnity is therefore felt and freely acknowledged. This duty has brought us to meet and confront the danger of a war with Great Britain and other States allied with the insurgents who are in arms for the overthrow of the American Union. You will perceive that we have approached the contemplation of that crisis with the caution that great reluctance has inspired. But I trust that you will also have perceived that the crisis has not appalled us.

Mr. Adams must have perused this letter many times as he waited for the meeting of the British Ministry,—which he learned had been called for October 23,—to act upon the question of the Civil War in America. Indeed, he had felt a strong impulse to call for his passports immediately after the Gladstone speech at Newcastle, but had concluded to wait a few days for formal action by the government to which he was accredited.

But now conditions and circumstances beyond the ken of diplomacy had conspired to put the inevitable moment indefinitely forward. Whether, as has been suggested, Gladstone, in his Newcastle speech, had intended to force his colleagues into a position the only outlet of which was recognition, or whether knowing their sentiments he had in mere exuberance let the cat out of the bag, he had committed a grave breach of official etiquette in thus speaking without express Cabinet sanction. It was a false move, upon which Palmerston and Russell seized with eagerness and,—it may be imagined,—private glee. Within a week Sir George Cornewall Lewis, a member of the Cabinet, made, at Palmerston's express direction, a public speech in which he adroitly gave the lie to Gladstone. The fateful Cabinet meeting of the 23rd was postponed, and a new proposal of Napoleon III that came at about this time,—a proposal looking to joint mediation or intervention,—was rejected, on the ground that the time was not yet ripe.

The British Ministry kept looking for the auspicious opportunity for several months thereafter. Many thought it had come in the middle of December, when the Fredericksburg disaster was described by the London *Times* correspondent as "a memorable day to the historian of the Decline and Fall of the American Republic." But on the last day of the year was begun the battle that was to show the British public,—what was sometimes forgotten,—that there were armies outside of Virginia and territories beyond the Alleghanies. Out of the mists which surrounded Stone's River,—out of the uncertainty due to counter-claims of victory by the rival commanders,—arose this definite fact: The Northern Army had occupied the town that it set out to take, and the Southern Army had retired almost to the borders of Tennessee and could not dispute the claim of its enemy to the greater part of the area of that Commonwealth.

Another postponement seemed necessary. By this time also the leaven of Lincoln's Emancipation Proclamation, which at first had been derided, was working in England; and, in their turn and time, Gettysburg and Vicksburg aided to produce a much-changed official atmosphere. The Foreign Minister who, against the law of the Kingdom, had let the *Alabama* and the *Florida* slip away to prey upon American commerce, was to strain that law a few months later to hold war-vessels that had been built for the South.

The danger to the Union from foreign sources had passed.

CHAPTER 3
THE ARMIES AND THEIR LEADERS

The armies that were soon to measure strength in Middle Tennessee were not strangers. They had raced with each other to the banks of the Ohio in the previous fall, they had confronted each other,—at times,—in fractional strength upon a score of fields. It was the advance division of the Army of the Ohio, which had checked the Confederate onset on the first day at Shiloh, where Grant was all but overwhelmed, and that command, in full strength, had done its share in driving the gray-clad battalions from the field the next day. The guarding of Middle Tennessee and the taking of East Tennessee had since then been its special charge and designed function, and in token thereof it had been named anew "the Army of the Cumberland," after the river that traverses those regions.

The army was composed principally of soldiers from the old Northwest Territory,—a region dedicated to human freedom in the ordinance of 1787. But while Ohio, Indiana, Illinois, Michigan, and

Wisconsin furnished the bulk of the troops, there were also regiments from Kentucky and several composed of East Tennessee Unionists. Pennsylvania had sent a contingent, and Missouri and Kansas were both represented. From the regular army of the United States, there were a formidable force of artillery, a few troops of cavalry, and a particularly fine brigade of infantry.

The Confederate Army of the Tennessee was composed largely of sons of the Commonwealth from which it derived its name, but almost every other State in the Confederacy was represented. A picturesque and romantic element was the famous "Orphan Brigade" composed of Kentuckians who fought for the South while their State adhered to the North, and who attested their heroism on many occasions during the war. The two armies were substantially equal in strength, for the Army of the Cumberland reported an available present of 43,400 men, while the Army of the Tennessee, which had the advantage of position, showed 37,700 ready for battle. The Southern Army was greatly superior in cavalry, for this arm of the service had not, as yet, received in the North the attention it warranted. On the other hand, the Northern Army was greatly superior in artillery. While the bulk of both armies was made up of veteran troops, each had considerable percentages of raw levies.

Gen. Braxton Bragg had the advantage,—somewhat doubtful in his case,—of long service with his Army of the Tennessee. He was a splendid organizer and disciplinarian, thoroughly versed in the technique of his profession, brave, honourable, devoted to his cause, and a strategist of no mean order. But he united a high, imperious temper and a saturnine disposition with a martinet's passion for the letter of military regulation and etiquette. As a consequence, he was frequently embroiled with those near him in stations of authority,—officers who did not hesitate to accuse him of finding convenient scapegoats for his own errors. His controversies with those under him form an interesting chapter of Confederate records. It is but just to him to add that there were those that fought under him who testified to warm admiration for his soldierly abilities and who entertained high personal esteem for his qualities as a man.

Bragg's army was divided into two corps. One of these corps was commanded by Lieutenant-General William J. Hardee, who had won a conspicuous position in the Army of the United States before he had come to offer his sword and talents to the Confederacy. He was the author of a book of tactics employed in the United States Army long after the Civil War,—a system said to have been founded on the drill regulations devised by Napoleon. The other corps was commanded by Lieut.-Gen, Leonidas Polk, who was Bragg's pet aversion, and who spent much of the next twelve months in writing to Richmond about his superior and extricating himself from the latter's orders of arrest.

General Polk had been educated at West Point, but had afterward entered the Episcopal Ministry. When the war broke out he was Bishop of Louisiana; but he speedily exchanged the surplice for the uniform, and attained high rank in the Southern Army. He was a man of considerable warlike talent, though perhaps short of first-grade.

One of Bragg's division commanders was Major-General John C. Breckinridge, of Kentucky, who, as Vice-President of the United States, had declared the count of the electoral vote whereby Lincoln was chosen President, and who had left his seat in the United States Senate,—months after the outbreak of hostilities,—to cast his fortunes with the South. Afterward, as Confederate Secretary of War, he accompanied Jefferson Davis on his flight from Richmond, and assisted Gen. Joseph E. Johnston in arranging the terms for the surrender of the latter's army to William T. Sherman,—terms that were repudiated by the Washington authorities.

Other notable figures in Bragg's army were the impetuous Gen. "Pat" Cleburne, who was to lose his life in the wild charge on the fortifications of Franklin two years later; Gen. John H. Morgan, the Kentucky partisan raider, and Gen. Joseph Wheeler, the cavalry leader, who had so managed the rear-guard in the retreat from Kentucky as to preserve intact the rich booty of the "Blue Grass" region borne by the retiring Confederates. Wheeler was one of the Southern generals who later saw service under the "old flag" in the Spanish-American war, commanding a division in Shafter's Army before Santiago.

Maj.-Gen. William S. Rosecrans was one of the contradictions of the war. A graduate of West Point, he had resigned from the army and was practising his profession of engineering, when the outbreak of hostilities called him to arms again. He had achieved considerable success in 1861, when, having taken up a work left unfinished by McClellan, he cleared the Confederates out of West Virginia, thereby placing in temporary eclipse the military reputation of Robert E. Lee. His assignment to the command of the Army of the Cumberland was chiefly due to his defence of Corinth during the fall, though he was criticised by Grant,—then his immediate superior,—for not having achieved greater results in this engagement. As a strategist Rosecrans was of the first order; indeed, one of his campaigns still stands as a model for the study of professional soldiers. But brave, warm-hearted, and impulsive, he was prone to lose his poise in battle, as the melancholy outcome of Chickamauga was later to prove.

Rosecrans had divided his army into right wing, centre and left wing,—for convenience designated as corps. The centre was commanded by Maj.-Gen. George H. Thomas, the idol of the army, and probably the most complete soldier that the Union produced. It was said of him that he never made a mistake. At Mill Springs he had given the Union cause its first generous beam of hope by his crushing defeat of Zollicoffer. In the recent campaign in Kentucky it was his soldierly instinct that had penetrated the plans of the enemy; his counsel, which followed, led to success,—which disregarded, led to failure. It was he who below Chattanooga was to gather around him the fragments of a broken army, the commander of which had fled the field, and fighting on, was to win lasting fame as the "Rock of Chickamauga." It was he who, at Nashville,—waiting amid a storm of criticism, abuse, and threats from those higher in authority,—sallied forth, when all was ready, to win the most complete victory of the four years' struggle.

The right wing of the Army of the Cumberland was under command of Maj.-Gen. Alexander McDowell McCook, a native of Ohio, and one of the "Fighting McCooks," so-called, because so many of his family fought for the Union. The left wing was commanded by Maj.-Gen. Thomas L. Crittenden, scion of a noted Kentucky family, which, with great liberality and rare impartiality, contributed stalwart representatives to both sides of the war. Among the division commanders was Philip H. Sheridan, who later was to defeat Early in the Valley of the Shenandoah, and, by throwing his columns across the line of Lee's retreat from Richmond, was to furnish the prelude for the final scenes of the war drama at Appamatox.

Nashville, the capital of Tennessee, had, after the Battle of Shiloh, been occupied as a secondary base by the Army of the Cumberland, and had been heavily fortified. Distant 150 miles from Louisville,—the primary base,—with lines of communication frequently interrupted by the ubiquitous Morgan and other Confederate raiders, it was difficult to accumulate sufficient supplies for a campaigning army; but by December ample stores were in hand. Murfreesboro, where the headquarters of the Army of the Tennessee had been established, was an important military and strategic place as it was the converging point of a large number of unusually good wagon-roads and by reason of its location on the Nashville and Chattanooga Railroad. Its facilities gave it dominance over a wide stretch of country, rich in supplies and recruits for the Confederates, and its possession was the first requisite in that movement for the relief of East Tennessee and its harassed Unionists,—a movement that had been so constantly urged by President Lincoln upon the Federal commanders in that region.

The hearts of those in authority in the Confederate Government never beat so high with hope as during those December days of 1862. Mr. Davis and his Cabinet, as they surveyed the situation, might well have felt that they had reason for confidence. The principal army of the Northern foe had been repeatedly and seriously defeated, and was about to suffer the awful reverse of Fredericksburg. In Tennessee and Mississippi,—while fortune had not been so uniformly kindly,— there were all the facilities, resources, and spirit for successful aggressive work. While much ground had been lost in the Trans-Mississippi Department, word had lately come that Hindman had succeeded in raising a fresh army in Arkansas,—a force that was expected to begin the task of redeeming that State and recovering Missouri. Pemberton confronted Grant with temporarily superior forces near Vicksburg. Confederate diplomatic efforts were at length promising to bear fruit, and the *Alabama* and other vessels were driving Northern commerce from the high seas. New Orleans had fallen; but Mobile, Charleston, Wilmington, and Savannah held out, to offer refuge for the blockade runners, which brought the precious military stores into the South.

It was under the spell of sentiment, inspired by such conditions, that the Confederate President paid a visit to his generals and their forces in Tennessee and Mississippi. Bragg felt so certain of himself and his ground that he readily fell in with the suggestion of Mr. Davis to detach some 10,000 troops to Pemberton, though Gen. Joseph E. Johnston, who was in command of the whole department, advised against this course. The presence of their President roused the enthusiasm of the soldiers at Murfreesboro to a high pitch, and many official and social ceremonies served to vary the festivities planned for the Christmas season. There were balls, receptions, theatrical entertainments, and one evening, in the presence of a brilliant throng, General Morgan took unto himself a wife,—the ceremony being performed by Bishop-General Polk,—and immediately left for Kentucky on another of the raids that did so much to harass, impede, and annoy the Union armies.

Rosecrans had learned of the detachment to Pemberton, of Morgan's departure, and also had been informed that Wheeler had been sent on a raid. He rightly concluded that the time to strike Bragg was when the Confederate cavalry was absent, and his three corps set out from Nashville on separate roads the day after Christmas. It soon developed that, if Wheeler had been ordered away, he had been recalled; for his troopers gave ample notice of the advance of the Union Army, and Bragg had plenty of opportunity to perfect a plan of resistance.

Thomas and Crittenden, however, encountered little difficulty on the march. McCook found Hardee in his path, and had to do some heavy skirmishing before he got up. But the evening of December 30 saw the Army of the Cumberland in position about three miles from Murfreesboro. In some way Rosecrans got the impression that Bragg had fallen back, and gave orders for entering the town. In the darkness some of Crittenden's troops began a movement,—a movement that must have resulted disastrously, if pushed; and shots had already been exchanged with the Confederate pickets, when the mistake was discovered and the order recalled. Though it had rained for several days, and though the night was bitter cold, the men of the left and centre were forbidden to light fires,—even for cooking,—lest they might betray their whereabouts. But fires were kindled all along the front of McCook's corps and far to the right thereof; for Rosecrans hoped to deceive Bragg as to his exact position. It may be conjectured that this hope was illusive, for Bragg had exceedingly accurate sources of information.

Each commander decided to attack on the morrow. Rosecrans planned to deliver battle from his left flank, crumpling up the right of his enemy, and taking up the attack with his centre in such a way as to enfilade and crush Bragg's entire army. McCook was instructed to resist strongly, but not to attack, except by way of diversion.

The position taken by McCook's corps had given Rosecrans much concern, and the night before the battle, at a conference with his principal officers, he had made several suggestions about it to the Ohio warrior. In conformity with the order of battle, McCook's right was strongly refused,—that is, bent back,—but, in general it was too near where the enemy were supposed to be to suit the commanding general. McCook, however, evinced such reluctance about giving up ground for which his men had already fought,—and which presented elements of natural strength that were not to be found further back,— that the matter was at length left to his own judgment. He, therefore, placed the bulk of his corps in conformity with the rest of the army, which was aligned upon a north-and-south line, threw back the right brigades of Willich and Kirk,—of Johnson's division,—so that they, with their artillery supports, faced almost directly south, and placed, as a reserve, in the corner thus formed Baldwin's brigade of the same division.

The rest of the battle front, while presenting in general an eastern face on a north-and-south line, was here advanced, here retired, as inequalities of ground or patches of forest seemed to offer favourable position. The whole Union Army was west of Stone's River, though the extreme left of Crittenden's left wing touched that stream at a ford.

Bragg's plan of battle called for a heavy concentration of force on his left flank, which was to take the initiative in an attack upon the Union right, and by a grand wheel, with the centre as a base, would take the invaders in flank and rear. Each unit was to take up the movement as the battle reached it, and it was hoped that by a rapid, spirited, and sustained attack it would be possible to force Rosecrans back of the Nashville pike,—his sole line of supply and retreat,—and hurling his commands one upon the other, accomplish the capture or destruction of the whole Union Army. In furtherance of his plan, Bragg placed almost two-fifths of his infantry at his left under Hardee, to whom was entrusted the initiation of the movement. But one division was left, under Breckenridge on the right, and separated from the rest of the army by the river.

The Confederate battle front,—could it have been viewed in its entirety,—would have presented a much more symmetrical appearance than that of its adversary; as the comparatively open and level country that it momentarily occupied permitted a more orderly alignment. McCown's division occupied the extreme left,—except for some cavalry,—and Cleburne's heavy columns were massed almost immediately in the rear.

Thus, it will be observed, the rival commanders had, with practically similar conditions to encounter, hit upon practically similar plans of battle. Could each plan have been carried out, the two armies would have presented the appearance of revolving upon a common axis, the right in each case retiring before the attack of the enemy's left. As it was, however, a great advantage,—as must be apparent,—was to attend that army which should first strike the enemy with its heavy masses in battle array. And the contingencies of the conflict ordained that that advantage should be gained by the Confederates.

CHAPTER 4
THE FIRST DAY'S BATTLE

Crittenden's corps on the left of the Army of the Cumberland,—which had been selected by Rosecrans to make the initial move in the fight,—was separated from Breckenridge's entrenched division, on Bragg's right, by two miles of distance and Stone's River, which in that immediate vicinity could be crossed at only one ford. Between the heavily-massed regiments on Bragg's left flank and Mc-Cook's corps, to the contrary, there were only a few hundred yards. Therefore, though McCown,—who had moved in the night,—found some difficulty in adjusting his line to suit Hardee's taste, the Confederates had ample time to strike the first blow. A dense fog shielded the movement from the Union pickets. McCown's troops swung off in a semi-oblique direction, leaving an ever-widening interval between him and Withers's division, of Polk's corps, into which at the proper instant Cleburne slipped. In a few moments the crackling of rifle-fire heralded the opening of the battle.

That the brigades on the extreme right of the Union Army were surprised upon that fateful morning has been repeatedly denied; but it is certain that they were not properly prepared for the storm that was about to burst upon them. August Willich was actually away from his command, and his men were at breakfast, with their arms stacked. The captain of the battery that was posted at the left of the brigade had sent his horses off to water, so little did he dream of impending danger. The men of the other brigade were scarcely,—if any,—better prepared, and upon them fell the brunt of the first assault.

Right on the heels of the pickets, whose shots were of little apparent effect, appeared a long line of gray-clad infantry that extended far beyond either flank of the hapless Union brigades. The advancing troops fired as they came, and many Northern soldiers were shot down before they could grasp their arms. General Kirk sent a vain summons to Willich for aid, and fell mortally hurt in an heroic effort to form his men. Old Willich himself, spurring in hot haste to rejoin his command, rode straight into the enemy's line. This scion of a royal house,—for he was reputed to be the natural son of William of Prussia,—had several months in a Southern prison in which to reflect upon whatever error he may have committed that morning. The two brigades did not flee without an effort at resistance;[Pg 46] indeed, both offered obstinate opposition for as long a time as possible, but they could not hold out against two divisions, of four brigades each.

Kirk lost 500 killed and wounded, and 350 captured; while Willich's loss was more than 400 killed and wounded, and about 700 captured. They were soon in headlong flight.

With the dispersion of these troops, but one brigade, of Johnson's division,—the reserve under Baldwin,—was left intact; and now the next division was threatened on the flank. With quick soldierly instinct the commander, Jefferson C. Davis, drew back his right brigade, under Post, and made other dispositions to co-operate with Baldwin. He had scarcely had time to complete these preparations, ere both Baldwin and Post were struck. At the same moment the Confederate grand wheel having got into full swing, two brigades of Withers's division, of Polk's corps, hurled themselves against Davis's two remaining brigades,—Carlin's and Woodruff's,—and against Sill's brigade of Sheridan's division, adjoining Davis on the left.

Here the Confederates met a check. Baldwin, it is true, had to retreat shortly, to escape being taken in right and rear; but Post repulsed an attack upon his front, and Carlin, Woodruff, and Sill threw back their assailants so violently that Polk ordered up his reserves. A second attack met the same fate, though General Sill was killed between the guns of a battery that he was directing. For the third time the gray infantry advanced to the fight, which now involved the whole of Sheridan's division. In frontal attack they were held, but one Union command after another had to retire, to avoid capture under flank attacks. Thus Sheridan's division was dislodged, as had been Johnson's and Davis's.

Up to this juncture the working out of Bragg's plan had fully equalled, if not exceeded, the expectations of the Southern commander. The whole right wing of the Union army had been hurled from position, and some of the commands composing it had been driven for miles. Thousands of Union prisoners and great stores of small arms had been captured, together with many pieces of artillery, which could not be hauled back in the headlong retreat over the rough ground and through the clumps of cedar in which the battlefield abounded. In its further development, or swing, the grand wheel was now threatening the Union centre, and the exultant Confederates entered with confidence upon another distinct stage of the fighting. If the right could be driven still further, or the centre pierced, the Nashville pike would fall into the possession of the Army of the Tennessee, which would then have at its mercy practically the whole Army of the Cumberland. But,—though the prize seemed so near,—it now became evident that new conditions were to be encountered, and that the contest was about to enter upon a new phase.

Confident in the belief that his right wing could and would resist any movement against it, Rosecrans had gone early in the morning to Crittenden's corps, to witness the initiation of his carefully conceived plan. It was 8 o'clock before the leading brigade of Van Cleve's division waded Stone's River at the near-by ford, and began climbing the hill on the other side, with a view to attacking Breckinridge. For a couple of hours firing had been heard on the right, but it gave no uneasiness to the Union commander, who believed that the instructions of the night before were being obeyed. Even when a message from McCook, asking aid in somewhat formal terms, came, Rosecrans was not disturbed, but sent back word that the right must be held.

It was not until two of Van Cleve's brigades had crossed the stream, and the third was making ready, that a frantic message gave Rosecrans an idea of the disaster that had befallen part of his army. And as he gave hurried orders, the crowds of fugitives,—cowards, skulkers, the slightly wounded, and brave men who had fought until beaten,—that began to stream through the woods brought confirmation of the evil tidings.

Rosecrans instantly recalled Van Cleve's division. One brigade,— Fyffe's,—that had not yet crossed, he hurried straight out on the Nashville pike, where his instinct told him the greatest danger lay, and where at that moment the enemy's cavalry was reaping rich spoil from the long wagon trains. The men of Beatty's brigade were sent, dripping with the water of Stone's River, right into the heart of the battle, which now raged almost in the rear of the centre. The third brigade,—Price's,—was held to guard the ford. The demonstration of this division against Breckenridge, though so quickly abandoned, had important effects on that general as well as on the fortunes of the day.

It was the supreme test for Rosecrans, and whatever his previous faults may have been, he now bore himself well. He hurried up ammunition, which was much needed at many points; directed the formation of new lines and the posting of fresh batteries; and whenever the emergency permitted, he took himself to the battle front, where his presence served to reanimate his sorely-beset soldiers. In spurring from one part of the field to another, his aide-de-camp and much-loved companion, Lieut.-Col. Julius P. Garesche, was beheaded by a cannon ball, and his blood sprinkled the uniform of his commander. But battles give scant time for mourning, and Rosecrans, without delay, ordered the further disintegration of Crittenden's corps, that re-enforcements might be sent where needed. Harker, of Wood's division, was hurried after Beatty,—to the right of Rosecrans's division of Thomas's corps,—while Hascall's brigade was held as a mobile body, under the eye of General Wood himself.

Upon Thomas now fell a burden of tremendous weight. He had early perceived the displacement of Sheridan, and had sent two brigades of Rosseau's division to re-enforce that commander and support his right. Then he turned to face one of the most dangerous and furious efforts made by the foe during the whole day. Hardee, with his whole force, was moving to take Sheridan in flank and in the rear; Cheatham, of Polk's corps, was advancing against Sheridan in front, and Withers was preparing to leap upon Negley. To give way here would be fatal, for back of Thomas and of what was left of the right wing Rosecrans was hastily arranging a new battle-line to hold the Nashville Pike.

The commander of the centre seemed ubiquitous. Though his charger never broke out of the slow pace that had given its master the nickname of "Old Trot," Thomas was apparently in all places at once,—now directing the firing to repulse a charge, now placing a regiment in line, and again marking a point to which his troops must retire and take up the fight anew.

The Confederate infantry now pressed forward in a frenzy of enthusiasm. The piercing "rebel yell" rose triumphantly above the roar of cannon and the bark of musketry, and many regiments pressed clear to the borders of the cedars in which the Union troops were posted, before they had to retire from a merciless fire.

Again and again Hardee and Cheatham brought their men to the charge. The exigencies of the battle twisted the Union line into strange shapes. Here a brigade was in a half-circle with a concave side to the enemy; another presented a convex front to attack. Miller's brigade of Negley's division was like a triangle without the base, and, aided by splendid artillery service, repulsed simultaneously assaults in front and on both sides. But many trains having been captured or swept away, Sheridan's men found themselves out of ammunition, and his division was withdrawn, leaving Negley's right and Rosseau's left "in the air." Into the interval poured the Confederate columns. Thomas was compelled to withdraw his two divisions to an improvised line, and

Negley and Rosseau reluctantly faced the rear.

The firing had been so heavy in these divisions that the cartridge-boxes of dead and wounded had been robbed for the precious ammunition. Rosseau made the movement under fire, but, reaching Thomas's temporary line, turned and delivered such a blast from rifles and artillery as threw back the pursuing enemy and left the field covered with bodies.

Shepherd's brigade of regulars especially distinguished itself here; for, firing by platoon from flank to flank,—as steadily as though at drill,—it cut down the enemy in front as a scythe mows grain, and drove away a greatly superior force, losing in a few minutes one-third of its whole number. Negley's division was almost surrounded, and had to cut its way,—sometimes at the point of the bayonet,—through the Confederates, who had reached its rear. In the movement this division had to abandon six guns.

Palmer's division, which was already fiercely engaged, was now in the greatest peril, as Negley's retirement left an unprotected flank. On the right Cruft's brigade was almost surrounded while repulsing a frontal attack; but Grose's brigade, held in reserve, changed front to the rear and cleared a way. Hazen, at the apex of what was known as the "Round Forest," met repeated heavy attacks, but, owing to superior position and artillery support, was able to hold his own, though losing heavily. As Palmer retired, his division established connection with the right and faced the enemy with renewed confidence.

The grand wheel had now traversed the full quarter of a circle. It had been carried out with remarkable consistency and with remarkable speed and power. Every command in Bragg's army, with the exception of his reserve, had felt the impulse of the great manoeuvre, had taken a place therein, in regular order, and, at first glance, it would have seemed with complete success. For the entire Union army, with the exception of a small part of the left wing, had been forced from position. Its battle-front, instead of facing squarely east, now faced south, and its curving line was in place behind the Nashville Pike,—its only avenue of safety,—which in some instances was in plain sight of the enemy and within reach of his artillery and musketry.

But though Rosecrans had lost heavily in men, guns, horses, and ammunition, Bragg had not escaped without cost. Some of his splendid brigades mustered but half of the strength with which they had begun the battle, and almost all the men were so exhausted as to be unable to go further. Moreover, they faced an army of men,—

men who disliked being beaten, who occupied an elevated position of great strength, who had secured fresh stores of ammunition, who, acutely conscious of their danger, were resolved not to yield further, and who actually, here and there, showed a disposition to make reprisals upon their valiant foe.

But Bragg had not entirely exhausted his resources. The Union left lay temptingly near him, and, if he could crush or turn it, the rest of Rosecran's army might still be his. Fresh troops were needed for such an attempt, but the five brigades of Breckinridge's division were at hand and they were summoned for the final effort. Breckenridge had been asked for re-enforcements early in the day, but he had seen Van Cleve's big division start in his direction, and, apparently, had not seen it return when it was sent flying to arrest the rout of McCook's corps. He had also been ordered to meet some re-enforcements, which Bragg had thought were coming to Rosecrans, but which did not appear; and consequently, had kept his division intact. Now he detached the brigades of Adams and Jackson, which, dashing through the river, threw themselves impetuously upon the Union forces in the "Round Forest." Upon Hazen's sorely-tried troops the brunt of the assault fell, but, using the railroad embankment as a protection, they managed to hold on. Soon Adams and Jackson turned back, shattered beyond further use.

Now Breckinridge in person led to the assault the brigades of Preston and Palmer; but Hazen was now aided by whatever regiments, battalions, and odds and ends of troops could be spared to him. Preston and Palmer were not only driven back, but they left some prisoners as a result of a countercharge by a Union regiment.

Here ended the first day's battle.

Chapter 5
The Night and the Next Day

The dusk of the short winter's day had already come on when the last desperate charges of the Confederate hosts were repelled. As though by common consent, the firing ceased almost simultaneously on both sides, and a period of comparative calm succeeded the storm of battle.

Never was a cessation of strife more welcome than to the two armies. The Army of the Cumberland had been so riven and torn during the struggle as to bear scarcely any resemblance to the compact organization of the morning. Divisions had been swept away from the rest of their corps, brigades had been torn away from divisions, regiments from brigades, and even battalions and companies from regiments. It was in very truth an improvised battle-line,—the line that had clung to the Nashville Pike during the closing hours of the engagement. A vast number of individual soldiers,—not by any means all skulkers, but, in many cases, men who had become separated from their own commands and had done valiant service wherever opportunity offered, with or without orders,—were wandering about back of the Union lines, seeking the camp-fires of their comrades.

To restore a semblance of order and alignment was the first task of officers,—great and small,—and it was hours before this could be accomplished in part. It was the intention of Rosecrans to forbid fires, for fear of drawing attacks from the enemy; but before any order could be issued, they were lighted all along the line, and the exhausted troops got an opportunity to boil coffee and toast bacon before sinking down to sleep.

On the Confederate side there was less confusion. The Army of the Tennessee,—though clearly fought out for the time being,—had preserved far more of the autonomy of its several commands, and as the camp-fires were kindled along its battle front, the impression was universal that the fight would be renewed on the morrow. Bragg himself was in a state of exultation, for though his cherished plan had not yet been carried out, he felt that success had merely been deferred.

There was a council of the principal Federal officers during the night at the commanding general's headquarters. Rosecrans, it is said, had in mind a retirement of a few miles to Overall's Creek, but this was given up when it was pointed out that the new position was scarcely as strong as the one now held, and offered few advantages. Then somebody suggested the question of retreat. There is a tradition to the effect that Thomas had fallen into a doze during the talking, but that he woke up when this unpleasant word was uttered.

"Retreat!" he exclaimed,—so the story goes,—"This army can't retreat!"

This assurance seemed to satisfy the timid ones, and the question was dropped forthwith.

New Year's Day, 1863, dawned clear and cold. During the night every effort had been made to strengthen the Union position, and to good effect; for Bragg had a cloud of skirmishers out with the dawn, and all day they searched the line in every part, at times being aided by the artillery. But not a crevice could be found, and the Confederate manoeuvres at no time developed into movements of importance. But Wheeler's Cavalry found plenty to do, and its capture of a wagon-train caused the liveliest rumours of disaster among the garrison that had been left at Nashville.

Despite, however, the activity of the horsemen of the enemy, Rosecrans managed to get through the lines a considerable store of rations, ammunition, and other supplies. So the day ended with the situation much as it had been when the day began, except that the soldiers on both sides had had an opportunity to restore themselves after the intense fatigue of the first day's fight, and that order had been evolved out of the chaos into which the Army of the Cumberland had been thrown.

One change in the situation,—at the time regarded as of little account, but which was to have momentous results,—had been made. During the day Rosecrans gave some scrutiny to Breckinridge's division of the Army of the Tennessee, which had retired to its original position on Bragg's right. As this force was posted, it was too far away to be watched closely, and Rosecrans, as a precautionary measure, directed Crittenden to throw Van Cleve's division, now under Gen. Samuel Beatty (for its own white-haired commander had been wounded), together with Grosse's brigade, across the ford to a position in Breckenridge's front. The movement, which had for its purpose little more than observation, was accomplished without interference on the afternoon of January 1, 1863.

CHAPTER 6
THE SECOND OF JANUARY, 1863

For the greater part of the next day the two armies, merely rested on their arms. With food and rest, the feeling of confidence, which had been somewhat shaken in the Union Army, began to revive, and the soldiers exhibited a cheerful tone. The Confederate forces, however, showed a contrary spirit. There was deep chagrin in all ranks, because the work that had been so bravely begun was not resumed and carried to a triumphant end; while criticisms of the general commanding began to be exchanged with freedom among the officers highest in rank. There is no doubt that this gossip reached Bragg's ears and that he was stung to the quick by it. It is possible, too, that it led him to order the movement that resulted in the final scene of the battle.

During his repeated examinations of the field, Bragg had noticed the Union detachment that had been thrown across the river in Breckinridge's front, and he now determined to dislodge it. In his official reports he lets it be understood that he merely wanted to drive away a force that was posted in an advantageous position for observation and that might, if re-enforced, be able to make a dangerous attack upon his army,—for it could enfilade his whole line. But, if dislodgement were all that was intended, it is hard to understand why Bragg should have organized such a heavy column for a slight task. It may well be suspected that the Confederate Commander saw an opportunity to crush the Union left and, in the confusion necessarily ensuing, to drive the whole Federal Army from the field in rout.

Bragg gave to Breckinridge 10,000 of his best fighting men, including 2,000 cavalry and ample supports of artillery. At the head of this formidable column, Breckenridge descended upon the Union troops in his immediate front, at 4 p. m., January 2. The blow fell with the swiftness and force of a hurricane. Both Van Cleve's division and Grosse's brigade had lost heavily in the previous fighting, and their ranks were too thin to offer effectual resistance. A few volleys of musketry and a few rounds of artillery were fired, and then they broke and fled to the ford, closely pursued by the yelling Confederate host.

By a singular chance, not a single Union general officer was near this part of the field at the time. They were, in fact, around the centre and right, against which Bragg, as a ruse, had opened a heavy artillery fire. The brigade nearest the ford was under the command of John F. Miller, a young Indiana colonel, who had not yet received his stars. It was apparent to him that Breckenridge's charge, unless checked, would result disastrously to the army; and he broached the subject of a countercharge to an officer of like grade of another brigade. He was assured of support. Miller sent an orderly to find some general officer to authorize the movement, and drew up his men in readiness. He had barely 1,500 with which he might hope to check 10,000, flushed with victory. In a few moments the crisis was at hand, and Miller was still awaiting orders. His brigade opened ranks to let through the fugitives, and then Miller, placing himself at the head of his men, spurred his horse into the water. He was in mid-stream, when the orderly returned with the news that General Palmer, the only general officer to be found, had forbidden the movement.

"It is too late now," replied Miller, and drawing his sword, he gave the order to charge.

The very audacity of this step was its success. It is probable that the Confederates believed Miller to be leading an overwhelming force, for they stopped, fired a few shots, and then began to retreat. With fixed bayonets, Miller's men pursued, and now, with quick perception of the opportunity, other Union commands joined in the charge. Perhaps a half mile had been traversed when the Confederates showed signs of rallying. But as their lines were halted and rearranged, the missiles of death from half a hundred cannon,—drawn hastily together by Major Mendenhall, Crittenden's chief of artillery, and posted on a hill which commanded the whole field,—suddenly fell among them. They fled again, leaving on the ground 2,000 dead and wounded,—the fruit of an action of less than an hour.

This ended the battle of Stone's River. For another twenty-four hours the two armies confronted each other with no fight of importance. During the night of January 3, Bragg retreated unmolested. He reported having received information that Rosecrans was being re-enforced, but in this again he may be suspected of a euphemism. As a matter of fact, the retreat had been advised at a council of his principal generals, two of whom,—Withers and Cheatham,—united in the blunt statement over their own signatures that he had only three reliable divisions left and that these were, to a certain extent, demoralized. Most of his officers also assured him, with equal frankness, that he ought to give up the command of the army,—advice that he did not heed; and Polk, for writing to this effect to the Confederate President, was placed under arrest; but he was afterward released.

CHAPTER 7
WHAT MIGHT HAVE BEEN,—AND WHAT WAS

The Battle of Stone's River produced profound disappointment both in the North and in the South. Claimed as a victory by both sides, the first fruits fell to the Army of the Cumberland, which had not only held the field but had compelled the retirement of its adversary and the relinquishment by the latter of strategic positions and domination over considerable areas. But as the weeks passed without developments of other striking results, the Northern people felt that the victory had been little more than technical, and that the battle was another of the practically indecisive contests so frequent at that period.

On the other hand, the Southern people were mortified and chagrined at a defeat suffered when their cause was prospering in almost all other quarters. They were not more given to analyzing strategic and tactical features than their Northern enemies, but they were able to realize that their second army in size and importance had lost thousands of soldiers, and that it has been driven out of Middle Tennessee, and away from the vicinity of the State capital, the recovery of which had always been a cherished object of their hearts. The opposition to Bragg, both in and out of the Army of the Tennessee, became intensified from the time the retirement from Murfreesboro was ordered.

It was perhaps natural that the outcome was thus viewed in the two sections, for it is in the light of what it might have been,—rather than what it was,—that Stone's River must be judged. Union victory upon that field did not, it is true, reveal results of transcendent importance, but Confederate victory,—at one time so near,—would have been followed by the weightiest and most far-reaching consequences. Had Bragg been able to drive his infantry across the Nashville pike on the last day of 1862, or had he been able to crush the Union left on the second of January, 1863, the capture or destruction,—whole or partial,—of his enemy would have been one of the least of these consequences. For the way to the Ohio would then have been open, and Cincinnati and other opulent Northern cities would have been at the mercy of Confederate arms. Vicksburg would not have been an historic name, for overwhelming forces could have been turned against Grant to crush him, or drive him from Mississippi. Tennessee,—second State in population below Mason and Dixon's line, and first in such food as armies consume,—would have been held to furnish the vital recruits and supplies to the Confederacy. East Tennessee would have waited in vain for the relieving Northern forces. Kentucky and Missouri might have been wrested from Union control, and Arkansas freed from the presence of the invader. Finally, Europe's recognition, with the manifold complexities for the North that must have ensued therefrom, could have been no longer logically denied to the Richmond government.

After Stone's River, Bragg's battered battalions retired 30 to 40 miles away,—to the line of Duck Diver,—and there maintained an attitude of defiance for 6 months. It took that period for Rosecrans to restore the ravages of battle in his army. Wheeler, Morgan, and Forrest,—the cavalry chieftains,—meanwhile, kept up a series of raids upon Rosecrans's long line of communications,—raids that sorely tried that commander, pestered as he was by constant injunctions from Washington to move forward. But in June, 1863, having at length accumulated sufficient supplies, the Army of the Cumberland started the campaign that was to drive the Army of the Tennessee out of the

State from which it took its name. Then came another halt; but in September the Union forces again advanced and the Confederates again retired.

At Chickamauga the Army of the Tennessee, reinforced by Long-street and Buckner, turned, and, inflicting a bloody defeat upon the Army of the Cumberland, locked it up in the fastness of Chattanooga. But Bragg was unable to gather substantial fruits from his victory. At Missionary Ridge, in December, the Army of the Cumberland led in the movement that broke the battle-front of its historic adversary. Thenceforth the Army of the Tennessee,—fighting bravely at every turn,—was obliged by the weight of opposing numbers to retire further and further into the South.

At Resaca, at Dalton, at Kenesaw Mountain, at Atlanta, and at a score of other places it showed the qualities of valour and endurance that had already won it deserved renown. But it never looked to the North again until the latter days of 1864, when Hood summoned it for its last great adventure,—that desperate leap past Sherman, which was to end in utter rout before the ramparts of Nashville.

The Army of the Cumberland lost in the Stone's River campaign 1,730 killed, 7,802 wounded, 3,717 captured and missing; a total of 13,249.

The Army of the Tennessee lost 1,294 killed, 7,945 wounded, 1,027 captured or missing; a total of 10,266.

APPENDIX

Notes to Introduction

"In the second half of this year (1862) the Confederates failed to gain control of Maryland and Kentucky, but made head strongly and at the end of it were at the height of their power, with the North badly defeated at all points save one. The writer considers that the battle of Stone's River, or Murfreesboro, on December 31st, was the military turning-point of the war, though the Confederates made various strokes at different times for political purposes, which, had they succeeded, might have attained their end, the chief of which was the campaign of Gettysburg. From a purely military point of view, however, nothing could save the Confederacy unless the results of Stone's River were undone. The year 1863 opened with the Confederates fought out; they had made their effort but could not maintain it, and had failed to secure the centre of the strategical line which was vital for both sides."—*The American Civil War*, Formby; London, John Murray, 1910.

Notes to Chapter 2

"...That my opinion was founded upon a false estimate of the facts was the very least part of my fault. I did not perceive the gross impropriety of such an utterance from a cabinet minister, of a power united in blood and language, and bound to loyal neutrality; the case being further exaggerated by the fact that we were already, so to speak, under indictment before the world, for not—as was alleged—having strictly enforced the laws of neutrality in the matter of the cruisers. My offence was indeed only a mistake, but one of incredible grossness, and with such consequences of offence and alarm attached to it, that my failing to perceive them justly exposed me to very severe blame...."—Gladstonian fragment, *Life of Gladstone*, Morley; New York. The Macmillan Company, 1911.

Notes to Chapter 3

"Further to mislead the enemy as to the point from which the attack was to be made, long lines of camp-fires were started on McCook's right and commands given by staff-officers to imaginary regiments in tones loud enough to be heard by the enemy's skirmishers, to induce the Confederates to think that our line extended much further to the right than it actually did. I have always doubted whether Bragg was misled or deceived by this subterfuge; and not unlikely he considered it a confession of weakness on our right and formed his own plans accordingly."—*The Murfreesboro Campaign*, Otis; Boston. Papers of the Military Historical Society of Massachusetts, Vol. 7, 1908.

Notes to Chapter 6

"At this juncture, Colonel John F. Miller, followed by a portion of Stanley's brigade, charged with his brigade across the river. Disregarding an order from a general officer, not his immediate commander, to desist from so hazardous an adventure, he dashed over and fell furiously upon the foe, already in rapid retreat. The right of Miller's line was supported by the Eighteenth Ohio, and portions of the Thirty-seventh Indiana and Seventy-eighth Pennsylvania, of Stanley's Brigade. Moving on the opposite bank, his left, was Grose's brigade, which had changed front and resisted the enemy, when Price and Grider gave ground, and in his rear were Hazen's brigade and portions of Beatly's division. Miller reached a battery in position and, charging with the Seventy-eighth Pennsylvania, Sixty-ninth and Seventy-fourth Ohio, and Nineteenth Illinois, the Twenty-first Ohio, striking opportunely on the left, captured four guns and the colours of the Twenty-sixth Tennessee Regiment. . . ."—*History of the Army of the Cumberland*, Van Home; Cincinnati, Robert Clarke & Co., 1875.

"Miller sent his staff officers and orderlies, Lieutenant (afterward Brigadier-General) Henry Chiney, Lieutenant Ayers, and Major A. B. Bonnaffin (I repeat that I am writing now what I saw with my own eyes and heard with my own ears) to scour the field and ask permission to cross the stream to Van Cleve's relief. Only one such officer could be found, General John M. Palmer (of Illinois) and from him came instead of the desired permission a positive prohibition—an order not to cross. The other two brigade commanders, belonging to the division, General Spear of Tennessee and Colonel T. R. Stanley, of the Eighteenth Ohio, were not present. General Negley, the division commander, was not to be found. . . .

"Miller found himself the ranking officer present with the division and realized that the decision fraught with so much importance lay with him. He was surrounded by a group of regimental commanders who alternately studied the field and his face.... He turned to the officers around him saying quietly:

"'I will charge them.'

"'And I'll follow you,' exclaimed the gallant Scott, wheeling and plunging his spurs into his steed to hasten back to his regiment (the Nineteenth Illinois). Colonel Stoughton of the Eleventh Michigan and other regimental commanders belonging to the Twenty-ninth brigade echoed Scott's enthusiastic adherence and they, too, started for their troops."—*God's War*, Vance. London, New York. F. Tennyson Neely, 1899.

The Third Day at Stone's River

BY GILBERT KNIFFIN

While the heroic commander of the Union Army, with fearless confidence in his remaining troops, was hurling the hard-hitting brigades of the left and centre upon Hardee's victorious advance during the first day of the fight at Stones River, kindling anew the dying embers of hope in the breasts of the retreating soldiers of the right, and by his exalted courage snatching victory from the jaws of defeat; while Thomas calm and brave, with perfect presence of mind, superintended every move in the desperate game of battle, watchful of every point, a tower of strength to his devoted men, and Crittenden, more cheerful than usual in the hell of carnage that raged along his front, brought regiment after regiment and battery after battery in support of the point where Hazen, and Hascall, and Grose, and Cruft were clinging tenaciously to their position, and beating back the desperate charges of Polk and Breckinridge, the cavalry were performing prodigies of valour in the rear and on the right.

General Wheeler, on his return from his exploits at La Verne, to the rear of Hardee's line on the morning of the 31st, found that the battle had opened. He immediately joined in the pursuit of Johnson's retiring division, while Wharton, in command of ten regiments of cavalry, and a battery of artillery, moved over towards the Nashville pike and turned his attention to the immense supply train of the army. A portion of this train, six miles long when stretched out upon the road, was moving across the country from the Wilkinson to the Nashville pike. The scene was one of the most indescribable confusion. Urged by impending calamity the canvas-covered wagons flew across the fields with the velocity of four-mule power, each driver plying whip and spur; sutler wagons bounding over the rocks, distributed their precious contents along the way. Stanley's thin line of cavalry, stretching from the woods in the rear of Negley to the right and left, rested its right flank upon the Wilkinson pike, where Colonel Zahm, with the First, Third, and Fourth Ohio Cavalry was stationed in rear of Overall's Creek.

Colonel Minty, in command of 950 cavalry, crossed Overall's Creek early in the morning and took position parallel to and a mile distant from the Nashville pike. The Fourth Michigan and First Tennessee dismounted, formed a skirmish line with Jenning's Battalion of the Seventh Pennsylvania and two companies of the Third Kentucky, under Captain Davis, supported by the Anderson Troop in their rear. Wharton advanced at full charge, after a few volleys from his artillery, but meeting with stubborn resistance drew off, but in a few minutes rallied and bore down, two thousand strong, upon Minty's little command. The Anderson Troop gave way and the Confederate troopers swept past the left. Hastily remounting, the remainder of the command fell back across an open field out of range of the artillery, leaving the train, with fully a thousand fugitives from the battle-field, in possession of the enemy.

At daybreak Zahm's brigade was drawn up in line of battle and two squadrons were sent to the right and front to reconnoitre. Soon the cannons' opening roar upon his left announced the beginning of battle. The rush of infantry to the rear gave token of disaster. Now came the exultant shout of victory and the sweeping charge of McCown's columns overlapping Johnson, and appearing on the right of the cavalry. Falling back, Zahm formed in line of battle a mile in rear, where the enemy opened upon him with artillery The first shell killed Major Moore, of the First Ohio. Again he fell back, when Willich's old regiment halted in its retreat and formed in support of the cavalry, when the two repulsed a charge, but only for a moment. The torrent of fugitives fled through the woods like leaves before the blast, and after them pressed the charging regiments of Ector and Raines' Confederate cavalry in resistless volume.

Meanwhile, Wharton's Cavalry Brigade was moving rapidly past Colonel Zahm's right, and the Confederate infantry pushing by his left at a distance of two hundred yards. An aide to General McCook came requesting succour for the supply train moving over toward the Nashville pike. Col. Gates P. Thruston, one of McCook's aides, gave a graphic picture of the capture and recapture of the precious supply train. "McCook's baggage train, starting for the rear, was soon in the hands of the enemy; our supply trains shared the same fate. Gen. Joe Wheeler's command appeared in rear of our flank on the Murfreesboro pike, and all soon became excitement and confusion there. Wharton, after a succession of captures, charged over the fields in rear far down toward our infantry lines, sweeping everything before him. By Rosecrans' orders Stanley's Cavalry hastened to the rescue. There was a succession of conflicts over a wide field, with varying fortunes. The whole area in rear between our right and left was a scene of strife and confusion that beggars description. Stragglers from the front, teamsters, couriers, negro servants, hospital attendants, ambulances added to the turmoil. Wounded and riderless horses and cattle, wild with fright, rushed frantically over the field.

While in the open ground, moving our ammunition train rapidly to the left, it was discovered by the enemy. In my anxiety for its safety I had already reported the importance of the train to every cavalry officer within reach, and appealed for protection. Colonel Zahm, of the Second Ohio Cavalry as he states in his report (official record), promised me all possible help, and promptly formed his regiment in line for that purpose. Major Pugh, of the Fourth Ohio Cavalry, at my request also placed his regiment on our flank, facing the enemy. The First Ohio and the Second East Tennessee and a battalion of the Third Ohio Cavalry were near at hand.

Alas, when the crisis came a few minutes later they were not in position to successfully withstand the shock. They were unprepared, and not in brigade line. Wharton's Confederates unexpectedly appeared in great force. His artillery opened fire furiously upon the Fourth Ohio Cavalry, and threw the regiment into some confusion. Soon apparently his entire command charged down upon us like a tempest, his troopers yelling like a lot of devils. They first struck the Fourth Ohio, which could make but little resistance. Col. Minor Millikin, the gallant commander of the First Ohio, led a portion of his regiment in a brilliant counter charge, but had to retire with fearful losses. In the onslaught the dear, fearless colonel, my intimate college friend, engaged in single combat with a Texas Ranger, and was slain.

There was no staying the Confederates. They outnumbered and outflanked us, and, to tell the melancholy truth, our defending cavalry finally retired in confusion to the rear and left the ammunition train to its fate—high and dry in a corn field. As may be imagined, our teamsters, the train guards, and the ordnance officer (yes, I must admit it), were not left far behind in the general stampede. We fired one volley from behind the protection of our wagons and then hunted cover in the rear of a friendly fence and in the nearest thicket. Our teamsters outran the cavalry. Most of them never reappeared. The Confederates began to collect and lead away our teams and wagons, and our condition seemed desperate, indeed, hopeless.

Happily, this appalling state of affairs did not last long. Some of our cavalry rallied, other Union detachments came to the rescue. Wharton had soon to look to his own flanks, and was kept too busy to carry off our train. The conflict fortunately shifted. Capt. Elmer Otis, with six companies of the Fourth Regular Cavalry, attacked Wharton's command with great vigour and success. Soon two battalions of the Third Ohio Cavalry came up from the rear. I hastened to appeal to the commander to aid our train guard in saving the train, and he at once covered our front and held the enemy in check until our badly-wrecked train, with its disabled wagons and scattered animals was reorganized and put in moving order. We repaired and patched up the breaks. Everybody, even officers and stragglers helped, and nearly every wagon was finally recovered.

The third attack referred to by General Thruston came from a force that Wharton had not yet met. Before they had time to take advantage of their success, Kennett was upon them. Col. Eli H. Murray, at the head of his gallant regiment, the Third Kentucky, charged down upon the train, sweeping Wharton's cavalry before him. Here the brave Captain Wolfley, with eighty men, and Captain Breathitt, with his battalion, charged with such velocity as to turn the tide of battle, driving the rear forward upon the front, where the Fourth Cavalry struck it with drawn sabres. The rout of the Confederates was complete. The entire train, with 250 prisoners, were recaptured. The hospital of Palmer's division, which had fallen into their hands, as well as the Fifth Wisconsin Battery, and one section of the First Ohio, were recaptured, and Wharton's Brigade routed and driven back two miles. The Third Ohio easily rallied and took part in the fray.

Captain Otis' sabre charge was brilliantly executed. Dashing forward with the velocity of a locomotive, the trained battalions fell upon the undisciplined mob huddled together at the head of the train where Murray had swept them in his irresistible onslaught. The train was moved close up in the rear of the left wing, where it remained unmolested during the remainder of the day. In a battle such as that at

Stones River, where a long line of troops is engaged simultaneously, it is impossible to give due credit to each regiment that deserves it. The writer witnessed scenes of personal daring which to recount would occupy the night in the description. There were many instances in which officers, casting aside their swords, seized the muskets of their fallen soldiers, and fought side by side with their men. Entire companies fought without officers. In great emergencies such as this there is positively no rank except that which valour bestows. Orders to fall back were in several cases unheeded, and the men held their places in line under the leaden hail, obstinately refusing to retreat. It was not merely a line of battle, but a Nation in arms, repelling, with a Nation's pride, this bold assault of its rebellious sons upon its life.

Darkness covered the battle-field. The roar of artillery, the rattle of musketry, the hoarse shouts of command had ceased, and in the silence that followed there fell upon the ears of the soldiers on picket the groans of men in mortal agony lying within the space that separated the lines. In rear of the pickets men sank upon the ground where they stood and shivered through the night without fires, for the faintest flash of light on either side became a target for alert artillerists. A cup of hot coffee, that *Dominus donari* to the weary soldier, on this night of all nights when he needed it most, was denied him. All through the night the ambulances passed to and fro on the road to the hospitals, where further torture awaited the wounded, unless the angel of death kindly relieved them of the ministrations of the surgeons.

A space twenty yards in front of the White House, near Overall's Creek, was covered with the mangled forms of men awaiting their turn upon the operating tables. Inside were groups of surgeons with sleeves rolled up to the elbows, their brawny arms red with blood, one handling the saw, another the knife, another the probe, while others bound up the bleeding stumps and turned the patient, henceforth the Nation's ward, over to nurses, who bore them tenderly away. In a corner lay a ghastly heap of arms and legs and hands and feet, useless forevermore. The busy fingers which had indited the last fond message to the anxious wife or mother would never caress them more. Does this horrible recital grate upon the ear? It is as much a part of the history of a battle as is the furious charge and repulse from which it resulted. Forty years have passed since that awful scene was witnessed. The stalwart young men left upon the firing line are old men now, and, in the judgment of some chiefs of bureaus, too old to longer serve the Government.

The writer, returning from a ride along the lines, where he had been under orders to see that all fires were extinguished, came upon a regular battery, in the rear of which, at the bottom of a trench of glowing coals, the artillerists were cooking supper. The savoury smell of broiling steak and steaming pots of coffee saluted his nostrils. Dismounting, he was at once invited to partake of a soldier's hospitality. His tired horse was fed, and in a moment he received at the hands of a grizzly veteran a cup of coffee and a cake of hard bread, covered with juicy steak, tender and succulent. His meal dispatched, he was about to remount and ride back to headquarters, when he was asked if he knew where the steak came from. He said he did not, but that it was the best he ever ate. "Come here, and I will show you," said the sergeant. He led the way a few yards distant where an artillery horse lay dead, killed by a cannon ball. His flank had been stripped of the skin, and the tender, juicy steak that had contributed to the enjoyment of the writer had been cut from the flesh.

At army headquarters a strange scene, revealing the characteristics of the prominent commanding officers, was presented. With prudent regard for the safety of his supplies, General Rosecrans had ordered the subsistence train back to Nashville, thus enabling him to manoeuvre his army without regard to front or rear. There was no indication that Bragg contemplated withdrawal, and the prevailing impression was that a heavy assault would be made upon some point of the Union line early in the morning. Where would the blow fall? Would the line at that point be strong enough to resist it? Has Bragg any troops that have not been engaged? Are reinforcements for him on the way? were questions more easily asked than answered.

Mounting his horse, the commanding general rode to the rear, accompanied by General Stanley and a few staff officers. Past the hospital, to Overall's Creek, the group of horsemen pursued their way. In the fields on both sides of the road the darkness was dispelled by bivouac fires lighted by the straggling soldiery of the right wing. Along the pike the long supply train moved slowly and steadily toward Nashville, while here and there a few wagons were cut out of it by a faithful commissary, the contents of which, after a hard night's work, he would succeed in transferring to the soldiers' haversacks.

Walker's and Starkweather's brigades had already passed to the front, where the former bivouacked in close column in reserve in rear of McCook's left, and the latter, posted on the left of Sheridan, next morning relieved Van Cleve's division, now commanded by Col.

Sam Beatty, which resumed its position in the left wing. Generals Van Cleve and Wood, each suffering from wounds in the foot, were sent in ambulances back to Nashville.

Headquarters were located in a double log house, which then stood on the east side of the turnpike about opposite the lower ford of Stones River. In a room on the left hand, General Thomas sat before a fire, asleep; the officers of his staff, stretched upon the floor, with their feet to the fire, were also asleep. Ready at a moment's warning to obey any order that might be given him, the old soldier was snatching a brief respite from care, in the friendly arms of Morpheus. To a question of General Rosecrans, earlier in the evening, he had made the characteristic reply: "The question of retiring from the battlefield is one of such delicacy that I am quite willing to leave it to the judgment of the commanding general."

On the right of the passageway a far different scene was presented. General Crittenden paced the floor with quick, impatient stride. "Communication is cut off," said one. "We must fall back," said another, and the words were deliberately uttered by a brave man. "My corps is not whipped," shouted Crittenden, "and we must not fall back." At this moment General Rosecrans entered the room and caught the expression as it fell from the lips of his heroic commander. "Gentlemen, we fight or die right here," said the chief as he passed them and took a seat by the fire.

The sun of the New Year rose bright and fair; an occasional gun gave token of the proximity of the two contending armies. During the night Rosecrans retired his left to a more advantageous position, the extreme left resting on Stones River above the lower ford and extending to Stokes' Battery, posted on a knoll on Rousseau's right. Beatty's division was posted across Stones River on the margin of the woodland that covered a gentle slope from the river to an open field in their front. Across the field, the Lebanon road, running nearly at right angles with the front of Beatty's line, was nearly in sight. Off to their right and front an elevation still held by Hanson's Brigade of Breckinridge's division, was crowned by Cobb's Battery of Artillery. The Confederate line, formed by Polk and Breckinridge on the right and Hardee on the left, extended from the point on Stones River where Chalmer's Brigade had bivouacked since the 28th, in a direction almost at right angles with its original line.

The body of the brave General Sill was found where it had fallen, and sent to Murfreesboro, where it was buried. At dawn on the 1st of

January the right flank of General Polk was advanced to occupy the ground vacated by the left flank of the Union Army. Neither commander deemed it advisable to attack, but each was watchful of every movement of the other. The picket lines of either side were thrust forward within sight of the main lines of the opposing force, on the alert to notify their commanders of any movement in their front. As two gladiators of equal strength, who, having fought until nature is exhausted, stretch their herculean forms upon the earth, each confident that his antagonist is as unable as himself to renew the contest, rise when refreshed and glare upon each other, watchful for advantage, so were these contending armies, drawn up in firm array, weaker in numerical strength, but more compact and infinitely stronger in indomitable will, on the morning of the New Year, each awaiting the order to advance and close in a final struggle. It was the crouching of tigers before the death grapple.

The rest afforded the weary troops of both armies, many of whom were smarting with wounds which were not sufficiently serious to render their removal to the hospital necessary, fell with the grace of a benediction upon the scene of strife. As the ponderous bells of a great city, at stated periods, rising above the hum of traffic fill the air with the uproar of deep, sonorous strokes, and smaller ones fill with their clangour the intervals of sound, so did the artillery ever and anon break upon the silence with sullen roar, while the sharp rattle of picket firing, now on the right, then on the left, recall the terrible strife of yesterday and foretell the impending conflict.

Night came, and the contending hosts sank to rest in the mud, upon their arms, in the rear of the stout picket lines, lulled to sleep by the booming of an occasional gun or the report of an exploding shell. The sun arose upon the second morning of the new year and glowed pleasantly upon Union and Confederate alike. The exercises of the day commenced as usual by picket firing along the lines, and was followed by an artillery duel between Estepp's Battery of Wood's division and Scott's Battery of Cheatham's division, in front of the Round Forrest, in which Estepp was worsted. Bradley took up the gauntlet and was fast getting the best of it when one of the batteries in his rear undertook to throw grape over his head, when he was forced to retire.

Reinforcements now came to both sides and a spirited contest ensued. Stokes, Loomis, and Guenther each in succession took part in the fight, which was confined exclusively to artillery. Robertson's Battery of Wither's division, from its position near the Burnt Brick House, and

Semple's Battery on the left, had accurate range of the Union batteries, and their guns were handled with skill. But the artillery fire soon ceased. Chalmer's Brigade had advanced early on New Year's morning, and his skirmishers now occupied the ground which Hazen had so stubbornly contended for on the first day of the battle. Price's Brigade, which assumed its position in Van Cleve's division, now commanded by Col. Samuel Beatty, was on the right of the division.

The line as thus formed was at right angles with the river, upon which its right flank rested, and nearly parallel to Breckinridge's original line. Below the right of the line the river suddenly changes direction, flowing about a half a mile in rear and nearly parallel with the line. The gently sloping ground was woodland on the right and open field on the left.

To strengthen the left flank, Colonel Grose's Brigade of Palmer's division, reduced by hard fighting on the 31st to 1,000 effectives, was ordered by General Crittenden to cross the river on the morning of the 2nd of January. These dispositions were barely completed and temporary breastworks constructed when, at four o'clock, a magnificent sight presented itself. General Bragg confidently expected to find the Union Army gone from his front on the morning of the 2nd of January. His cavalry had reported the Nashville pike full of troops and wagons moving toward Nashville. On the return of the cavalry expedition he sent Wharton to assume command of the cavalry on the Lebanon road, consisting of his own and Pegram's Brigade, while Wheeler, with his brigade, returned to the vicinity of the Nashville pike to observe the movements of the Union Army in that direction.

Before Wharton had taken his position, the force east of Stones River had attracted Bragg's attention, and reconnaissances by staff officers revealed the line of battle formed by Beatty's division and Grose's Brigade. From the position occupied by this force, Polk's line, which, it will be remembered, had advanced as far as the position vacated by Rosecrans' left on the night of the 31st, was enfiladed. Bragg says: "The dislodgement of this force, or the withdrawal of Polk's line, was an evident necessity. The latter involved consequences not to be entertained. Orders were accordingly given for the concentration of the whole of General Breckinridge's division in front of the position to be taken, the addition to his command of ten Napoleon guns (12-pounders), under Captain Robertson, an able and accomplished artillery officer, and for the cavalry forces of Wharton and Pegram to join in the attack on his right."

General Breckinridge was sent for and the object of the movement explained to him. He was ordered to drive the Union line back,
crown the hill, entrench the artillery, and hold the position. General Breckinridge was opposed to the attack as ordered by General
Bragg, and tried to dissuade him from it, predicting disaster, as the
ground occupied by the main portion of the Union troops on the
bluff on the opposite bank of the river was considerably higher than
that over which the attacking force must march, and it was possible
for Rosecrans to mass artillery and sweep the whole field. In urging
his opinions he drew, with a stick, on the ground the position of the
contending forces.

Considerable time was occupied in the discussion, but Bragg remained firm, and finally ended the discussion by an imperative command to move at once to the attack. As General Breckinridge rode
forward to his command he met General Preston, commanding his
Third Brigade, and said: "This attack is made against my judgment
and by the special orders of General Bragg. Of course we must all do
our duty and fight the best we can. If it should result in disaster, and I
be among the slain, I want you to do justice to my memory, and tell
the people that I believed this movement to be very unwise, and that
I tried to prevent it."

To distract the attention from the real point of attack a heavy artillery fire was ordered to be opened from Polk's front at the exact hour
at which the movement was to begin. At other points along both lines
all was quiet, and at half-past three General Breckinridge reported that
he would advance at four o'clock. The effective strength of Breckinridge's division on the morning of the 31st was 7,053. Adding two
batteries and deducting 730 men disabled in the three brigades of
Palmer, Preston, and Adams, in the assault of the 31st in front of the
Round Forrest, left 6,576 infantry and artillery, 3,000 cavalry, and sev-
en batteries of artillery with which to make the attack. Hanson's fine
brigade of Kentuckians, who had signalized their valour at Shiloh and
Baton Rouge, 1,000 strong, had up to this time been disengaged.

The movement of Breckinridge's command was observed by General Crittenden from the bluff on the opposite bank of Stones River,
above the lower ford, from the moment that the advance commenced.
To reach Beatty's line it was necessary to cross an open space six or
seven hundred yards in width, with a gentle ascent, in full view from
the opposite shore, as well as from the front line of Beatty's division. In
the assault that followed a brief cannonade, Hanson's left was thrown

forward close to the river bank, with guns loaded and bayonets fixed, under orders to fire once, then charge with the bayonet.

This charge of General Breckinridge will live in the memories of those who witnessed it, coupled in precision of formation, in rapidity of movement, and in grandeur of execution, if not in results, with the charge of the armies of the Cumberland and Tennessee at Mission Ridge, the storming of Lookout Mountain by Geary's division of Hooker's Corps, and the no less thrilling spectacle in front of Kenesaw, when the brave and lamented Harker and McCook, with 2,000 men, were launched against a fortified position, bristling with artillery, between the two contending armies. On the right of Price's Brigade the Eighth Kentucky, commanded by Lieutenant-Colonel May, received the first attack, made by Colonel Lewis' Sixth Kentucky, Confederate, followed in quick succession by a charge from Hanson's and Pillow's Brigades; then in successive strokes from right to left the blows fell all along Beatty's line.

Overborne by the numerical strength of the Confederate brigades, the gallant men of this veteran division, 2,500 strong fighting bravely, were hammered back by overwhelming force. For full ten minutes they stood in line, pouring a galling fire upon the oncoming line, which, leaving its course marked by the writhing forms of its fallen braves, pressed forward, overlapping the right, where they were met by Lieutenant-Colonel Evans with the reserves of the Twenty-first Kentucky, and by Colonel Swayne, with the Ninety-ninth Ohio. These regiments, changing front to the right, held their ground firmly and administered volley after volley upon the skirmishers of the Confederate Sixth Kentucky, who pushed forward toward the ford. The front line falling back, followed rapidly by the entire Confederate line, loading as they retired, and turning to fire upon their assailants, became intermingled with the reserves, when, in a confused mass, assailants and assailed, fighting hand to hand, moved in a resistless volume toward the river.

The reserve regiments, the Ninth Kentucky, Lieutenant-Colonel Cram; Nineteenth Ohio, Lieutenant-Colonel Manderson, and the Eleventh Kentucky, Major Mottley, undaunted by the disaster upon the right, advanced through a thick undergrowth of wild briars, and came suddenly upon Adam's and Preston's Brigades, which, driving Fyffe's Brigade and the Seventy-ninth Indiana before them, were moving with rapid strides toward Grose's position on the extreme left. Meanwhile the brigades of Hanson and Pillow had gained positions to their right and the movement toward the ford threatened to cut these regiments still remaining on the left off from retreat.

At Colonel Manderson's suggestion, Colonel Grider now ordered his brigade to fall back to the river. Colonel Grider, bearing his regimental flag in his hand, rallied his brigade three times in succession while retiring, and checked the advance of the Confederate line by volleys of musketry. The pursuit of Beatty's three brigades led the Confederate columns to the right of Grose, and as soon as it could be done with safety Livingston opened upon the advance with his artillery, but in obedience to an order from General Rosecrans crossed the river and reopened from the opposite shore.

The space between the river bank and the ridge occupied by Grose's Brigade was now a scene of the wildest disorder. Instances of the most exalted courage were displayed. It was here that Corporal Hochersmith, colour guard of the Twenty-first Kentucky, and Sergeant Gunn, of the same regiment, won the gold medals voted them by the legislature of their native State. When confronted by a squad of Lewis' skirmishers, who demanded his flag, the brave corporal said: "You can take me but not my colours," and threw the flag over their heads into the river, where it was seized by Sergeant Gunn and borne in safety through a shower of balls to the opposite shore, where the regiment immediately rallied around it.

It may well be understood that General Crittenden, under whose observation his old division had been driven from its position back across the river, was by no means an uninterested spectator of the scene. It had all passed so rapidly as to afford no time to reinforce the line when first assaulted, and when it had commenced falling back the west side of the river was evidently the best position to reform and reinforce it. His men had no sooner gained the low ground near the river than, turning to his chief of artillery, he said: "Now, Mendenhall, you must cover my men with your cannon." Never was a more tremendous response to so simple a request.

In his report, Captain Mendenhall says:

Captain Swallow had already opened with his battery. I ordered Lieutenant Parsons to move a little forward and open with his guns, then rode back to bring up Lieutenant Estepp with his Eighth Indiana Battery. Meeting Captain Morton, with his brigade of Pioneers, he asked for advice, and I told him to move briskly forward with his brigade and send his battery to the crest of the hill near the batteries already engaged. The Eighth

Indiana Battery took position on the right of Lieutenant Parsons. Seeing that Lieutenant Osborne was in position between Parsons and Estepp, I rode to Lieutenant Stevens, Twenty-sixth Pennsylvania Battery, and ordered him to change front to the left and open fire; then to Captain Standart, and directed him to move to the left with his guns, and he took position covering the ford.

I found that Captain Bradley had anticipated my wishes, and had changed front to fire to the left, and opened upon the enemy. This battery was near the railroad. Lieutenant Livingston crossed the river and opened fire again. During this terrible encounter, of little more than an hour in duration, forty-three pieces belonging to the left wing; the 'Board of Trade' Battery, and nine guns from General Negley's division—fifty-eight pieces of artillery—played upon the enemy.

The effect of the storm of iron that swept the front of these batteries is indescribable. It tore through the mass of men as they swarmed down the slope, mowing down scores at each discharge. Not less than one hundred shots per minute were fired with unerring aim. Branches of trees, lopped off by cannon balls, pinioned men to the earth. For a few minutes they held their ground; then a wild terror seized upon them and bore them away. General Hanson fell among the first. His brigade lost over 400 in killed and wounded; the loss in the division was 1,400. There was no thought now of attacking Grose; there was but one thought paramount in the hearts of all, and that was to get to a place of safety. They no sooner turned than Beatty's men were upon them, pouring in volley after volley upon the retreating enemy. Hazen's Brigade crossed further down the stream; Jeff C. Davis on his left, Miller and Morton at the ford, and moving rapidly forward the line swept up the slope.

The artillery fire ceased, and the minnie rifles, taking up the refrain continued it until darkness closed the scene. Three guns of Wright's Battery, abandoned by Breckinridge, to whose division it belonged, stood upon the crest of the hill. The horses, killed by the tempest of iron that had fallen here, lay heaped together; the gunners, mangled by exploded shells, dotted the ground around the battery. As the Union line pressed forward on each side a boy clad in Confederate gray (Private Wright), mounted upon one of the guns, stood guard over the wreck. Swinging a hatchet above his head he shouted: "The first Yankee that touches one of these guns dies." Saluting him with a rousing cheer the line pressed on, leaving this second Cassabianca master of the situation.

Although the Confederate forces, yielding to the irresistible logic of Mendenhall's guns, had considered not so much upon the order of going as upon its rapidity, until beyond the range of the artillery, many of them rallied behind Robinson's Battery and Anderson's Brigade in the narrow skirt of timber, from which they emerged to the assault. The Union line advanced and took position upon the ground from which Beatty had been driven an hour before. The picket lines of both armies occupied opposite sides of the open field, over which Breckinridge had advanced, and darkness covered the battle-field. During the night General Cleburne moved his division over to its original position on the right, in support of Breckinridge, and General Hardee resumed command of that portion of the line.

Apprehending the possible success of a flank attack upon his left, Bragg had caused all the tents and baggage to be loaded on wagons and sent to the rear. On Saturday morning, the 3rd of January, the soldiers of both armies had been in battle for four days and nights; their provisions, if cooked at all, were scanty and unfit to eat; their clothing soaked with rain and stiff with mud, with no fires to dry them and to warm their chilled bodies, they had responded with a will to every command. With death beckoning them to his clammy embrace they had advanced with unfaltering tread, leaving their trail marked by the dead forms of their comrades.

Even now there was no word of complaint. It rested with the generals in command of the contending armies whether another holocaust of lives should be offered before either would acknowledge himself vanquished. No thought of retreat had at any time entered the minds of Rosecrans, Thomas, or Crittenden. With one exception, neither of the division commanders in the centre or on the left wings had favoured it. McCook, after his bloody repulse on the 31st, had advised falling back upon Nashville upon purely military grounds, but had readily acquiesced in the decision of the commanding general to "fight or die right here." The fugitives in his command who had not pursued their shameless way to Nashville had rallied to their standards and were anxious to restore their tarnished laurels.

The losses during the three days of battle were nearly evenly divided. General Bragg acknowledged a loss of 9,000 in killed and wounded, 25 per cent of his army of 38,250, while General Rosecrans' report shows a loss of 8,778, over 20 per cent of killed and wounded of his force of 43,400. It is impossible to do full justice to the heroic constancy of the soldiers of the Union, whose valour wrung victory from defeat on the morning of the 31st of December, and who all through that terrible day bared their breasts to the storm of battle. To the living the great wealth of a Nation's gratitude is due, but to those to whom death came in the cause of National unity, his

"Voice sounds like a prophet's word
And in its solemn tones are heard
The thanks of millions yet to be."

It came like a *pæan* of victory to the ears of the long suffering President and to the sorely taxed patience of the loyal people of the United States. It fell with the dull thud of a mortal wound upon the hearts of the Southern people. Gone and forever dispelled were the fond delusions that one Confederate was equal to three Yankees. Henceforth it was known by each that victory would perch upon the banner of the strongest force, and that the god of battle was on the side of the heaviest artillery. As the blood of the martyr is the seed of the church, so was that spilled at Stones River the inspiration by which the magnificent Army of the Cumberland bore its banners through two years more of carnage to final victory. They renewed their vows of fidelity to the flag of their country upon the field of Chickamauga and upon the bloody slope of Mission Ridge, and through a hundred days of battle to Atlanta, at Franklin, and Nashville. Marching through Georgia with Sherman to the sea, the devoted soldiery followed their leaders with unfaltering courage, billowing every battlefield with the graves of their fallen comrades.

Army of the Cumberland and the Battle of Stone River

By Gilbert Kniffin

The Army of the Ohio, after crowding into the space of six weeks more hard marching and fighting than fell to the lot of any other army in the United States during the summer of 1862, was, on the last of October, encamped in the vicinity of Bowling Green, Kentucky. General Bragg and Kirby Smith, turning Buelll's left flank, had invaded Kentucky, gained the rear of Buell, threatened his base at Louisville, and but for the *vis inertia* which always seemed to seize upon the Confederates when in sight of complete victory, would have captured Louisville. The battle of Perryville resulting in the hasty exit of the combined armies of Bragg and Smith through Cumberland Gap into East Tennessee, the deliberate sweep of Buelll's columns in their rear, the halt at Crab Orchard, and the return march towards Nashville are part of the events of an earlier chapter in the history of the rebellion.

The occupation of East Tennessee by the Union Army had from the commencement of hostilities been an object dear to the great heart of President Lincoln. He had hoped for its accomplishment under General Sherman. It had been included in the instructions to General Buelll, but eighteen months had passed and the Confederate flag still waved in triumph from the spire of the court-house at Knoxville. The retreat of the Confederate Army into East Tennessee in what was reported as a routed and disorganized condition had seemed like a favourable opportunity to carry out the long-cherished design of the Government. The movement of large armies across the country upon a map in the War Office, although apparently practicable, bore so little relation to actual campaigning as to have already caused the decapitation of more than one general.

The positive refusal of General Buelll to march 60,000 men into a sterile and hostile country across a range of mountains in pursuit of an army of equal strength with his own, when by simply turning south-ward he could meet it around the western spur of the same range, although it has since been upheld by every military authority, caused his prompt removal from command of the army he had organized and led to victory. The army had been slow to believe in the incapacity of General Buelll, and had recognized the wisdom of his change of front from Cumberland Gap towards Nashville, but there were causes for dissatisfaction, which, in the absence of knowledge as to the difficul-ties under which he laboured were attributed to him.

A full knowledge of all the circumstances would have transferred them to the War Department. Major-General William S. Rosecrans, the newly-appointed commander of the Army of the Cumberland, graduated at West Point July 1, 1842, as brevet second lieutenant corps of engineers. He resigned from the army April 1, 1854, and entered civil life at Cincinnati as a civil engineer and architect. His energy and capability for large undertakings, coupled with an inherent capacity for command, caused him to be selected as superintendent of a cannel coal company in Virginia and president of the Coal River Navigation Company.

The discovery of coal oil at this period at once attracted his at-tention, and he had embarked in its manufacture when the tocsin of war called him into the field. His first duty was as volunteer aid to General McClellan, where his military experience rendered him very efficient in the organization of troops. He became commander of Camp Chase, colonel on the staff, chief engineer of the State of Ohio, and colonel Twenty-third Ohio Volunteer Infantry, commanded later by Rutherford B. Hayes and Stanley Matthews, and was appointed brigadier-general U. S. A., May 16, 1861. After conducting the cam-paigns in West Virginia to a successful issue he was ordered South and assigned to command of a division in the Army of the Mississippi under General Pope. He participated creditably in the siege of Cor-inth, and after its evacuation, and the transfer of General Pope to the eastern army assumed command of the Army of the Mississippi and District of Corinth.

His heroic defence of that post and pursuit of Van Dorn's defeated army following closely upon his military record in West Virginia again attracted the attention of the President and pointed him out as eminently fitted to succeed General Buell. General Rosecrans ordered to proceed to Cincinnati did not specify the command to which he was to be assigned. His commission as major-general, dated September 16th, was of much later date than the commissions of Buelll, Thomas, McCook, and Crittenden. General Thomas ranked him five months—McCook and Crittenden two months. On opening his orders at Cincinnati he found an autograph letter from General Halleck directing him to proceed to Louisville and relieve General Buelll in command of the Army of the Ohio. The usual method has always been to issue simultaneous orders to both officers, thus affording time to the officer to be relieved in which to arrange the details of his office, but Halleck was a law unto himself, and in relieving an army officer usually did it in a way to render it equivalent to dismissal from the service.

Rosecrans afterward referred to his visit to Buelll's headquarters as more like that of a constable bearing a writ for the ejectment of a tenant than as a general on his way to relieve a brother officer in command of an army. The difficulty of rank was bridged over by antedating Rosecrans' commission to March 16th. In a subsequent interview with General Thomas, when that splendid soldier expressed the pleasure it would give him to serve under a general who had given such satisfactory evidence of fitness to command, but felt doubts as to his right to do so on account of the disparity of their rank, General Rosecrans frankly revealed the means by which his commission had been made to date from the period of his operations in Western Virginia, and that as it now stood, General Thomas need have no fears of compromising his dignity as a United States officer. The explanation was entirely satisfactory, and no question of the superior rank of the commanding general was ever raised. After a rest and visit to his family of only sixty hours, General Rosecrans proceeded to Louisville, and assumed command of the army on the 28th of October, and on the 30th joined it at Bowling Green.

Here the first interview took place between the General and his corps commanders. Major-General George H. Thomas, strong, grave, benignant, majestic in deportment, had now been with the army a year; revered by the entire army, loved by his old division, he was a man to be trusted. Major-General Thomas L. Crittenden, a son of Senator Crittenden, of Kentucky, bold, impetuous, and of knightly grace of manner, possessed of that cheerful courage which finds its best expression on the battle field, the idol of his old division, whose gallant conduct at Shiloh had won for its brave commander promotion to the rank of major-general. Major-General Alexander McD. McCook, the antipodes of Thomas, of never-failing good humour and undoubted courage, apt to neglect proper precautions for the safety of his command, but ever ready to assume all the responsibility of failure, over-confident, generous, yielding in his disposition, yet enjoying the confidence of the men whose heroism at Shiloh had won the eulogies of Sherman, added a second star upon his broad shoulders, and saved him from reproach after the repulse upon the field at Perryville.

In physique the three corps commanders were as unlike as in personal character. Thomas had a massive, full-rounded, erect and powerful figure, six feet in stature. His features heavy but well carved, with a strong, combative nose, his upper lip and square jaws and chin covered with a growth of sandy beard slightly silvered, bushy brows set like a canopy over clear blue eyes, a broad, white forehead, and curly golden hair in luxuriant profusion, covering a large, well-formed head. Out of fifty-four years of life he had worn the uniform of a United States officer twenty-two years, and in all that time he had borne himself as an officer and a gentleman. Altogether a soldier, simple and unaffected, honest, truthful, patient, obedient to orders and requiring obedience, he never swerved an iota from the path of duty; acting upon well-matured opinions, he was a friend to be loved and an enemy to be feared.

Crittenden was tall, slender, and straight as an arrow. His clean-cut features were handsomely modeled, his eyes dark and full of expression, were full of mirth when there was no cause for anger—then they shone with a dangerous light—a thin black beard worn full and pointed at the end, long flowing locks of raven hair falling nearly to his shoulders, beneath a black felt hat turned up at the sides, booted and spurred, with sword dangling at his side, and mounted upon his blooded horse, he was indeed a knight "without fear and without reproach." A long experience in the diplomatic service and in refined society had imparted a high degree of grace and polish of manner, which united to fair intellectual attainments and a magnetic smile which greeted all, from the simplest private soldier to the highest officer in his command, won the admiration and boundless affection of all who knew him.

McCook, low in stature, was inclined to be fleshy, a full face innocent of beard, with the exception of a slight moustache, a broad low forehead, regular features easily wrought into a smile, light hair and a well-shaped head gave him a boyish appearance. Closer observation revealed the presence of more character. There was in the steadiness of gaze, the massive jaws, and the respectful demeanour of his subordinate officers, reason to believe that the youthful major-general had fairly won the twin stars that shone upon his shoulder. He had graduated from West Point with the brevet rank of second lieutenant, had served in several campaigns against the Indians, been instructor in infantry tactics at West Point, where the breaking out of the war found him at thirty years of age. Ordered to Columbus, Ohio, as mustering and disbursing officer, he was appointed colonel of the First Ohio Infantry, which he led in the first battle of Bull Run, receiving commendation where so many failed to deserve it. Reward came in the form of a commission as brigadier-general, with orders to report for duty to General Buelll. The heroic conduct of his division at Shiloh added another star, and, but for the censure of General Buelll for bringing on the battle of Perryville without orders, there was no reason why he should not be entrusted with the command to which his rank entitled him.

Notwithstanding General Rosecrans was a stranger to the army, to the command of which he had been assigned, his name had long been familiar to both officers and men, for war literature had sounded his praises. They had followed him through his campaigns in Western Virginia, had heard the sharp volleys of his musketry on their left at the siege of Corinth, and more recently the country had been electrified by his brilliant victory over Van Dorn. The contrast between Generals Buelll and Rosecrans was not more marked in personal appearance than in methods. The former was cold, impassive, and polite; the latter boisterous, warm-hearted, and brusque. The frigid dignity which hedged the person of Buelll, enclosing department headquarters as within a wall of ice, behind which silence reigned, and through the guarded portals of which none ventured unbidden, was swept away by General Rosecrans, who transformed its solemn precincts into a busy workhouse, where chiefs of staff departments, surrounded by an army of clerks, wrought at their respective vocations, placing the new commander *en rapport* with the most minute details of his army.

Most of his staff accompanied him from the Army of the Mississippi. They had proved themselves capable and trustworthy, and the general naturally desired the presence of old friends in his military family. But there was at least one officer of the old department staff with whom the entire army parted with sincere regret—Colonel

James B. Fry, Buelll's adjutant-general and chief of staff. The kindness of manner, the inexhaustible patience and good humour and never-failing knowledge of military affairs which this officer possessed had gone far to soften the asperities and dispel the chill which hung about department headquarters.

Brigadier-General D. S. Stanley reported for duty as chief of cavalry early in December, and at once assumed command.

General Stanley graduated at West Point in the class of 1852, and was assigned to the Second Dragoons with the rank of second lieutenant. After three years' service on the plains he was transferred to the First Cavalry as first lieutenant, then under command of Colonel E.V. Sumner. Joe Johnston was lieutenant-colonel, and John Sedgwick and William H. Emory majors. In 1857 he accompanied Colonel Sumner on an expedition against the Cheyenne Indians, in which he was engaged in a sharp fight on Solomon's Fork of the Kansas River, in which the Indians were defeated. In 1858 he was engaged in the Utah Expedition, and in the same year he crossed the plains to the northern boundary of Texas. In a sharp and decisive battle with the Comanches Lieutenant Stanley displayed such courage and skill in handling his command as to receive the complimentary orders of General Scott.

The opening of the rebellion found him stationed at Fort Scott, Arkansas, where, in March, he received his commission as captain in the Fourth Cavalry. His command was included in the surrender made by General Twiggs, but the heart of the brave officer beat loyal to the flag of his country, and he resolved upon a march northward to Kansas City, Mo. Uniting his force with that at Fort Smith, the column moved through the Indian country. A Confederate force sent against them was, on the eighth of May, captured and paroled. On the fifteenth of June they occupied Kansas City, and marched at once upon Independence, where Captain Stanley was fired upon while carrying a flag of truce. He joined General Lyon in his expedition against Springfield, which was occupied July twelfth.

He participated in the various engagements in Missouri in the summer of 1861, displaying in an eminent degree the dash and conspicuous courage which so distinguished him in his subsequent career, and in September he reported with his regiment to General Fremont at St. Louis. He marched against Price from Syracuse, and in November moved against Springfield. Captain Stanley was appointed brigadier-general in November, 1861, and in March, 1862, was assigned to the command of the Second division of Pope's army in the expedition against New Madrid and Island No. 10, the Fort Pillow Expedition, and in the siege of Corinth. Here his acquaintance with General Rosecrans began, ripening into sincere attachment under the fire of Price's guns at Iuka, and the yet fiercer blaze of Van Dorn's hard-fighting battalions at Corinth in October.

His conspicuous gallantry on this occasion added a second star to the insignia of his rank and caused him to be selected by his old commander in arms to organize and lead the cavalry of his new command. In person General Stanley was tall and erect. A handsome face and long, flowing beard, slightly silvered, engaging in manner and full of enthusiasm for the success of the cause in which he held his own life as nothing in comparison, he soon impressed his personality upon the cavalry of the Army of the Cumberland and made it a reliable branch of the service.

December, 1862, was a busy month. The year was fast drawing to a close, and both Union and Confederate generals had little to report save plots and counter-plots. On the part of each there was little that was encouraging. The early spring had found Middle and West Tennessee in the possession of the former. Two large armies occupied all prominent points, and the beaten Confederates encamped in Mississippi were confronted by an army too powerful for them to attack.

Early autumn witnessed the enforced retirement of Buelll's army to the line of the Ohio River, while the Confederates reaped the harvests in Kentucky and Middle Tennessee.

The tenth of October found Grant embarked upon his march southward to Vicksburg, driving Pemberton before him. Sherman arranging for co-operation by water, the Army of the Cumberland encamped near Nashville, with Bragg's twice defeated army in its front, and Hindman's beaten troops flying before the victorious divisions of Herron and Blunt from the battle field of Prairie Grove.

East Tennessee being left comparatively free from molestation by the abandonment of pursuit through Cumberland Gap, General Kirby Smith was at liberty to reinforce points more strongly threatened. He had no sooner succeeded in collecting his stragglers and reorganizing his army, reinforcing it by several new regiments, than, in compliance with orders from the Confederate War Department, he dispatched Stevenson's division to the relief of Pemberton at Grenada, and McCown, with his division, to report to Bragg at Murfreesboro.

Orders for a forward movement were issued by General Rosecrans on Wednesday, the twenty-fourth of December, and on Christmas morning the camps were alive with preparation. The day was spent in writing to loved ones far away among the snow-covered hills of the great Northwest. Tattoo found men discussing the chances of coming battle. Here and there was a soldier giving the last finishing touch to the gleaming gun-barrel. The surgeon, in his tent, sat before a table on which in glittering display lay the implements of his craft. The long, keen knife, the saw, the probe, were each in turn subjected to close inspection and carefully adjusted in the case. Field officers paid a last visit to their faithful chargers and exhorted grooms to feed early and not to forget to bring along an extra feed lest perchance the following night would find the troops far in advance of the wagons. Quarter-masters, that hard-worked and little-appreciated class of officers, toiling through the long night with their loaded wagon trains getting into position for an orderly march; commissaries, upon whose vigilance all depended, carrying out orders for three days' rations in haversacks and five days' more in wagons.

A busy day was followed by a busy night. The clatter of horses' hoofs upon the turnpike roads leading out of Nashville to the en-campments sounded all through the night. Now a solitary orderly galloped down from division headquarters bearing a message to a bri-gade commander. Soon a group of officers rode gaily by from a late carousal at the St. Cloud; then came a corps commander with staff and escort from conference with the chief, his last injunction ringing in his ears, "We move tomorrow, gentlemen. We shall begin to skirmish probably as soon as we pass the outposts. Press them hard. Drive them out of their nests. Make them fight or run. Strike hard and fast; give them no rest. Fight them! fight them! fight them! I say," as the uplifted right hand emphasized each sentence upon the palm of the left hand. Thomas received the orders with a grim smile of approval; McCook's sharp eyes twinkled with enjoyment; Crittenden straightened his trim figure, and his eyes shone as he stalked out of the room, followed by his aides, as if in haste to begin his part of the programme. There was glorious assurance in the manly stride, the determined look, and in the triple armour with which he is clad who hath his quarrel just; and his must have been a dull ear, indeed, who did not note, in the merry jest and tuneful song that floated along the ranks, the augury of victory.

At the head of their respective columns rode Thomas, accompanied by his staff officers, with the brave and accomplished Major George E. Flynt at their head. There was Von Schroeder, Mack, Mackey, and the rest. McCook, with Langdon, Nodine, Thruston, Campbell, and Williams. Crittenden, followed by Starling, Loder, Mendenhall, Buford, John McCook, Knox, and the writer of this chronicle. Brave hearts beat high that day. On the right, far in advance of the infantry, rode Stanley, with trusty Sinclair by his side, while his cavalry swept on out the Nolensville pike, driving Wheeler's pickets before them.

Sturdy John Kennett, with a brigade of cavalry at his heels, advanced upon the broad turnpike road straight toward the enemy, nor stopped until nightfall, notwithstanding constant skirmishing, when, on reaching an eminence that overlooked La Vergne, a large force was encountered. The plain below was dotted with groups of cavalry. Suddenly a puff of smoke and a shell well aimed along the line of the road, carried death in its track. Another and another followed in quick succession, clearing the road as fast as men's legs could carry them. The head of Palmer's infantry column came up and halted at the side of the road. General Crittenden and his staff rode forward to watch the artillery duel now in progress—for Newell's battery had unlimbered at the first shot and was firing rapidly.

Mr. Robert H. Crittenden (a brother of the general), and the writer, his boon companion, riding side by side, advanced beyond their companions in full view of the artillerists, presenting a conspicuous mark. Quick as lightning a shell came hissing through the air and passed in the narrow space of a yard between their horses. It is needless to add that, their curiosity being gratified, they lost no time in seeking the friendly cover of a log-house by the roadside. Newell planted his shots from two three-inch Rodmans with such dexterity as to silence the enemy's battery of four guns.

Colonel Enyart, with the First Kentucky and the Thirty-first Indiana Infantry, supported on the right by Colonel W. C. Whitaker with the Sixth Kentucky and the Thirty-first Indiana Infantry, supported on the right by Colonel W. C. Whitaker with the Sixth Kentucky and Ninth Indiana, preceded by Colonel Murray with the Third Kentucky Cavalry, now moved to the left and advanced through the cedars towards Stony Creek, where they were met by a force sent to intercept them. The order to charge with the bayonet was followed by a swift rush across the creek, the routed Confederates flying before the gleaming steel, and the army bivouacked for the night before La Vergne.

After five days' fighting into position the army formed line of battle in front of Murfreesboro. Summoning his corps commanders the

General promulgated his plan of battle. General McCook was to occupy the most advantageous position, refusing his right as much as practicable and necessary to secure it, to receive the attack of the enemy, or, if that did not come, to attack sufficiently to hold all the forces in his front. Generals Negley and Palmer to open with skirmishing, and engage the enemy's centre and left as far as the river. Crittenden to cross Van Cleve's division at the lower ford, covered and supported by Morgan's pioneer corps, 1,700 strong, and to advance on Breckinridge. Wood's division to cross by brigades at the upper ford, and moving on Van Cleve's right, to carry everything before them to Murfreesboro. This movement would, it was supposed, dislodge Breckinridge, and gaining the high ground east of Stones River, Wood's batteries could obtain an enfilading fire upon the heavy body of troops massed in front of Negley and Palmer.

The centre and left, using Negley's right as a pivot, were to swing around through Murfreesboro and take the force confronting McCook in rear, driving it into the country towards Salem. The successful execution of General Rosecrans' design depended not more upon the spirit and gallantry of the assaulting column than upon the courage and obstinacy with which the position held by the Right Wing was maintained. Having explained this fact to General McCook, the commanding general asked him if, with a full knowledge of the ground over which he had fought, he could hold his position three hours—again alluding to his dissatisfaction with the direction which his line had assumed, but, as before, leaving that to the corps commander—"I think I can," said McCook, and the conference ended.

General Braxton Bragg, a graduate of West Point, a master in military science, a commander whose endurance and hard fighting qualities in the field were more conspicuous than his generalship in the management of campaign, was in command of the Confederate army at Murfreesboro. He had taken up the execution of the plan of battle where it had dropped from the dying hand of Albert Sydney Johnston, and was advancing to carry it out at Shiloh, when his brigades were recalled by Beauregard, sick in an ambulance three miles in the rear. He had, by a brilliant flank movement of three hundred miles through a mountainous region, gained Buell's rear in Kentucky, only to emerge from the farthest corner of the State without a decisive battle. Recriminations had grown out of this campaign which threatened to sap the influence of the commanding general.

General Polk had been threatened with court-martial, and Hardee expressed the opinion that if Bragg persisted in bringing charges, Polk could, if he would, "rip up the Kentucky campaign—tear Bragg to tatters." These compliments, however, passed only between prominent officers; the army was in good state of discipline, although out of an aggregate 85,372 only 47,930 were carried on the rolls as effectives, and 30,000 were absent, with and without leave.

Bragg had in his army about the same proportion of raw troops to veterans as were found in that in his front, and both armies were equally well armed. Men who had tested each other's metal at Pea Ridge, Shiloh, and Perryville, and in innumerable skirmishes, were again arrayed for a final conflict. Here was Bragg, sullen, hard-featured, unapproachable; Polk, benignant, dignified, majestic; Hardee, the superb rider, the strict disciplinarian, the steady, persistent fighter; Breckinridge, elegant in manner, eloquent in speech, courteous, courageous, the idol of the Kentucky brigade, and, like the men who composed it, dimly conscious possibly of the crime against his favourite dogma of States rights, and the ingratitude of a people whose cause they had espoused against the expressed will of their native State.

Among the division commanders were Cheatham, whose headlong charges at Shiloh and Perryville thousands of maimed soldiers both North and South had cause to remember; Cleburne, stubborn and stout of heart, blunt, impassive and heavy, who was destined two years later to pour out his life's blood upon the breastworks at Franklin; McCown and Withers of lesser note, and a host of brigade and regimental commanders who had won their rank under the eyes of their grim commander.

General Rosecrans, having arranged his plan of battle, had risen early to superintend its execution. General Crittenden, whose headquarters were a few paces distant, mounted at 6 A. M., and with his staff rode to an eminence, where the chief, surrounded by his staff officers, sat on their horses listening to the opening guns on the right. The plan of General Bragg was instantly divined, but no apprehension of danger was felt. Suddenly the woods on the right in the rear of Negley, appeared to be alive with men wandering aimlessly in the direction of the rear. The roar of artillery grows more distinct, mingled with continuous volleys of musketry. It cannot be that the veteran brigades of the Right Wing are being driven back. McCook is surely only falling back to secure a position that he can hold for the promised three hours.

The rear of a line of battle always presents the pitiable spectacle of a horde of skulkers—men who, when tried in the fierce flame of battle, find, often to their own disgust, that they are lacking in the element of courage. But the sight of whole regiments of soldiers flying in panic to the rear was a sight never seen but on that solitary occasion, before or since, by the Army of the Cumberland. Captain Otis, from his position on the extreme right, who arrives breathless, his horse reeking with foam, to inform General Rosecrans that the Right Wing is in rapid retreat. The astounding intelligence is confirmed a moment later by a staff officer from General McCook, calling for reinforcements. "Tell General McCook," roared the chief, "to contest every inch of ground. If he holds them, we will swing into Murfreesboro and cut them off."

Then Rousseau, with his reserves, was sent into the fight, and Van Cleve, at the head of Crittenden's old Shiloh division, came dashing across the fields, with water dripping from their clothing, to take a hand in the fray. Harker's brigade was withdrawn from the left and sent in on Rousseau's right, and the Pioneer brigade, relieved at the ford by Price's brigade, was posted on Harker's right. The remaining brigades of Van Cleve's division, Beatty's and Fyffe's, formed on the extreme right, and thus an improvised line half a mile in extent, presented a new and unexpected front to the approaching enemy. It was a trying position to Van Cleve's men to stand in line, a living wall, while the panic-stricken soldiers of McCook's beaten regiments, flying in terror through the woods, rushed past them, the sharp rattle of McCown's musketry behind them lending wings to their flight.

The Union lines could not fire, for their comrades were between them and the enemy. Rosecrans seemed ubiquitous. All these dispositions had been made under his personal direction. Finding Sheridan coming out of the cedars into which Rousseau had just retired, he directed him to the ammunition train, with orders to fill his cartridge boxes and return to the support of Hazen's brigade on the edge of the Round Forrest. Captain Morton, with the Pioneers and the Chicago Board of Trade Battery, pushed into the cedars, and disappeared from view simultaneously with Harker. The general course of the tide of stragglers toward the rear struck the turnpike at the point where Van Cleve stood impatiently awaiting the order to advance. All along the line men were falling, struck by the bullets of the enemy, who soon appeared at the edge of the woods on Morton's flank.

The order to charge was given by General Rosecrans in person, and, like hounds from the leash, the division sprang forward, reserving their fire for close quarters. It was the crisis in the battle. If this line was broken all was lost. Every man rose to the occasion and proved himself a hero. Steadily, as a majestic river moves on its resistless way, the line swept forward, sending a shower of bullets to the front. The left was now exposed to attack, and, riding rapidly to the ford, General Rosecrans inquired who commanded the brigade. "I do, sir," said Colonel Price.

"Will you hold this ford?"

"I will try, sir."

"Will you hold this ford?"

"I will die right here."

"Will you hold this ford?" for the third time thundered the general.

"Yes, sir," said the colonel.

"That will do"; and away galloped the general to where Palmer was contending against long odds for the possession of the Round Forrest in the centre of the line. All along the line from Van Cleve's right to Wood's left, the space gradually narrowed between the contending hosts. The weak had gone to the rear; no room now for any but brave men, and no time given for new dispositions; every man who had a stomach for fighting was engaged on the firing line. From a right angle the Confederate left had been pressed back by Van Cleve and Harker and the Pioneers to an angle of forty-five degrees in less than that number of minutes.

This advance brought Van Cleve within view of Rousseau, who at once requested him to form on his right. Harker, entering the woods on the left of Van Cleve, passed to his right, and now closed up on his flank. The enemy had fallen back stubbornly fighting, and made a stand on the left of Cheatham. Brave old Van Cleve, his white hair streaming in the wind, the blood flowing from a gaping wound in his foot, rode gallantly along the line to where Harker was stiffly holding his position, with his right "in the air." Bidding him to hold fast to every inch of ground, he rode to Swallow's Battery, which was working with the rapidity of a steam fire-engine, "Don't let them get your guns, Swallow!" he shouted, as he dashed by on his way to the left, where Sam Beatty, heavy and impassive, was pounding away with his minie rifles at a line of men who seemed always on the point of advancing.

The brigades of Stanley and Miller having fallen back, as previously described, and the entire strength of Cheatham and three brigades of Withers and Cleburne having fallen upon Rousseau, he had fallen back into the open field, where he found Van Cleve. Loomis's and Guenthers' batteries, double-shotted with canister, were posted on a ridge, and as the Confederate line advanced, opened upon it with terrible force. Men fell like ripened grain before a reaper, but the line moved straight ahead. The field, swept by a storm of iron hail, was covered with dead and wounded men. The deep bass of the artillery was mingled with the higher notes of the minie rifles, while the brief pauses could be distinguished the quickly-spoken orders of the commanding officers, and the groans of the wounded. It was the full orchestra of battle.

But there is a limit of human endurance. The Confederate brigades, now melted to three-fourths their original numbers, wavered and fell back; again and again they reformed in the woods and advanced to the charge, only to meet with a bloody repulse. Four deliberate and sustained attempts were made to carry the position, and each failed. While these events were following each other in rapid succession, and some of them occurring simultaneously, the Left Wing had not only held its position, but had furnished three brigades to repel the advance of Bragg's left upon the rear of the army.

While Colonel Hazen was gallantly defending the left of the line from nine o'clock in the morning until two in the afternoon, the fight raged no less furiously on his immediate right. Here a line composed of two brigades of Palmer's division and one of Wood's, filled out by the remains of Sheridan's divisions, who, after they had replenished their ammunition, formed behind the railroad embankment at right angles with Hazen's brigade, which alone retained its position upon the original line. Farther to the right was Rousseau, with Van Cleve and Harker on his right. I leave to more graphic pens to describe the grand pyrotechnics of the battle field at this supreme moment when victory hung evenly balanced. Past the crowd of fugitives from the Right Wing the undaunted soldiers of the Left and Centre had swept "with the light of battle in their faces," and now in strong array they stood like a rock-bound coast beating back the tide which threatened to engulf the rear.

Along this line rode Rosecrans with face illuminated by the light of exalted courage; Thomas, calm, inflexible as a mighty judge, from whose gaze skulkers shrank abashed; Crittenden, cheerful and full of hope, complimenting his men as he rode along the lines; Rousseau, whose fiery impetuosity no disaster could quell; Palmer, with a stock of cool courage and presence of mind equal to any emergency; Wood, suffering from a wound in his heel, stayed in the saddle, but had lost the jocularity which usually characterized him. "Good-bye, General, 'we will all meet at the hatter's' as one coon said to another when the dogs were after them," he said to Crittenden early in the action, but at ten o'clock a minie ball struck his boot and lacerated his heel—his good humour was gone for the day. "Are we going about it right now, General?" asked Morton, as he glanced along the blazing line of muskets to where the Chicago battery quivered with the rapidity of its discharges.

"All right, fire low," said the chief as he dashed by. Colonel Grose, always in his place, had command of the Ammen brigade, the "glorious Tenth" of Shiloh memory, with which, and, with Hazen's and Cruft's brigades, the gallant and lamented Nelson had swept, like an avenging Nemesis, upon the right of Beauregard's victorious army, driving it back to its base at Corinth.

After the formation of this line at noon it never receded; as has been stated, the right swung around until, at two o'clock, about one-half of the lost ground had been retaken. The artillery, more than fifty guns, was massed in the open ground behind the angle in the line; twenty-eight guns had been captured, when they poured a continuous torrent of iron missiles upon the Confederate line. They could not fire amiss. The fire from Cox's Battery was directed upon Hanson's brigade across the river, where Cobb, with Napoleons, returned the compliment with zeal and precision. Schaefer's brigade having received a new stock of cartridges, formed on Palmer's right, where later the brave commander received his death wound, the last of Sheridan's brigade commanders who had fallen during the day.

At four o'clock it became evident to the Confederate commander that his only hope of success lay in a charge upon the Union left, which, by its overpowering weight, should carry everything before it. The movement of Cleburne to the left in support of McCown had deprived him of reserves; but Breckinridge had four brigades unemployed on the right, and these were peremptorily ordered across the river to the support of General Polk. The error made by General Polk in making an attack with the two brigades that first arrived upon the field, instead of awaiting the arrival of General Breckinridge with the remaining brigades, was so palpable as to render an excuse for failure necessary.

This was easily found in the tardy execution of Bragg's order by

Breckinridge, and resulted in sharp criticism of the latter. The Third Kentucky, now nearly annihilated, and its Colonel, Sam McKee, killed, was relieved by the Fifty-eighth Indiana, Colonel George P. Buelll. The Sixth Ohio, with the gallant Colonel Nicholas L. Anderson at its head, took position on the right of the Twenty-sixth Ohio, with its right advanced so that its line of fire would sweep the front of the regiments on its left. The Ninety-seventh Ohio and One Hundredth Illinois came up and still further strengthened the right of Hazen's position. They had not long to wait for the attack. These dispositions had barely been made when a long line of infantry emerged from behind the hill. Adam's and Jackson's fresh brigades were on the right, and Donelson's and Chalmers's, badly cut up but stout of heart, were on the left.

Out they came in splendid style, full six thousand strong. Estepp's case-shot tore through their ranks, but the gaps closed up. Parsons sent volley after volley of grape shot against it, and the Sixth and Twenty-sixth Ohio, taking up the refrain, added the sharp rattle of their minie rifles to the unearthly din. Still the line pressed forward, firing as they came, nor wavered in the onward march, until met by a simultaneous volley of musketry which stretched hundreds of their number mangled upon the earth. They staggered back, but, quickly reformed and reinforced by Preston and Palmer, advanced again to the charge.

The battle had hushed on the extreme right, and the dreadful splendor of this advance is indescribable. The right was even with the left of the Union line, and the left stretched way past the point of woods from which Negley had retired. It was such a charge as this that broke the lines of Wallace and Hurlbut at Shiloh, and enveloped Prentice in its strong embrace. It had no sooner moved into the open field from the cover of the river bank than it was saluted with such a roar of artillery as shook the earth. Men plucked the cotton from the bolls at their feet and stuffed it in their ears.

No human force could withstand the tornado of iron that swept against it. Huge gaps were torn in it at every discharge. Men lay in heaps before and behind it. Shells exploding sent showers of mangled forms into the air. They staggered forward half the distance across the fields, when the infantry lines blazed in their front, and a shower of minie balls was added to the fury of the storm. They wavered and fell back. The field was won. Night fell upon a field strewn with the mangled forms of men, who, but twenty-four hours before were buoyant with life and hope, upon the faces of dead men turned upward to the sky; upon long lines of infantry faint for lack of food and gasping for water; upon a horde of panic-stricken men wending their way in solemn procession to the rear, "where the subsequent proceedings interested them no more," and upon Walker's and Shackelford's brigades marching to the front, Garesche, Schaefer, Sill, Roberts, McKee, and genial, happy hearted Fred. Jones, and a host of others were dead or suffering mortal agony.

The first day's fight was over.

The Regular Brigade of the Fourteenth Army Corps, in the Battle of Stone River, or Murfreesboro', Tennessee,

BY FREDERICK PHISTERER

To His Comrades,

The Survivors of the Regular Brigade,

Army Of The Cumberland,

In Remembrance of Past Days,

And to Place on Record a True Account

Of the

Participation of the Brigade

In the

Battle of Stone River.

July 1st, 1883.

When General Rosecrans took command of the Army of the Ohio there were in that army five battalions of regular infantry in two different divisions; when he reorganized this army he determined to bring these battalions together, to give them a regular battery, and form of them a Regular Brigade. The 15th, 16th and 19th were already at Nashville; the orders organizing the brigade found the two battalions of the 18th near Gallatin, Tenn., as a part of General Stedman's Brigade. On receipt of the orders, the 18th marched, on the 23rd of December, 1862, from Pilot Knob to Nashville, Tenn., arriving there on the 25th day of December, 1862, and, joining the other battalions and the battery, it completed the formation of the brigade, which, as then organized, consisted of:

The 1st Battalion of the 15th Infantry: Companies A, B, C, D, E, F, G and H; commanded by Major John H. King.

The 1st Battalion of the 16th Infantry: Companies A, B, C, D, E, F, G and H, 1st Battalion, and Company B, 2nd Battalion; Major A. J. Slemmer commanding.

The 1st Battalion of the 18th Infantry: Companies A, B, C, D, E, F, G and H, of the 1st, and A and D, of the 3rd Battalion; Major J. N. Caldwell in command.

The 2nd Battalion of the 18th Infantry: Companies A, B, C, D, E and F, of the 2nd, and B, C, E and F, of the 3rd Battalion; commanded by Major Frederick Townsend.

The 1st Battalion of the 19th Infantry: Companies A, B, C, D, E and F; Major S. D. Carpenter commanding.

Battery H, 5th U. S. Artillery, commanded by 1st Lieutenant F. L. Guenther.

Lieutenant-Colonel O. L. Shepherd, 18th U. S. Infantry, the senior officer, was placed in command of the brigade.

When the Army of the Ohio—then become the Army of the Cumberland, or the 14th Corps—advanced from Nashville, Tenn., toward its objective point, the enemy, the Regular Brigade broke camp on the 26th, encamping on the evening of that day on the Petersburg Turnpike; on the 27th it encamped near Nolansville, Tenn.; on the 28th, at night, it marched across the country to Stewart's Creek, and on the 30th to a point on the Murfreesboro' and Nashville Turnpike about four miles from Murfreesboro', Tenn.

On the morning of the 31st of December the brigade left its bivouac at an early hour and advanced on the Nashville Turnpike to a point a little less than three miles northwest of Murfreesboro', and, with its division, was posted in reserve. The division consisted of Scribner's, John Beatty's, Starkweather's and the Regular Brigade, and was commanded by Major-General Lovell H. Rousseau. Starkweather's Brigade had been left at Jefferson's Crossing on Stone River. The division was part of the centre, commanded by Major-General George H. Thomas. The formation in the brigade was from right to left as follows: 15th, 16th, 18th, 1st and 2nd Battalions, and the 19th.

To fully understand the events now following, it will be necessary to preface them with a short résumé of the opening and progress of the battle from 6.30 a. m. until noon; from the right of the army to the left of Palmer's Division of the left wing.

The left of Palmer's Division, Hazen's Brigade, rested on the Nashville Turnpike, about two and a half miles northwest of Murfreesboro', facing south by east—the other brigades of this division faced almost east; Negley's Division, of the centre, next in order, faced south by east; Sheridan's, of the right wing, faced almost east; Davis' faced south by east, and Johnson's, the right of the army, east and south, and a portion of it on the right flank west by south. A line drawn from the extreme right due north would have crossed the Nashville Turnpike near General Rosecrans' headquarters, about one mile northwest of Hazen.

All the divisions, excepting Palmer's and the left of Negley's, had to cross a dense cedar forest about three-quarters of a mile deep before they could reach the Nashville Turnpike to their left and rear.

The extreme right of Johnson's Division was attacked about 6.30 a. m., and the engagement extended gradually toward our left, the attacking columns of the enemy moving in echelon from their left to their right; the attack struck Johnson's flank, and, although portions of the division made a gallant stand, the weight of the attack was too much for the division. Johnson having been flanked and driven back, it became Davis' turn to be taken in rear and right flank, and forced back after considerable resistance.

The next division, Sheridan's, was forewarned, and offered a most determined resistance, falling back and changing front to the west as its flank and rear became vulnerable; ammunition falling short, the rebel force on his flank increasing, Sheridan commenced his retreat about 9.30 a. m., falling back slowly and fighting. Negley necessarily had now to refuse his right, change front to the west and northwest, and, running out of ammunition about 11 a. m., commence his retreat out of the cedars. This exposed the right of Palmer's Division, compelling him, after a sharp fight, to change front to the west and fall back on the railroad, pivoting his division on the left of Hazen's Brigade, until it was at right angles with its former position; this took place about noon.

The general front of the line, which in the morning was south by east, was now west by south; the new line formed about noon ran along the railroad and turnpike, and in front of it were open fields from Hazen's left to a point about one-eighth of a mile southeast of General Rosecrans' headquarters from which point the now reorganized right wing was posted in the forest in a semicircle facing south and west, with the right, refused, facing north by west and resting near the turnpike. Between the right wing and Palmer's Division there were Van Cleeve's Division of the left wing, the Pioneer Brigade, Negley's and Rousseau's Divisions.

During the remainder of the day these positions were not materially changed, except that Van Cleeve's and Negley's Divisions were later withdrawn and placed in reserve.

To return to the Regular Brigade: About 9 o'clock A. M. it became apparent that the tide of battle was most decidedly against the right wing of the army, and Rousseau's Division was ordered to the support of General McCook. The Regular Brigade with its battery moved by the right flank into the dense wood of cedars, alluded to above; when near Sheridan the head of the brigade changed direction to the right, and line of battle was formed in the cedars facing west. Meanwhile it had become evident that on this ground no use could be made of the battery, and that no good position could be obtained for the infantry; the advance was therefore discontinued and the battery with the brigade ordered by General Rousseau to the open field between the cedars and the turnpike, near where it started from.

Guenther's Battery first took position on a slight rise outside of the woods, but moved shortly to a knoll between the turnpike and railroad, shelling the woods in the direction of the advance of the enemy. The two right battalions, the 15th and 16th, not receiving the orders to halt, continued their advance, deployed skirmishers, and soon became engaged with a rebel force sweeping down in the rear of Sheridan. This force appeared to be clothed in the Union Blue, and for a time there was an uncertainty as to its character; the skirmishers being soon driven in, the status of these troops was quickly developed and the battalions had a hot and fierce fight for a short time, in which they were assisted by the 6th Ohio Volunteer Regiment on their right.

Majors King and Slemmer having finally received information of the movement of the brigade, prepared to rejoin it, falling back through the woods, and halting twice to repulse the enemy. Other forces coming to the support of the right, and Sheridan having changed front and refused his right, enabled these battalions to rejoin the brigade. Among the killed in this affair was Captain Bell, of the 15th. The other battalions, though under fire, did not come into action, but covered the movements, and followed in support of their battery, all taking, finally, position on a rise or knoll near the turnpike.

At this point the 19th was shifted from the left to the right wing between the 15th and 16th, thereby equalizing the strength of the two wings more nearly. While in this position, the line facing southwest, the brigade, the battalions of the 18th, and the battery especially, were exposed to an enfilading artillery fire, and Captain Denison, of the 2nd Battalion, was mortally wounded, and Sergeant White, of Co. F. 3rd Battalion, 18th infantry, was killed by a solid shot. The brigade was not long in position when Sheridan's troops began to come out of the woods, followed shortly after by the enemy, whose further advance was resisted by it.

At a point where a short thicket about half way between the battery and the woods and nearly opposite the battery and right of the brigade covered to some extent its approach, Wither's Division formed and made a desperate charge on Guenther's Battery. The enemy advanced boldly and bravely; Guenther turned his admirably served guns on him, and with the fire of his supports broke the column, which made four gallant efforts to continue the charge, but melted away under the dreadful fire; their battle flag went down three times in succession. Portions of Scribner's Brigade flanked the enemy's left, and, upon the repulse of his charge on the Regular Battery, Scribner's and John Beatty's Brigades, Van Cleve's Division, the Pioneer Brigade and other organizations, led by Generals Rosecrans and Rousseau in turn, charged upon the enemy, driving him well back into the cedars.

The remnants of the right wing having meanwhile been reorganized, reformed nearly all on the right, advanced and took positions, held by them until the close of the battle. The enemy's advance on our right and his flanking operations had now been successfully resisted, but Negley was still in the woods, flanked and almost surrounded. Extraordinary efforts were then made by the enemy to crush the centre and left; reinforcements were brought from their right and thrown upon the left of Negley and against Cruft, Grose and Hazen. Negley, out of ammunition, was compelled to almost cut his way out; Grose's and Cruft's Brigades of Palmer's Division, on Negley's left, necessarily had to follow in his wake, in a measure covering his retreat; Hazen's right, on Cruft's left, fell back and changed front from southeast to northwest, pivoting on his left.

To enable these troops to fall back, to afford them protection, to gain time to execute the now absolutely necessary movements in order to rectify positions of troops and to form a new line from Hazen's left toward the right, Rousseau's Division was again ordered into the cedars. General Thomas himself gave the orders for the advance of the Regular Brigade, saying to its commander: "Shepherd, take your brigade in there," pointing southwest toward the cedar forest, "and stop the rebels." The brigade, without the battery, for which there was no suitable position in this movement, was at once put in march, advancing to the front (south) along the railroad and turnpike.

After reaching the further side (south) of the open ground, it was suddenly directed to the right to enter the cedar forest, and after a change of direction slightly to the right, it was halted along the edge of the cedars facing southwest and west. During this movement the 2nd Battalion of the 18th executed a change of front to the south, by companies on its left company, as if at ordinary battalion drill, then marched by the right flank into the cedars; the other battalions moved up by their flanks and shortest routes, preserving proper intervals. This, all accounts agree, was about noon. The line was then advanced about fifty yards, until our retreating troops were in sight. The 15th held the right; the 2nd Battalion of the 18th the left, which rested less than one hundred yards from the south end of the woods; each battalion occupied the best position the rocky ground in its front afforded, and the brigade covered a front of a little over one-fourth of a mile.

Let us review the situation: Negley and Grose were retiring; Cruft was covering Negley's retreat and following him; Hazen's right was falling back; the enemy's force was victorious and reinforced by three brigades—according to a Murfreesboro' rebel paper and Bragg's report—which were fresh and intact and commanded by Jackson, Preston and Adams, and in this breach stood the forlorn hope of the army, the Regular Brigade. Hazen's right retiring, left the left flank of the brigade uncovered, but John Beatty's Brigade covered that point and the rear in reserve; on the right of the brigade, Scribner came up to cover that flank and to connect with troops still further on the right. As soon as the front of a battalion was clear of our retiring troops, its fire commenced; this waiting for our men to retire, and, meanwhile, receiving the enemy's fire without being able to reply, was the most trying time of all.

The firing commenced at the left as soon as Cruft's men—so reported by a staff officer—had withdrawn, and soon rose into a continuous roar. Capt. Oscar A. Mack, on General Thomas' staff, who approached the brigade with orders, and was severely wounded, declared the din of the fire to have been appalling. The first line of the enemy were scattered like chaff; their second line brought to a halt and held.

The report of the men, especially, is that there was a third line, which coming up, fixed bayonets and with the remnants of the other two lines prepared for a charge. General Negley, with some of his men, united with the 15th, our right, and with them resisted the advance of his pursuers. Part of Scribner's Brigade formed on Negley's right; John Beatty covered the left and rear of the brigade.

Officers and men were falling all along the line, but not a man turned his back to the enemy; every one stood up to his work and strove to be worthy of the hope placed in him, and to do credit to the Regular Brigade. General Thomas' orders had been obeyed; the enemy's onslaught on the centre had been repulsed, and his victorious troops brought to a halt; the rebels had been stopped, and the key of the battlefield secured, but at a loss of nearly half of the infantry force of the brigade. The new lines along the turnpike and railroad having been formed, troops moved into position, artillery posted to protect and cover the new lines, the right of the brigade received orders to fall back; the movement was executed under the protection of the battery, but unmolested by the enemy, from right to left in perfect order, one battalion moving after the other by the right of companies through the cedars to the rear.

Lieut. Ludlow's section of the battery had been detached to the front and right to cover the retreat of the right of the brigade. It was a bitter disappointment to obey orders then, but as the object of the advance of the brigade had been achieved, its further exposure would have been useless, and could only have resulted in its annihilation; still, this was not understood at the time by the officers and men of the brigade. When the heads of companies debouched from the woods, they were exposed to a tornado of artillery fire from rebel batteries to our left. From the position of the brigade in the cedars to a short distance outside, it was a gentle decline, the ground then again commenced to rise as far as the pike and railroad; about one hundred yards from the woods, on higher ground, the brigade reformed and faced the enemy; as there was no pursuit, it fell back of our new lines and joined again its battery in proper supporting position. Here roll was called, reports were made, and now the loss of the brigade was fully understood. John Beatty's and Scribner's Brigades fell back with the left and right of the Regular Brigade, and the artillery opened on the woods as soon as the brigade was out of them.

When the action opened in the cedars, Major Slemmer, of the 16th, was badly wounded, and Capt. Crofton took command; almost immediately after giving the command to retire, Major Carpenter fell, mortally wounded, struck by six bullets, and the command of the 19th devolved on Capt. Mulligan; on the retreat between the cedars and the railroad, Major King, of the 15th, was disabled, and Capt. Fulmer assumed command; in the cedars; in the 1st Battalion of the 18th, Capt. Kneass was killed and Lieut. McConnell mortally wounded; in the 2nd Battalion of the 18th, Lieut. Hitchcock was killed and Lieut. Simons mortally wounded; in the 15th Capt. Wise was mortally wounded; Major Townsend had his horse shot under him; the adjutant of the 1st Battalion of the 18th had his horse wounded; and the adjutant of the 2nd Battalion had his killed under him. When the brigade was again in its supporting position, its left wing was committed for the remainder of the battle to Major Townsend, the right wing, deprived of its field officers, needing more the attention of the brigade commander.

This closed the enemy's and our operations for that day as far as active participation by the Regular Brigade was concerned; the battery, however, continued to play on the enemy's position, and when later in the afternoon an attack was made to the left of the brigade, it assisted in the repulse of the enemy in that quarter. During the night parties were organized to collect the wounded of the brigade; the pickets of the enemy and of the brigade were within speaking distance, and one of the parties was captured; another party claimed to be an informal flag of truce, asking for the privilege to collect our wounded, and thus after some parleying was permitted to return.

During the night also our lines were straightened out; positions changed; the right of the first division of the left wing posted on the left of the turnpike, by which movement our front was thrown back about three hundred yards; and the left wing formed on a new line toward Stone River; this gave us a shorter line, more reserves, and allowed the Regular Brigade, at about 4 o'clock a. m., of the 1st of January, to fall back to a little piece of woods near General Rosecrans' headquarters, there to bivouac and seek rest.

Early on the 1st of January, 1863, the brigade, with its battery, was ordered to the right to support McCook's wing, against which demonstrations were made, and several positions were held by it without coming into action. Shortly after two o'clock the brigade was ordered to Stewart's Creek; having marched about four miles, it received orders to return double quick, and marched nearly the whole distance at that gait. Night coming on, the brigade bivouacked again to the left of the pike, near General Rosecrans' headquarters.

On the morning of the 2nd of January, before breakfast, the brigade advanced under heavy artillery fire to the support of the left wing, remaining as its support in different positions during the day and night; the battery, being in action off and on during the day, assisted in the enemy's repulse by the left wing in the afternoon of the day.

On the morning of the 3rd, the fourth day of the battle, the battery opened fire upon one of the enemy, which was annoying our troops, and soon silenced and drove it from its position. During the forenoon the brigade and battery advanced again to its position, the key of the field, held on the 31st of December, threw up slight intrenchments and held them for the remainder of the battle. The heavy rains during the day filled the ditches partly with water and rendered them almost untenable, while the surrounding ground was fast turning into a bed of mud; the men, at their option, could stand or recline in water or mud, but not a word of discontent escaped their lips in this trying and painful, as well as arduous and dangerous service. About 6 p. m., under the cover of the brigade and other batteries, an attack was made to the front by parts of John Beatty's and Spear's Brigades; this attack, though spreading to the front of the brigade, required on its part only increased watchfulness to prevent surprise in case of a reverse; the battery, however, was actively engaged in shelling the enemy's position in the woods to our front, south.

Before daylight of the morning of the fourth, the brigade pickets reported the retreat of the enemy. The day, Sunday, was spent in the sad duty of collecting the dead of the brigade, who were interred at night by moonlight and with military honours just in front of the intrenchments.

Thus ended the battle of Stone River, or Murfreesboro'; and here it may be proper to relate a few of the many incidents occurring in and during it, showing the spirit which pervaded the officers and men of the brigade, ready to laugh one moment, the next to suffer, and, if need be, to die.

During the fight at noon of the 31st of Dec., the colour-bearer of the 2nd Battalion of the 18th was killed by a shot in the head and fell with and on the colours; the colour-guard at once raised the flag, when the top became entangled in a low cedar; the Adjutant of the battalion, then still mounted, finally called Lieut. Bisbee to the aid of the colour-guard and the colours were at last free again and thrown to the breeze; it was a moment of great anxiety to all near, for it was understood that there was to be no losing of the colours. When the left reformed after leaving the cedars, Major Townsend, when on the rise took the colours and rode along the new line for all to see that and where the stand was to be made.

Capt. Douglass, of the 18th, described the rebel artillery fire in the open field, as if a blacksmith shop full of rotten iron was being thrown at the command. When the brigade was reformed near its battery, there was a large pile of knapsacks back of it, and many men rested against it from time to time; pretty soon a rebel battery commenced firing solid shot at it, making the knapsacks fly in all directions, but doing no other harm. For a while it was a pastime to watch the solid shot coming through the air, and one ball was especially noticed, going apparently straight toward a man crossing the large open field to the rear, coming from the hospital probably; the ball seemed to strike in front of and close to the man, ricocheted and passed over the man, who at the same time made a profound obeisance; to all appearances the ball would have decapitated him, had the man been erect; a shout of laughter, seemingly from all parts of the field, at the ludicrousness of the scene, relieved the anxious feeling of suspense.

But what a closing and beginning of a year was that! A large number of officers and men, in fact all, were without rations on the 1st and 2nd, and parched corn, horse and mule steaks were in demand and appreciated; the double quick back from near Stewart's Creek was doubly hard on empty stomachs; at last, on the evening of the 2nd, some bacon, flour and coffee were received and helped to tide the command over the worst; though the men were hungry, they were in the best possible spirits. When on the 2nd the brigade advanced by the right of companies double quick to the front, one man, seeing a solid shot rolling along very leisurely, put his foot out to stop it; the opposing forces did not overcome each other, and, the shot being stronger, the man found himself nicely tripped and rolling along with the ball, much to his surprise, and, not being injured, to the merriment of his comrades.

The battalion quartermasters, with the teamsters, servants, cooks and sick, defended their trains against the charges of rebel cavalry repeatedly, repulsing the enemy every time, and saving and preserving their trains. Of the three rebel brigades of Jackson, Preston and Adams, General Bragg, the commander of their army, says:

How gallantly they moved to their work, and how much they suffered in the determined effort to accomplish it, will best appear from the reports of subordinate commanders, and the statement of losses therewith.

This shows some of the work done by the Regular Brigade, and later by its battery repulsing the determined charge of these troops on to the left of the line of battle. General Thomas, when asked why he sent the brigade into the cedars, a regular holocaust, replied that it became a necessity to do so.

The casualties in the brigade were fearful, and almost all were suffered at noon of, and all occurred on, the 31st of December.

The statement on the following page is taken from official sources, and shows the casualties in the brigade in detail:

In his official report, General Rosecrans gives his loss as follows: Killed, 92 officers, 1,441 enlisted men; total, 1,523; wounded, 384 officers, 6,861 enlisted men; total, 7,245.

Total killed and wounded, 8,778 officers and men, or 20.22% of the entire force in action; the loss of prisoners, he states, will fall short of 2,800 officers and men.

The loss of the brigade compared with the loss of the army is as follows: Officers killed in the army, 92; in the brigade, 5; = 5.4% of army loss. Officers wounded in the army, 384; in the brigade, 21; = 5.4% of army loss. Enlisted men killed in the army, 1,441; in the brigade, 89; = 6.1% of army loss. Enlisted men wounded in the army, 6,861; in the brigade, 468; = 6.8% of army loss. Captured and missing in the army, 2,800; in the brigade, 47; = 1.6% of army loss.

The loss of the army in killed and wounded was about 20% of the force in action; the loss of the brigade in killed and wounded was 37% of its strength in action.

The effective force of the army in the battle was, all told, 43,400 officers and men; the effective force, of the brigade taken into action was, all told, 1,566 officers and men, or 3.6% of the strength of the army; while the loss of killed and wounded of the brigade is 6.6% of that of the army.

The loss of killed and wounded in Scribner's Brigade was reported as 208 officers and men, or about 2.3% of army loss; in John Beatty's Brigade as 281 officers and enlisted men, or about 3.2% of army loss; while the three brigades were virtually the same in strength of effective force.

Only two brigades in the whole army report a larger loss of killed and wounded than the Regular Brigade; both were about 200 men stronger than that brigade, and suffered losses before and after the

31st December, while the loss of the Regulars was all on that day; the brigades were Carlin's, of the right wing, loss 627—but lost on the 30th 175 men, and a few more after the 31st; Grose's, of the left wing, 585—but lost before the 31st 10 men, and on the 2nd of January, the brigade report states, met with a severe loss, not as large as on the 31st, however.

These figures tell the tale, and it is doubtful if in any other engagement of the war any organization under similar circumstances suffered as large a loss.

The total number of men received by the general Government in its armies during the war, for various periods, was 2,859,132; these, reduced to a three years' standard, would make 2,320,272 men.

The average effective number of each 1,000 men in service has been computed at 693 men; this, applied to the number of men of the three years' standard, would, in round numbers, give an effective force of 1,608,000 men.

The total losses of the war, as near as it can be done with incomplete returns, has been computed to be: Killed in action, 44,238, or about 1.9% of the effective force; wounded in action, 280,000, or about 12% of the effective force; while the Regular Brigade lost on the 31st of December alone: Killed in action, 94, or 6% of its effective strength; wounded in action, 489, or 31% of its effective strength. Of course, the above computations can be applied only in a general way, inasmuch as after 1861 the actual number of men in the United States service, on an average, was, in round numbers, only about 850,000 per year.

In his report of the battle, General Geo. H. Thomas says:

In the execution of this last movement, the Regular Brigade came under a most murderous fire . . . . . but with the cooperation of Scribner's and Beatty's Brigades and Guenther's and Loomis' Batteries, gallantly held its ground against overwhelming odds.

General Rousseau, in his report, speaks of the brigade as follows:

On that body of brave men the shock of battle fell heaviest, and its loss was most severe. Over one-third of the command fell, killed or wounded. But it stood up to the work and bravely breasted the storm, and, though Major King, commanding the 15th, and Major Slemmer (old Pickens), of the 16th, fell severely wounded, and Major Carpenter, commanding the 19th, fell dead in the last charge, together with many officers and men, the brigade did not falter for a moment. These three battalions were a part of my old 4th Brigade at the battle of Shiloh. The 18th Infantry, Majors Townsend and Caldwell commanding, were new troops to me, but I am proud now to say we know each other. . . . . The brigade was admirably and gallantly handled by Lieut.-Col. Shepherd. . . . . . Of the batteries of Guenther and . . . . . I cannot say too much. . . . . . . Without them we could not have held our position in the centre.

Surgeon Eben Swift, Medical Director, Department of the Cumberland, reports:

Much of the heaviest loss sustained today fell upon our Regular Battalions, brigaded under command of Lieutenant-Colonel O. L. Shepherd, in holding the cedar brake on the right of the centre against the columns of the enemy sweeping down upon them after having forced back our entire right wing.

W. D. Bickham, who was on the field himself, in his book, *Rosecrans' Campaign with the Army of the Cumberland*, published in March, 1863, makes the following record:

The Regular Brigade, Lieut.-Col. Shepherd at the head of the column, moved steadily into the thickets, and formed with Colonel John Beatty's Brigade on the left, and Scribner's in close support. Directly a dropping fire, like the big drops which precede a storm, indicated the proximity of the enemy. . . . . But the enemy pushed hard. The gallant regulars resisted with the staunchness of their professional *esprit*, and refused to yield an inch. . . . . . The file firing of the regulars at this point was fearfully destructive.

"Pont Mercy," a correspondent of the New York *Tribune*, wrote from the battlefield:

There is a record, however, which shall be more amply made, when the Biography of the gallant Regular Brigade is ready for history. . . . . Almost one-half the casualties were regulars, while they numbered less than one-fourth of the entire division. The missing indicates discipline and skill of officers with unmistakable emphasis. It was so in the sanguinary battle of Gaines' Mills on the Peninsula.

The Regular Brigade of the West had indeed sent greeting to their comrades in the East.

As already stated, the dead of the brigade were buried in front of the position held by it nearly throughout the battle; the intention was to erect a monument over their remains, and officers and men subscribing liberally, a large sum was collected—about $4,000. The dead heroes rest now at the same point in the National Cemetery, established by the General Government; and on the 12th of May, 1883, a monument made by the sculptor, Launt Thompson, was erected over their resting-place.

The foregoing is not a fancy painted history of the brigade in this battle; it is not embellished with rhetorical allusions to fire and smoke, shot and shell, grape and canister, the roar of the cannon, the rattling of the musketry, the groans of the dying and wounded; it is a simple and plain statement of facts in unembellished terms; although the groans of the wounded and dying, the rattling of the musketry, the roar of the cannon, grape and canister, shot and shell, and fire and smoke were constant accompaniments of the shifting scenes of this bloody and destructive drama of the history of our country.

ROSTER

OF COMMISSIONED OFFICERS OF THE REGULAR BRIGADE,

AT THE BATTLE OF STONE RIVER, TENNESSEE.

Brigade Staff

Lieutenant-Colonel O. L. Shepherd, 18th Infantry, Commanding Brigade.[5]

Captain N. C. Kinney, 18th Infantry, Quartermaster.[6]

1st Lieutenant Anson Mills, 18th Infantry, Commissary of Subsistence.[7]

1st Lieutenant Robert Sutherland, 18th Infantry Act'g Assist. Adjut.-Gen'l.[6]

1st Battalion, 15th U. S. Infantry.

Major John H. King, Commanding Battalion.[3,5]

1st Lieutenant F. D. Ogilby, Adjutant.[4]

Captain Jesse Fulmer.[6]

Captain W. W. Wise.[1]

Captain J. Bowman Bell.[1]

Captain Henry Keteltas.[6]

Captain Joseph S. Yorke.[3,6]

1st Lieutenant Horace Jewett.[7]

1st Lieutenant Charles Wickoff.[7]

The following statement is taken from official sources, and shows the casualties in the brigade in detail:

	NUMBER ENGAGED		NUMBER KILLED		NUMBER WOUNDED		NUMBER CAPTURED		TOTAL LOSS	
	Commissioned Officers	Enlisted Men	Commissioned Officers	Enlisted Men	Commissioned Officers	Enlisted Men	Commissioned Officers	Enlisted Men	Commissioned Officers	Enlisted Men
Field and Staff of Brigade	4									
1st Battalion, 18th U.S. Infantry	36	301								
		293								
		398								
		373								
		398								
Battery, 5th Artillery	3	120								
Total	79	3486								
Aggregate		1560								

1st Lieutenant Sol. E. Woodward.[6]
1st Lieutenant W. B. Occlestone.[3,4]
1st Lieutenant R. P. King.[6]
1st Lieutenant James Y. Semple.[4]
2nd Lieutenant William Galloway.[6]
2nd Lieutenant Roman H. Gray.[4]

1st Battalion, 16th U. S. Infantry

Major A. J. Slemmer, Commanding.[3,4]
1st Lieutenant John Power, Adjutant.[3,6]
Captain R. E. A. Crofton.[7]
Captain R. P. Barry.[3,6]
Captain James Biddle.[6]
Captain N. L. Dykeman.[3,6]
Captain J. C. King.[3,6]
1st Lieutenant A. W. Alleyn.[6]
1st Lieutenant E. McConnell.[6]
1st Lieutenant W. H. Bartholomew.[3,4]
1st Lieutenant W. W. Arnold.[6]
1st Lieutenant J. C. Howland.[3,6]
1st Lieutenant R. E. Kellogg.[7]
2nd Lieutenant S. E. St. Onge.[6]
2nd Lieutenant W. J. Wedemeyer.[7]

1st Battalion, 18th U. S. Infantry.

Major J. N. Caldwell, Commanding.[5]
1st Lieutenant R. L. Morris, Adjutant.[4]
1st Lieutenant Dan'l W. Benham, Quartermaster.[7]
Captain Henry Douglass.[3,7]
Captain William S. Thurston.[6]
Captain David L. Wood.[3,6]
Captain Charles L. Kneass.[1]
Captain Robert B. Hull.[3,6]
Captain William H. H. Taylor.[6]
1st Lieutenant Joseph L. Proctor.[6]
1st Lieutenant Thomas T. Brand.[5]
1st Lieutenant Samuel I. Dick.[4]
1st Lieutenant Joseph McConnell.[2]
1st Lieutenant Gilbert S. Carpenter.[3,7]
2nd Lieutenant Merrill N. Hutchinson.[5]
2nd Lieutenant Ebenezer D. Harding.[6]

2nd Lieutenant John J. Adair.[3,6]

2nd Battalion, 18th U. S. Infantry
Major Frederick Townsend, Commanding.[6]
1st Lieutenant Frederick Phisterer, Adjutant.[6]
1st Lieutenant Wm. P. McClery, Quartermaster.[6]
Captain Henry R. Mizner.[7]
Captain Charles E. Denison.[2]
Captain Henry Belknap.[6]
Captain Ai B. Thompson.[3,5]
Captain Wm. J. Fetterman.[4]
Captain Henry Haymond.[3,6]
Captain Ansel B. Denton.[6]
1st Lieutenant Morgan L. Ogden.[3,6]
1st Lieutenant Herman G. Radcliff.[4]
1st Lieutenant James Simons.[2]
1st Lieutenant Henry B. Freeman.[7]
2nd Lieutenant William H. Bisbee.[7]
2nd Lieutenant John F. Hitchcock.[1]
2nd Lieutenant Wilbur F. Arnold.[4]

1st Battalion, 19th U. S. Infantry
Major S. D. Carpenter, Commanding.[1]
1st Lieutenant Howard E. Stansbury, Adjutant.[6]
Captain James B. Mulligan.[6]
1st Lieutenant A. H. Andrews.[6]
1st Lieutenant Jacob D. Jones.[6]
2nd Lieutenant Joseph J. Waggoner.[4]
2nd Lieutenant Wm. R. Lowe.[6]
2nd Lieutenant Alfred Curtis.[6]
2nd Lieutenant Chas. F. Miller.[4]
2nd Lieutenant Geo. W. Johnson.[6]
2nd Lieutenant Arthur B. Carpenter.[6]

Battery H, 5th U. S. Artillery
1st Lieutenant F. L. Guenther, Commanding.[7]
2nd Lieutenant Israel Ludlow.[6]
2nd Lieutenant J. A. Fessenden.[7]
Medical Department
Assistant Surgeon Webster Lindsley, Acting Brigade Surgeon.[4]
Acting Assistant Surgeon Patton.[6]
Acting Assistant Surgeon Henderson.[6]

Notes

1. Killed in battle of Stone River.
2. Died of wounds received at Stone River.
3. Wounded at Stone River.
4. Died in service since Stone River.
5. Retired.
6. Resigned, discharged, mustered out, and out of service.
7. still in the U. S. Army, active list

BATTLES AND ENGAGEMENTS
PARTICIPATED IN BY THE REGULAR BRIGADE.

Stone River or Murfreesboro', Tenn., Dec. 31, 1862 to Jan. 3, 1863.
Eagleville, Tennessee, March 2, 1863.
Hover's Gap, Tennessee, June 26, 1863.
Chicamauga, Ga., September 19 to 21, 1863.
Mission Ridge, Tenn., November 25, 1863.
Buzzard Roost and Tunhill, Ga., Feb. 25 to 27, 1864.
Rocky Faced Ridge, Ga., May 5 to 9, 1864.
Resaca, Ga., May 13 to 15, 1864.
New Hope Church, Ga., May 28, June 1 and 4, 1864.
Kenesaw Mountain, Ga., June 22 and 30, 1864
Neal Dow Station, Ga., July 3 and 4, 1864.
Peachtree Creek, Ga., July 20, 1864.
Atlanta, Ga., July 27 and 31, and August, 1864.
Utoy Creek, Ga., Aug. 7, 1864.
Jonesboro', Ga., September 1, 1864.

ENGAGEMENTS AND BATTLES PARTICIPATED IN
BY THE BATTALIONS BEFORE ORGANIZATION OF
THE REGULAR BRIGADE.

15th, 16th and 19th U. S. Infantry

Shiloh, Tenn., April 7, 1862.
Corinth, Miss., May, 1862

1st and 2nd Battalions, 18th U. S. Infantry

Lick Creek, Miss., April 26, 1862.
Corinth, Miss., May, 1862.
Springfield to Texas, Ky., October 6, 1862.
Perryville or Chaplin Hill, Ky., October 8, 1862

The Battle of Stone's River Near Murfreesboro', Tenn.

By Alexander F. Stevenson

Preface

The story of the great battles of our civil war will grow in inter-est as the years pass on. Believing that every participant should, as far as circumstances permit, write down and make public such incidents as have come to his notice, I have, at the request of many comrades, undertaken the task of writing a history of the battle of Stone's River. My authorities are the reports, both Union and Confederate, in the archives of the War Department, together with the maps accompany-ing them.

I am aware that this account differs from others heretofore pub-lished; but I know that the latter do not place the Confederate troops in the positions actually held by them. In order to elucidate the progress of the battle I have compiled a map from a number of sources.

The Confederate positions are taken from the maps of Generals Bragg, Polk, and others, and are ascertained to be correct by the regi-mental and brigade reports.

The positions of the Union troops are taken from regimental and brigade reports.

It is a source of regret that many acts of personal heroism, and the incidents accompanying them, have not been given in detail in the reports.

It would be a pleasure to me to incorporate in a future edition, should this narrative find favour with my comrades, such well-authen-ticated incidents of heroism as may be communicated to me.

Too many of our most gallant men lie in nameless graves; the story of many brave and daring acts has never been told; and it becomes the sacred duty of all survivors to give to the world at large the circumstances of the heroic deaths of those that fell.

To reconcile all the reports of the different division, brigade, and regimental commanders with each other is an impossibility; there are honest mistakes, and there are also instances where the pens of the writers were mightier than their swords.

My thanks are due to Lieutenant-General P. H. Sheridan; Hon. Robert T. Lincoln, Secretary of War; U.S. Senator John A. Logan, and Colonel Robert M. Scott of the War Record Office, for valuable Union and Confederate reports and maps furnished or loaned to me, and without which I would not have attempted to write what I believe to be a true account.

Alexander F. Stevenson.

Chicago, Illinois, February, 1884.

CHAPTER 1

THE ADVANCE ON MURFREESBORO', TENN.

On the 24th day of October, 1862, an order was given by the Secretary of War creating the Department of the Cumberland. In it General W. S. Rosecrans was ordered to relieve General D. C. Buelll of the command of the troops designated as the Fourteenth Army Corps, but which was known as the Army of the Cumberland. In compliance with this order General Rosecrans took command of the department at Louisville on the 30th. On the 2nd of November he arrived at Bowling Green, and on November 7th a general order was issued, dividing the army into the Right Wing, under General A. McD. McCook; the Centre under General G. H. Thomas; and the Left Wing under General T. L. Crittenden.

The city of Nashville, occupied by Negley's and Paine's divisions (the latter commanded by General John M. Palmer), was still surrounded by the rebels and frequently threatened with assault. The morale effect of taking the capital of Tennessee was urged by many rebel leaders as a reason for trying capture it; while the property owners vigorously protested, and claimed that the destruction and loss of their property by the cannonade and fight would counterbalance any supposed stimulating effect on the inhabitants of the State. A serious attempt to capture the city was, therefore, never made. General Rosecrans, however, was determined to hold Nashville, and General

Thomas was ordered to guard the railway from Louisville to Nashville with two of his divisions, then to push immediately towards the latter city, and aid in forwarding supplies to the troops defending it. General Thomas thereupon established his headquarters at Gallatin, and with his usual care and vigilance began this task.

On the 17th day of November, 1862, the first troops of the advancing army came to the relief of the besieged divisions at Nashville, and a few days afterwards General Rosecrans established his headquarters in that city. After becoming acquainted with the strength of his own army, as well as that of the enemy, he foresaw the weakness of his cavalry in comparison with Bragg's, and asked the War Department for an increase in this branch of the service; but without success. Immediately before the advance the following changes were made in different commands, for various reasons, such as seniority, ill-health, etc.

General J. M. Palmer was ordered to take command of Nelson's famous division, then commanded by W. S. Smith; General T. J. Wood, of Hascall's division; General J. C. Davis, of McCook's First division. General R. W. Johnson, a ranking officer, took command of Sill's division. General Sill was placed in command of Greusel's First brigade, in Sheridan's division, and General R. B. Mitchell relieved General Negley in command of Nashville. The Right Wing, under General McCook, passed through Nashville, and went into camp near Mill Creek, a few miles south of that city. General Crittenden crossed the Cumberland, and, by way of Silver Springs, likewise went into camp, not far from McCook. About the 22nd day of December General Thomas reached Nashville, and made the following disposition of his command: Rousseau's and Negley's divisions, and Walker's brigade of Fry's division, were ordered to be ready for active service; Mitchell's division, composed of Brig.-Gen. J. D. Morgan's and Col. Dan. Mc-Cook's brigades, was left as a garrison in Nashville, while Reynolds's division and two brigades of Fry's division were placed along the railway to Louisville, to guard it against the assaults of the rebel cavalry under General Morgan and others.

Colonel Roberts, of the Forty-second Illinois, commanding a brigade under General John M. Palmer during the siege, disliked the idea of doing garrison duty, and applied to the commanding general to assign his brigade where they could meet the enemy in battle, and General Rosecrans thereupon ordered him to report to General Sheridan, and to take the place of the brigade commanded by Colonel McCook. As the true excellence of Colonel Roberts as a soldier is but little known or remembered now, it may not be improper to give a short description of him here, as an additional evidence that his heroism in this battle is not a mere fanciful story, but true in every detail

Tall in stature, with a grand muscular frame, he had an appearance that indicated great strength of character. His bravery, courage, and daring, could not be excelled by any man, as he was absolutely without fear. When on the Mississippi River, above Island No. 10, he displayed at once the nature of his character.

The gunboats and transports on the Mississippi River desired to pass this island; but it was impossible to do so, owing to a battery so placed that its guns were but a few inches above the water, threatening annihilation to any vessel attempting the pas- sage. It was known as the Upper Battery, or No. 10 Fort. Colonel Roberts asked permission to take it. This was at first refused, as being absolutely foolhardy; but, persisting in his request, he finally obtained leave to undertake his daring exploit. He waited for a stormy night. On the 1st of April, 1862, a terrible storm swept over this region. The elements burst forth in their greatest fury; the waves of the Mississippi River were lashed into foam; at midnight the gale turned into a hurricane, boats were torn from their moorings by the terrible winds, and it seemed certain that venturesome small craft would be utterly destroyed in the stormy depths. But this was Roberts's hour for action, and he asked for five boats, with the necessary oarsmen.

Selecting then about forty men, exclusive of officers, from the Forty-second Illinois, they embarked and drifted with the strong current towards the battery. The rain poured in torrents. In the boats all was silence. The oars and oar-locks had been muffled; not a word was spoken. Each moment it seemed as if the waves breaking over the boats, and filling them, were preparing a watery grave for these gallant men. These were grand, solemn, and terrible moments,—the enemy's battery in front, the angry waves around them, while brilliant flashes of lightning illuminated the awful scene. Still they drifted steadily on. Suddenly there was an intensely bright flash in advance; it lighted up the whole surrounding country, and a roar followed as though a hundred guns had been fired in quick succession. The hearts of brave men even ceased to pulsate for an instant, as they expected the rebels' cannon-balls to crush the frail yawls into fragments. But, thank God! it had been the heavens' artillery, and its light had. shown them how close they were to the enemy's battery and where the sentinels were posted.

Still they drifted nearer, the oarsmen ready to pull with all their strength, when the command should be given; nearer they came; but a few rods intervened, when the order came in low tones, but sufficiently loud for anxious ears to hear: "Now, boys!" and the boats shot like arrows through the waves. For the men to jump to the embankment was but the work of an instant. The sentinels fled in dismay, as though demons had risen from the waters. The alarm being given, the rest of the rebels ran for dear life. Strong files and hammers quickly did their work, and in a minute's time every gun was spiked, and not a life was lost. The guns thus disabled were two 64-pounders, three 80-pounders, and one 9-inch pivot-gun.

You can readily imagine how eager a man like Colonel Roberts must have been to meet his country's enemies in battle. Roberts's brigade, on reporting to General Sheridan, was designated as the third of that division.

Nothing important occurred until about Christmas. Everyone was busy in getting ready for the coming battle. Occasionally an order came to get the command ready, and even on Christmas morning it was believed that our march would begin that day. Here an incident occurred that shows how ignorant and forgetful we are that the Angel of Death stands close to the soldier's side.

Colonel Roberts had invited to his headquarters a few friends to take a Christmas dinner,—frugal, to be sure, when compared with those we had at home. Among them were Colonel Harrington, Lieutenant Tallioferro, and Lieutenant-Colonel Swanwick. When a toast was drunk to the success of our arms in the approaching battle, Colonel Roberts rose, with his grand physique, speaking full of enthusiasm and eloquence of our great cause, thrilling his hearers as a man with a splendid voice only can. He ended with these words: "I will take all chances of rebel bullets."—"So will I,"—"So will I," quickly joined Harrington and Tallioferro, and the glasses rung amid renewed cheers.

But, alas! not a week had passed, and these three brave, enthusiastic, and patriotic men lay naked, on the bloodstained battlefield of Stone's River, robbed even of their clothing to the skin. [1]

During the night of December 25th the order came to move forward, and in the early morning of December 26th the army began its

1. In honour of the Confederate General A. P. Stewart, it ought to be mentioned that he called attention to this stripping of the dead, and asked that an order forbidding it be issued.

march towards the south.

It was then still uncertain where the enemy would make a stand?, and the different corps had to march in such a manner that they could support each other in case of encountering superior numbers. Many believed that the enemy would make a halt on the steep banks of Stewart's Creek; while others considered that the familiar grounds of his winter-quarters at Murfreesboro' would be chosen as offering superior advantages for defence.

General Stanley, chief of cavalry, assigned Minty's brigade, under Colonel Kennett, to Crittenden's Corps, Zahm's brigade to McCook's, and the remainder of the cavalry he commanded himself, with the exception of the Fourth U.S., which was detailed for escort and courier duty; the whole effective force not exceeding three thousand men. General Crittenden's Corps, composed of Palmer's, Wood's, and Van Clove's divisions, advanced on the direct road,—the Murfreesboro' pike,—with directions to move but slowly until McCook's Corps should reach Triune, and ascertain whether Hardee would offer battle there or retreat, and whether the retreat would be towards Murfreesboro'. In commencing the march on this rainy Friday, General Palmer's division had the advance.

After skirmishing with the enemy's cavalry all day, the division bivouacked with the remainder of Crittenden's Corps, near La Vergne, about fifteen miles from Nashville. On Saturday, Dec. 27th, about 11 a.m.,[2] General Wood's division took the lead. The village of La Vergne, a short distance from the front, being occupied by Confederate General Maney's brigade and General Wheeler's cavalry, General Hascall was ordered to drive the rebels from it. Cavalry being considered of little use in this wooded part of the country, Hascall formed his command in two lines, and in a few minutes' time had driven the enemy from the houses. His pursuit was constant and vigorous, and he followed the rebels with such rapidity that the Third Kentucky dashed on the bridge spanning Stewart's Creek, five miles from La Vergne, and extinguished the fire set to it by the enemy ere much damage had been done, and thus saved an important link on the road to Murfreesboro'.

About the same hour, 11.30 a.m., General Palmer likewise received orders to move forward, following Wood, with directions to send one brigade to the Jefferson pike, and seize the bridge where it crosses

2. The movement was commenced late, for the reason that McCook was still some distance from Triune.

Stewart's Creek. This task was assigned to Col. W. B. Hazen, who had, the evening before, joined his brigade. Ninety men of the Fourth Michigan Cavalry, under Captain Maxey, being ordered to report to him, he directed them to put spurs into their horses as soon as they had succeeded in driving the enemy, and not to stop until they had reached the bridge, while the infantry and artillery were ordered to follow as quickly as possible. The enemy was overtaken within three miles of the bridge, whereupon a chase ensued till the bridge was reached and saved.

That night Crittenden's Corps bivouacked in the vicinity of Stewart's Creek. December 28th, being Sunday, the army rested. On December 29th General Crittenden advanced again. Wood's division, with Wagner's brigade leading, moved on the left; while Palmer's division, Colonel Grose's brigade leading, advanced on the right of the Murfreesboro' pike, Grose's men wading waist-deep through Stewart's Creek rather than wait till they could pass over the bridge. Van Cleve's division moved in the rear as a reserve, while General Negley, who had reached Stewart's Creek the evening before, crossed it about one and a half miles west of Palmer, and then moved on Crittenden's right flank. The enemy opposed the advance of Crittenden, but was driven back until Wood and Palmer, about sundown, succeeded in taking a position about two and a half miles from Murfreesboro', where they established their line of battle, Wood on the left and Palmer on the right of the pike; Palmer being joined by Hazen later in the evening. Scarcely had they halted when an order came from General Crittenden to Wood and Palmer to advance on the enemy.

Wood protested, but sent Colonel Harker, with his brigade, across Stone's River to attack the enemy at that point. (Breckenridge.) General Palmer protested also most vigorously, and, pointing to the entrenched camp of the enemy but a few hundred yards distant, declared it a folly to make a night attack against an enemy in a fortified position, whose strength was unknown, and on grounds entirely unfamiliar to any one of the federal officers. Palmer's and Wood's protests were so vigorous, and these two gallant generals agreeing to bear all the responsibility, General Crittenden suspended the order for one hour. General Rosecrans arriving in the meantime, it was ascertained that he had received a signal dispatch, purporting to come from General Palmer, to the effect that the rebels had evacuated Murfreesboro' and were in full retreat, and that this was the reason for ordering Crittenden to advance. Finding, on inquiry, that no dispatch of that nature had been sent by Palmer, the order was countermanded, and Colonel Harker succeeded in withdrawing his line from across Stone's river without serious loss. Van Cleve's division remained as a reserve. General Crittenden made his headquarters at the toll-gate near the front that night, and was afterwards joined by General Rosecrans.

As soon as the enemy had been driven from Stewart's Creek the Pioneer brigade, 1,600 strong, under Captain J. St. Clair Morton, was ordered forward to construct bridges; after constructing two over Stewart's creek they arrived, on December 30th, near the front, and went into camp about three miles from Murfreesboro'.

General Thomas, with Rousseau's and Negley's divisions and Walker's brigade, marched on the Franklin pike to Brentwood, then, by way of the Wilson pike, to Nolensville; marching from there, Negley arrived at Stewartsboro', about nine miles from Murfreesboro', on the evening of December 27th, and Rousseau, owing to the continual rains, a day later. On the 29th Negley's division advanced in support of Crittenden's right flank, as above indicated, and halted about three miles from Murfreesboro'; Rousseau remaining in camp at Stewartsboro' with all of his division except Starkweather's brigade, which was sent to the Jefferson pike crossing of Stone's River to observe the enemy. Walker's brigade reached Stewartsboro' that same night.

On the morning of December 30th Rousseau's three remaining brigades marched towards Murfreesboro', halting three miles from it; Negley having been ordered before his arrival to oblique to the right and to take a position on the right of Palmer, in a south-westerly direction, towards the Wilkinson pike, a little north-east of Harding's house, where the Nineteenth Illinois in approaching met the enemy, and immediately commenced to skirmish with the rebel sharp-shooters.

General McCook had likewise commenced his movement on the 26th day of December, in the direction of Nolensville. General Davis, with the First division, took the Edmonson pike to Prim's blacksmith-shop, and then moved by a country road to Nolensville; General Sheridan, with the Third division, took the direct road to Nolensville; General Johnson, with the Second division, following him on the same route.

Triune was reached on December 27th, and a reconnoissance was ordered to be made by General Willich, of Johnson's division, on the 28th, to ascertain in what direction Hardee had retreated. It was found that he had gone south about six miles on the Shelbyville pike, and then taken a road that leads into the Salem pike to Murfreesboro'.

Leaving Baldwin's brigade, of Johnson's division, at Triune, the corps marched, on the 29th day of December, on the Bolejack road, to Murfreesboro'. General Davis, leading with his division, reached Wilkinson's cross-roads (five miles from Murfreesboro') long after dark. On the same evening word was sent to Baldwin's brigade to speed towards Murfreesboro'.

On the morning of the 30th the corps again moved forward, General Sheridan's division in front and Colonel Roberts's brigade in the advance. With the exception of some small skirmishing on the right or south of the Wilkinson pike, in which Major Rosengarten, encountering infantry, lost his life, nothing important occurred until the advance regiment, the Twenty-second Illinois, reached a place about two and a half miles from Murfreesboro', where the Nineteenth Illinois had been thrown out as skirmishers to the south of the Wilkinson pike, guarding Negley's right. The confederate sharpshooters, by their accurate aim, had wounded quite a number, and the Nineteenth Illinois seemed sorely pressed, as no one could show his head from behind the trees in that timber without being sure that a moment afterwards a bullet would pass very near it.

When the Twenty-second, therefore, came to their relief, a general shout arose, and Colonel Roberts, but a few rods behind the skirmish line, gave this gallant regiment the order to drive the rebels out. Having received no orders where to halt, he kept advancing until he had gone far beyond Negley's line on his left; but a short distance further, and he would have encountered the rebels in their breastworks. A few moments before this General Sheridan came in full speed down the Wilkinson pike, and halting the Forty-second Illinois, which was immediately in rear of the Twenty-second, he sent word to Roberts to come back and form a line on the immediate right of Negley, resting his own left on the Wilkinson pike.

The Twenty-second and Forty-second Illinois were thereupon placed in line of battle immediately to the right of Negley, with skirmishers as far as possible in advance, the command facing east, the Twenty-seventh and Fifty-first Illinois being in reserve.

Sill's brigade took up a position early in the morning to the right and rear of Roberts's, facing towards the south, advancing about as far as Harding's house about noon. In so doing an artillery duel occurred between Bush's battery and that of Waters, of Manigault's brigade, in which the rebel battery had to seek cover. Schaefer's brigade was held in reserve. General Davis, following General Sheridan's division, had in the meantime placed his command on the right of General Sill's brigade, also facing south, and about three hundred yards south of Wilkinson's pike and parallel with it General Johnson's division was kept in reserve.

About 2 o'clock p.m. an order came from General McCook to advance General Sill's brigade and General Davis' division, with special orders to General Johnson to look well to his right. The movement for Sill's brigade was in the nature of a left wheel for about ninety degrees of a circle from their original position, which brought them in a line a little in the rear of Roberts's line, also facing towards the east. General Davis marched his division directly forward, and then obliqued a little to the left, so as to place his extreme left slightly to the rear of the extreme right of General Sill, forming with his line a right angle to that of Sill. General Johnson sent General Kirk's brigade to the right of Davis's division, with instructions to refuse his own right so as to protect his right flank; and, later in the evening, General Johnson sent General Willich's brigade to the right of Kirk, directing him to throw out a heavy line of skirmishers as far as possible to the front.

Colonel Baldwin's brigade was held in reserve over a mile in rear of Willich's front. As some changes were made during the night, it is best to give the line of battle as it stood an hour before daylight on December 31st, giving first the Right Wing, or the troops on the right or south side of the Wilkinson pike, and afterwards the Left Wing and Centre.

The Fifty-first and Twenty-seventh Illinois were in the front line, their left resting on the pike, and the Twenty-second and Forty-second Illinois in reserve. These regiments (Roberts's brigade) all faced east; the first two in the cedars, the latter in the open field north of Harding's house. To the right of the Twenty-seventh Illinois stood Sill's brigade, first the Eighty-eighth Illinois in the open field; then Bush's battery to its right, slightly in advance, on account of the ground, the Thirty-sixth Illinois; to its right, again bending back a little, and extending to a cornfield south of the timber, the Twenty-fourth Wisconsin; while the Twenty-first Michigan stood as a supporting column to the Eighty-eighth Illinois and in rear of it.

Houghtalling's and Hescock's batteries were placed on elevated positions not far from Harding's house, and west of it; while the Second brigade, under Colonel Schaefer, was held in reserve till early in the morning, when the Fifteenth Missouri and Forty-fourth Illinois were moved into the timber in rear of the Thirty-sixth Illinois as a supporting column. From Sill's right the line of battle made an angle to the west, held by Woodruffs brigade, of Davis's division. At the angle between Sill and Woodruff three guns from Carpenter's battery were placed; to its right the Eighty-first Indiana, then the Twenty-fifth Illinois. Here again the line made an angle towards the south, in which the other three guns from Carpenter's battery held a commanding position, and on the right of these stood the Thirty-fifth Illinois. The line was long and without reserves, but protected by a fence, behind which the troops found shelter. Colonel Carlin's brigade was on the right of the Thirty-fifth Illinois, facing in a south-south-easterly direction; in the front line the Thirty-eighth Illinois and One-hundred-and-first Ohio; between them, somewhat retired, Hotchkiss' Minnesota battery, supported by the Fifteenth Wisconsin on its left, and the Twenty-first Illinois on its right.

This brigade was somewhat in advance of those to its left and right, and had, on the previous evening, driven the rebels very close to their line of battle, when Colonel Alexander, with the Twenty-first Illinois, made a brilliant dash at Captain Robertson's Confederate battery, placed temporarily west of Widow Smith's house, driving the cannoneers from their pieces. But when about eighty yards from the fence near this widow's house, the rebel infantry, in largely overwhelming numbers, and well protected by the fences and out-houses, poured upon them such a terrific fire that the gallant men had to return, leaving many of their brave comrades either dead wounded in the hands of the enemy. This attack was ordered by General Davis himself.

In the early morning, therefore, the line was drawn back about two hundred yards, the respective regiments keeping nearly their former positions. On the right of Carlin was Colonel Post's brigade; but, as this brigade changed its position before the enemy reached this part of the field, it is unnecessary to save the position of its regiments and battery till they came into action. To the right of Colonel Post was General Kirk's brigade, the left regiment facing south and the others in an easterly direction, as follows: on the left the Seventy-seventh Pennsylvania; then the Thirtieth Indiana; then the Twenty-ninth Indiana,—all in heavy woods; to its right Edgarton's battery, in open ground, and on its right the Thirty-fourth Illinois, its right resting on the Franklin road.

The line of battle here again made a right angle. General Willich's brigade was placed to the right and rear of General Kirk; facing south, immediately in rear of the Thirty-fourth Illinois, stood the reserve companies (five each) of the Thirty-ninth Indiana, and to its right the Thirty-second Indiana; on the right of the Thirty-second Indiana was a lane; on the west side of this lane, also facing south, stood the Forty-ninth Ohio; to its right Goodspeed's battery; two guns facing south and four to the west; in rear of the Forty-ninth Ohio the Eighty-ninth Illinois, and to the right of it the Fifteenth Ohio, facing towards the west.

To the rear of Willich's, more than a mile away, was placed Baldwin's brigade, as a reserve.

The Left Wing and Centre stood in the following lines: Van Cleve's division was placed on Stone's river, near a ford, about three miles from Murfreesboro' in rear of the left of our line, with orders to cross Stone's river early on December 31st, and to move against the enemy on the east side of the river. General Hascall's brigade, of Wood's division, was in his front on the extreme left, with orders to cross the river as soon as Van Cleve was over; this brigade guarding the ford over which it was to cross with the One-hundredth Illinois and Fifty-eighth Indiana. Colonel Barker's brigade was on the right of Hascall's, its right resting in a small piece of wood east of the Nashville R.R., and Colonel Wagner's brigade was in line to the right of Harker, its right resting on the Nashville pike about two and one-half miles from Murfreesboro'. Each of these brigades changed their line of battle before they met the enemy, and it is therefore of no importance how each regiment stood in the early dawn of that memorable day.

On the right of the Nashville pike, perhaps a little in advance of Wagner's right, was Colonel Hazen's brigade, of General Palmer's division; in the front line on the left the Forty-first Ohio; on the right, the Sixth Kentucky, supported by the One-hundredth Illinois on the left, and the Ninth Indiana on the right. The left of the brigade rested about five hundred yards north-west from the intersection of railway and pike, and the line of the brigade formed nearly a right angle with the pike and extended near the woods on the right. Two hundred and fifty yards to the right of Hazen was the left of Colonel Cruft's brigade; in the front line the Second Kentucky on the left, and the Thirty-first Indiana, with Standart's battery, on the right; the Ninetieth Ohio in rear of Second Kentucky, and First Kentucky in rear of Thirty-first Indiana. In rear of the interval between these two brigades stood Colonel Grose's brigade in reserve. About three-eighths of a mile in rear of Colonel Grose was Rousseau's division, the reserve of General Thomas's Corps.

The Pioneer brigade, with Stokes' battery, was near the river, and a little further from Murfreesboro' than Van Cleve's division, engaged in improving the fords across the river. Following the line of battle to the right came finally the two brigades of General Negley's division.

To the right of Cruft was Colonel Miller's brigade, facing southeast in the following order, from left to right: Hewitt's battery, Twenty-first Ohio, Marshall's battery, Seventy-fourth Ohio, Thirty-seventh Indiana, and Seventy-eighth Pennsylvania; to his right Colonel Stanley's brigade, who changed his line as soon as General Sheridan took his third position along the Wilkinson pike, and thus came in his front. The regiments and battery were placed as follows, from left to right: Schulz's battery, Sixty-ninth Ohio; Eleventh Michigan, in the front line, the latter resting near the Wilkinson pike, in rear of the Sixty-ninth; the Eighteenth Ohio, and some distance in the rear, the Nineteenth Illinois as a reserve.

Everyone was eager for the fight, but anxious as to when and where the first blow would be struck. Some believed the enemy would retreat, little knowing How General Bragg was manoeuvring to make an almost crushing assault in the very beginning of the battle.

CHAPTER 2

THE MOVEMENTS OF THE CONFEDERATE ARMY

Before the advance of the Union army the Confederate pickets extended from Murfreesboro' to within two miles of our lines; the Centre of the Confederate army composed of Cheatham's and Withers's divisions, under Lieutenant-General Polk, and Palmer's, Preston's and Hanson's brigades, of Breckenridge's division, was at Murfreesboro'. The Right was at Readyville, twelve miles east of Murfreesboro', under General McCown; while the Left, consisting of Cleburne's division and Adams's brigade, of Breckenridge's division, was at Triune and at Eagleville, the latter twenty miles west of Murfreesboro', under Lieutenant-General Hardee. The simultaneous advance of our troops on several roads, quickly reported to General Bragg, convinced him that this was a general movement of the Union army, and that a battle would have to be fought. He gave directions, therefore, to impede the Federals' progress as much as possible, choosing in the meantime the most favourable positions for his army. He formed his line of battle about two miles from Murfreesboro'.

In so doing the left of the Confederate line—Loomis's brigade, of Withers's division—rested on the north side of the Franklin road, a few rods east of the house of Widow Smith, extending in a north-easterly direction; on his right was Manigault's brigade, extending in north-north-west direction; on his right Walthall's brigade, commanded by General J. Patten Anderson, turning in an easterly direction of about forty-five degrees from Manigault's line; and on his right Chalmers's brigade, whose right extended to Stone's river, near the crossing of the pike and the Nashville railroad. These four brigades all belonged to Withers's division. These troops threw up breastworks as speedily as possible, constructing them from stones and logs in the immediate neighbourhood.

From five to eight hundred yards in rear of this first line, as above indicated, conforming themselves to the ground, was placed Cheatham's division, in the following order: Vaughan's brigade on the extreme left, in rear of Loomis's; Maney's in support of Manigault's; General A. P. Stewart's in rear of Anderson's, but placed in a still more easterly direction, not far from the river, so as to be easily available in case General Chalmers should be attacked; and General Donelson, as a second line to Chalmers, his left resting on the ridge about three hundred yards south-east from Widow James's house.

To simplify commands, and to prevent loss of time, General Cheatham received the command of the two left brigades of Withers, as well as his own two brigades in rear of them, while General Withers received the command of the four brigades to the right.

These two divisions constituted a corps, under the command of Lieutenant-General Polk. About two hundred yards in rear of Chalmers's right, but on the east side of Stone's River, Breckenridge's division was placed, Hanson's brigade on the left; then Palmer's, then Preston's; and on the extreme right, resting its right on the Lebanon road, about one and one half miles from Murfreesboro', Adams's brigade. A short distance in advance of Adams's, and on the right (east) side of the Lebanon road, Jackson's brigade took position for a short time. Parallel with Breckenridge, but also from seven to eight hundred yards in rear of it, was Cleburne's division, both divisions forming a corps, under command of Lieutenant-General Hardee. There being an important eminence about six hundred yards in front of Hanson's line, General Breckenridge ordered Hanson, on Monday evening, December 29th, to take possession of it, and the latter placed there Cobb's battery, supported by the Sixth and Ninth Kentucky and the Forty-first Alabama. On December 30th Semple's battery of Napoleon guns was placed on another elevation, to the left and rear of the former, while Cobb's battery was, at the same time, reinforced by a section of Lumsden's battery, and also a section of Slocomb's Washington artillery.

General McCown's division, of Kirby Smith's Corps, finally held a position near the Nashville pike, behind Stone's River, as a reserve.

After Crittenden's Corps had forced General Wheeler's cavalry back of the rebel line of battle Wheeler rested for a few hours. About midnight, December 29th, General Bragg ordered him to proceed to the enemy's rear; and this dashing officer started at once on a raid that cost the Federal Government several hundred thousand dollars, and showed the wisdom of General Rosecrans in asking for more cavalry ere the advance should be made. Wheeler's command consisted of the First Alabama, Third Alabama, Fifty-first Alabama, Eighth Confederate, Holman's and Douglas's two battalions, and a part of Wiggin's battery, reinforced by Colonel Carter's First Tennessee Cavalry. Starting at a sharp trot, General Wheeler reached Jefferson by daylight, and destroyed a large train of wagons, with contents.

A few hours later he captured A small train on the road towards La Vergne; reaching that hamlet at noon, he burned an immense amount of army stores. From this place he proceeded to Rock Springs, when he overtook another train, leaving it in smouldering ruins. He then rode to Nolensville, and set fire to a large number of wagons filled with army stores, and paroled also a number of prisoners taken with the different trains. After resting a few hours at Nolensville, he left at 2 o'clock a.m., arriving at the Murfreesboro' and Nashville pike, just north of Overall's Creek, at a time when the Right Wing was already fighting. He at once attacked the Union forces, but was repulsed.

McCook's Corps coming on the Triune road towards Murfreesboro', General Bragg, on December 29th, ordered General McCown to fill a supposed gap between the left of Lieutenant-General Polk's Corps and the Franklin road; but there being none, McCown placed his division on the left of Loomis's brigade, and about one hundred and fifty yards in front, along a lane which runs at nearly a right angle with the Franklin road, as follows: Rains's brigade on the extreme left, on his right Ector's, and McNair's brigade in an oblique line between Ector's right and Loomis's left.

The Union troops not attacking December 30th, and General McCook swinging his corps towards the east and south in a rather long line, General Bragg sent orders, about 8 o'clock that evening, to General Cleburne to withdraw his line in rear of General Breckenridge, and to move it to the extreme left of the army, in rear of Mc-

Cown's division. In obeying this order he placed his division about five hundred yards in rear of McCown, as follows: Liddell's brigade on the extreme left; then Johnson's Brigade, whose left rested near the McCullough house; on his right, Polk's, whose' right rested on the Franklin road; and three hundred yards in rear of Polk's stood Wood's brigade. Many of the troops did not get into position until midnight, and the ammunition trains could be heard for several hours afterwards, though straw and hay had been placed on stony places to prevent the Federals from hearing the massing of troops in front of McCook. Lieutenant-General Hardee was then ordered to take command of these two divisions.

The precautions taken by the Confederates did not succeed, however, in keeping the watchful generals of the Union army in ignorance. About 2 o'clock that night gallant General Sill came over to General Sheridan's headquarters (consisting of a large log and a small fire), and informed him that there was great activity in the camp of the enemy beyond, and the two generals instantly walked quickly to the picket line on the extreme right of Sill. It required but a few minutes' listening to convince General Sheridan that an early and a desperate attack might be expected, and he requested General Sill to accompany him to General McCook's headquarters to inform that general of the approaching danger.

It was reported immediately after the battle—and there are evidences that the report is true—that General Sheridan, in terms as positive as a junior general can speak to his superior, called General McCook's attention to the fact that his line was very long and not well supported; that it was very near the enemy's line, and that it seemed to him an absolute necessity to draw it farther back and to concentrate the same in such a manner that support could be sent to any part of the field needing assistance. He further, it is said, called his attention to the fact that the enemy was massing new troops on the (rebel) left, and that there was little doubt that he would attack General McCook's extreme right early in the morning with overwhelming numbers. But General McCook declined to make any change whatever, claiming, as appears by his report, that his orders from General Rosecrans were positive as to his line, forgetting, perhaps, that a corps commander has always some discretion left him when circumstances demand action; while General Rosecrans, in his report, states that, lot having been over the ground, he relied on General McCook, who had passed over it, and left everything to him.

While this controversy cannot be solved now, this much is certain,— that General McCook did not consider it necessary to go to the front himself; that he did not send messengers to General Rosecrans that night, calling his attention to the massing of more troops in his front, and asking for permission to change his line, if General Rosecrans's orders were imperative; nor are there any indications in the reports that he sent messengers to warn General Johnson and General Davis of the enemy's movements, and to require additional vigilance on the part of Willich, Kirk, Post, and others.

No one will speak ill of General McCook from malice, for he is a man of generous impulses, kind in his disposition, fond of good company, running over with laughter and good cheer, and every one will cheerfully bear testimony to his bravery in action. In command of a division he would have been a success; as commander of a corps he was not; for to win battles it is not alone necessary to be brave, but the general must have great energy, quick decision, and a presence so fall of courage, enthusiasm, and rage if need be, that a panic-struck soldier will halt when he sees his general, and turn for the enemy at the mere waving of his sword. If General Sheridan had been in command of the corps that day the battle of December 31st would have resulted differently.

General McCook seems to have underestimated the valour of the southern men, and to have lacked in ability to obtain correct information about the enemy's position, movements, and strength. The report of a citizen who lived on the Franklin road, about the position of the rebel army, which is mentioned at length by General McCook, was false. The general also says at the close of his report:

I am well satisfied that Hardee's Corps, supported by Mc-Cown's division, attacked Kirk's and Willich's brigades; while Withers' division attacked Davis's and Cheatham's division attacked Sheridan.

This statement is evidently a great error; for, if it had been true, there would have been left only one brigade of infantry (Jackson's), with eight hundred and seventy-five men, to fight the whole Left Wing and Centre. But, notwithstanding this anxiety about his right being turned, and believing thirty-five thousand men to be standing opposite his fifteen thousand, General McCook kept his reserve, Baldwin's brigade, about one and one-half miles from his front line, and permitted the division commander, General Johnson, to make his headquarters an equal distance from his front.

After the return of Generals Sheridan and Sill from General Mc-Cook they sat on a log for hours during the night, discussing the serious position in which their troops were placed.

About 9 o'clock the previous evening, at the same time Cleburne's men commenced their march from the extreme right to their extreme left, General Rosecrans called together his corps commanders, to communicate to them his plan of attack; and, singularly enough, the plans of Generals Rosecrans and Bragg were the same,—"to attack and break the opponent's right." General Rosecrans had massed Van Cleve and Wood on his left; Bragg had Cleburne and McCown; but the hour of attack by Bragg was earlier. He had the advantage of having ordered his troops on December 29th to cook rations for three days, while unmolested by the Union army; while, on the other hand, Rosecrans's army had to advance, continually prepared to give battle, through roads sometimes knee-deep with mud. Fatigued, therefore, by hard marches, with the expectation of harder work before them, General Rosecrans could not well do otherwise than to order the attack to commence at about 7 in the morning, after the men had had their scanty breakfast.

The instructions of General Bragg to his corps commanders were to execute a right wheel, with the pivot on Chalmers's right, near Stone's River, and to let the extreme left brigade attack first; then the next, and so on till the Federal army was driven to the Nashville pike. The night preceding the battle passed drearily. The men in the front could only rest with their muskets in hand, while those in reserve had to make their bed either in deep mud or on rough stones. Were it not for the fatigue of the continual march but few would have closed their eyes in sleep. At 4 o'clock our men were aroused; but no fires were permitted near the front. In the left wing of the Confederates the greatest activity continued.

CHAPTER 3

THE BATTLE OF DECEMBER 31ST, 1862

A few minutes past 6 o'clock, when there was just sufficient light to distinguish objects nearby, a gray mass of silent troops commenced to move as noiselessly as possible in a westerly direction. These were Rains's and Ector's brigades, closely followed by McNair's,—all of McCown's division.

Clearing the fence in their front, and crossing the road, they were soon in the open field, and as they came into line all three commenced a right wheel, marching in an oblique manner towards Kirk's and Willich's brigades. The outposts were on the alert, for Kirk's brigade had been under arms for some hours; part of the horses of Edgarton's battery, however, had just been sent to the rear for water.

As soon as the rapid firing of the pickets indicated the approach of the enemy, General Kirk rode to the front, and, seeing a large mass of the enemy come nearer with steady step, brushing the skirmishers before them like cobwebs, he sent an aid to notify General Johnson, and ordered the Thirty-fourth Illinois, which was nearest to the rebel line of march, quickly forward, and to hold the enemy. With firm step and earnest mien the regiment advanced, and fired with great rapidity. The enemy halted for an instant, but, as the rebel mass pressed forward in vastly superior numbers, General Kirk rode quickly back to Willich's brigade, to ask that a couple of regiments be sent to his assistance. But neither General Johnson nor General Willich were near the front, and the commanding officers of regiments, in the absence of their superiors, refused to move, nor were they prepared to do so. Gallant General Kirk then returned quickly to his brigade, and shortly afterwards fell from his horse mortally wounded.

The Thirty-fourth Illinois was therefore the first regiment that felt the rebel assault; it was immediately in front of the right regiment of Ector's brigade. The rebels steadily advanced, and, the Thirty-fourth not giving way, they came to a hand-to-hand fight in many instances. There were brave men among them,—men who would have worn an eagle before the close of the war if death had not overtaken them. When the Tenth Texas dismounted cavalry of Ector's brigade came closer to our line, the colour-bearer of the Thirty-fourth waved his flag, urging his regiment to charge the enemy. The gallant men responded; they fought but a score of feet from the rebels with all the might and fury of brave soldiers.

Singularly enough it so happened that the flag of the Tenth Texas was immediately opposite that of the Thirty-fourth Illinois, and the colour-bearer of the Texas regiment jumped forward, seized the flag of the Thirty-fourth, while the brave Illinoisian grasped that of the Texas regiment. Instantly a struggle ensued between the men, each filled with desperate valour to save his own, and take the enemy's flag. Suddenly shots fired by the colour-guard of each regiment struck the opponent's colour-bearer to the ground; quickly new men sprang forward to seize the treasured emblems, and again and again the men fell dead or wounded, till the last colour-guard was disabled; at this moment the Illinois regiment was forced to retreat to avoid capture.

What a grand, sad sight it must have been to have witnessed this fight for the standard! No blush of shame need rest on that regiment whose flag was lost when so ably defended. Captain Edgarton's battery tried to stop the onward march; but so close were the Confederates, and so quick their advance, that they were within thirty yards when the second round was fired. The rebels, receiving at this moment orders to charge, ran towards the battery with such a yell that it seemed as though the demons of the lower regions had been let loose. No horses were ready to take the battery off the field, and, the infantry retreating quickly, it fell into the enemy's hand; but its brave captain fought his guns till surrounded by thousands of the enemy. Willich's brigade, like Kirk's, had been in line before daybreak; but, as the light grew stronger, General Willich believed that no attack would be made, and as General Johnson had not been near the line, nor sent him any orders, he rode quickly to division headquarters for directions.

The troops stacked their arms, and leave was given them to cook their breakfast. Thus lulled into seeming security, the first few shots did not alarm them; but when, presently, the pickets' firing came nearer and nearer, they quickly ran to their arms and sought to form into line. Five minutes more would have sufficed to present to the enemy a battle front that could not be easily driven back; but, before Willich's men could put on their accoutrements and take their muskets in hand, the rebels had reached their line. This brigade had in its ranks excellent material, but not being quite ready, and without brigade commander, the fighting was done in an individual way, and without a head to direct it. It could and did arrest the onward march of the Confederates for a moment, but only for a moment; then they pressed forward with a yell, and the command, becoming demoralized, fell back in disorder. The regiments retreated in a north-westerly direction, towards Overall's creek where the Wilkinson pike crosses it, leaving two guns of Goodspeed's battery on the field. [1]

---

1. Capt. Goodspeed states, in a recent conversation, that the rebel attack was entirely unexpected. He had, the day before, called the attention of one of his superior officers to his peculiar position, but was told that he must obey orders. As soon as he saw the rebel assault, and the danger to his battery, he ordered his guns, as quickly as they could be got ready, to a little knoll towards the west, a good position for artillery. After he had sent two guns, one of his sergeants came, on a run, hatless and out of breath, to inform him that the rebel cavalry were at that knoll, and that his two guns had already been captured.

McNair's brigade, immediately to the (rebels) right of the Tenth Texas, attacked the Twenty-ninth and Thirtieth Indiana regiments, placed in the woods. Observing their right give way, these regiments likewise fell back in a north-westerly direction, firing as they retreated, and doing considerable injury.

The Seventy-seventh Pennsylvania, the left regiment of Kirk's,— likewise in the woods, but not assaulted by McNair, his line passing to its right,—moved forward, and, there being no enemy in its front, it marched a little in advance of Edgarton's battery and halted. A few moments afterwards a battery came in full trot from the east, near this regiment. The Pennsylvanians, believing it to be a Federal battery, waved their flag. It was, however, Douglas's battery of Ector's brigade. Its commanding officer observed that this regiment was labouring under a mistake, and in order to further deceive them, he unlimbered one hundred and twenty-five yards distant, with the front towards the west, in *echelon*. Again the regiment waved its flag, and many men cheered; but in an instant they were undeceived.

"Double canister!" was the command at the battery, and, as soon as the guns were loaded, the order came: "Action to the right! Commence firing!" In ten seconds the battery was turned on the regiment, and the shots came tearing through it. The Seventy-seventh gave one volley with a hearty goodwill, and then fell back towards Post's brigade, firing as they retreated.

General Cleburne's division commenced to move forward to the attack soon after General McCown had left his line; it marched straight forward till it passed Widow Smith's house on the right, and then commenced a right wheel. Owing to the fences and the roughness of the ground the movement caused a great deal of crowding in some places, while gaps occurred in others. As the command came nearer to the Franklin road Carlin's skirmishers received them with marked attention, but unpleasant consequences. Cleburne therefore ordered out his sharpshooters to drive them from the fences along the lane. When this was done the division again continued its wheel, making a complete change to the right, on reaching the Franklin road. Here the division halted and moved a short distance to the left, to permit Wood's brigade to come into line between Brigadier-General Polk's right and Widow Smith's house.

After Ector and McNair had driven Willich and Kirk they reported that their brigades had suffered considerably, and that they were nearly out of ammunition. McCown thereupon ordered a halt. General Cleburne having, by this time, reached the Franklin road, General McCown, on consulting him, marched his troops towards the left, or west, giving Cleburne the whole front, as follows: Liddell on the extreme left; on his right, Johnson, whose centre regiment, the Twenty-fifth Tennessee, was opposite the lane that leads from the Franklin road northerly towards Griscom's house; Polk on his right, and Wood on the extreme right of the division, opposite part of Carlin's brigade, and the Thirty-fifth Illinois, of Woodruffs. As soon as McCown reached the left of Cleburne both moved forward. During the short time that Cleburne halted, to permit McCown to get to Liddell's left, Colonel Post, seeing that he was outflanked on the right, withdrew his line towards the rear and his right. He ordered the Seventy-fourth and Seventy-fifth Illinois regiments to a position behind a fence close to the timber, east of the lane, while Pinney's battery, with the Fifty-ninth Illinois on its left and Twenty-second Indiana on the right, were placed on a slight elevation west of the lane.

Neither General Johnson nor Colonel Baldwin seem to have been aware of the defeat of Kirk and Willich till stragglers came, terror-stricken, towards them. Immediately orders were given by General Johnson to Baldwin to advance. The Sixth Indiana, on the left, moved to a rail fence near the edge of the timber, and the First Ohio was placed to the right, in the open field, seventy-five yards in advance. Between them a section of Simonson's battery unlimbered, the other sections remaining farther to the rear. One hundred and fifty yards back of the First Ohio stood the Fifth Kentucky, and, still farther to the rear, the Ninety-third Ohio.

Scarcely had the line been formed when the rebels commenced their attack. Liddell's brigade moved forward like a solid block. The First Ohio and the Sixth Indiana—the latter well sheltered behind the fence—fired with the greatest energy, and the Confederates began to stagger and fall back, when part of McNair's brigade, coming up on Liddell's left, fired into the First Ohio from the flank, and the latter, being then exposed, gave way and fell back on the Fifth Kentucky. The latter regiment, being by this time also outflanked on the right, changed front to the right on rear company; but all was in vain. A rapid retreat had to be ordered, to prevent capture by overwhelming numbers, and two guns of Simonson's battery were left behind.

The Ninety-third Ohio was eager for the fight; time and again its brave commanding officer, Col. Charles Anderson, sought to lead them against the enemy. He complains bitterly, in his report, that he was refused the privilege of coming to the rescue of his companions, and was ordered to leave the field without offering any resistance. Farther to the right the Thirtieth Indiana, aided by the Seventy-ninth Illinois, bravely led by Colonel Sheridan P. Read, and which had come on the double-quick from the wagon train, made an effort to stem the overpowering tide, in which Colonel Read was killed; but the Confederate troops were too full of enthusiastic zeal, and our own troops too much discouraged, to keep up this unequal contest for a long time. All of Johnson's division fell back, fighting here and there, where fences or rocks permitted them to make a stand, until, more like a mob than organized troops, they reached the Mecca of the retreat,— the Nashville pike; while others ran like mad men through the timber, shouting: "We are sold again! We are sold again!"[2]

In the line of their retreat, and not far from the Wilkinson pike, was the whole ammunition train of the Right Wing, protected in part by the Second cavalry brigade, composed of First, Third, and Fourth Ohio, and also the Second East Tennessee, of the cavalry reserve. The rebel cavalry, being ordered in pursuit of our extreme right, began to shell them and then charged. The Second East Tennessee instantly ran like sheep, and the stampede demoralized the First and Fourth Ohio to such a degree that they followed them, leaving the Third Ohio alone, which then likewise fell back. Our infantry was speedily overtaken by the rebel cavalry. Officers too brave to run, or who tried to rally their men,—though in vain,—were ordered to deliver their swords; while hundreds of soldiers, bewildered, and not knowing in which direction to turn to reach our line, were taken prisoners and quickly sent to the enemy's rear.

After the Third Ohio cavalry had fallen back a short distance a staff officer of General McCook, probably Captain Thurston, galloped to Major Paramore, commanding the left wing of that regiment. "There," he said (pointing to a wagon train), "is the whole ammunition train of the Right Wing; it must be saved at all hazards." The rebels, seeing the Third Ohio hold their ground, left them alone, but pursued the fleeing troops. When they had passed, Major Paramore ordered his men to charge on the rebel cavalry's rear; and it was done with excellent effect, for at that very moment, when the Third Ohio came thundering down, a rebel was demanding the sword of Colonel Gibson in command of the brigade after Willich's capture. The result was, that

---

2. It was believed by many private soldiers that Buelll had sold out to Bragg at Perryville; hence these exclamations.

the rebel cavalry ran, and that the ammunition train and many of our men were saved from rebel capture. Another gun of Goodspeed's battery, however, fell here into the enemy's hands.

Colonel Post, with his brigade in front of and to the left of the Sixth Indiana, was impeding the progress of Confederate General Johnson's brigade and of the Third Arkansas, the right regiment of Liddell's. Pinney's battery, the Fifty-ninth Illinois, and Twenty-second Indiana fired like men; but they could not stand against the superior numbers in their front. The Seventy-fourth and Seventy-fifth Illinois, protected by the fence, likewise held their ground for some time, but finally the whole brigade was compelled to fall back towards the Wilkinson pike.

To the left of Colonel Post the battle raged very severely. Confederate General Polk's brigade (one thousand three hundred and fifty strong) and Wood's (one thousand one hundred) received orders from General Cleburne to drive the enemy out of the cedar glen; they advanced, and soon came face to face with Colonel Carlin's splendid brigade and the Thirty-fifth Illinois, of Woodruffs. Well protected behind rocks and trees, and commanded by such men as Colonel Carlin, Colonel Alexander, of the Twenty-first Illinois, Colonel Heg, of the Fifteenth Wisconsin, and Colonel Stem, of the One-hundred-and-first Ohio, the Federal troops could be expected to make a grand fight, and gloriously did they meet these expectations.

When Confederate General Wood crossed the Franklin road with his brigade, supported on his left by General Polk they moved into a dense cedar glen, filled with rocky crevices. Believing that Confederate General McCown had passed over this ground, and driven the Federals from it, the usual precautions were not taken. The regiments moved fearlessly forward, apprehending but little danger, when suddenly a terrific volley from the One-hundred-and-first Ohio and Thirty-eighth Illinois, hidden in the crevices and out of sight, rolled back the advancing line. Urged forward again, new volleys greeted them, and they recoiled.

Confederate General Wood then advanced again; but, being unable to see the hidden foe that caused so much injury, he ordered his line to fall back.

With loud cheers the One-hundred-and-first Ohio and Thirty-eighth Illinois rose from those crevices, and followed the retreating enemy. Soon the latter were ordered to halt, and again a heavy fire of musketry began. Being largely outnumbered, these two regiments were compelled to fall back towards the second line of their brigade.

Confederate Generals Wood and Polk then pressed forward with a great deal of vigour, and an almost hand-to-hand fight occurred between the opposing lines. Hidden in the rocky sink-holes, standing behind trees or dense bushes, the soldiers of the Fifteenth Wisconsin, Thirty-eighth Illinois, Thirty-fifth Illinois, sought to make their fire effective, and disable the enemy, but a few yards distant. The ground was too full of crevices, fallen timber, and bushes to admit of skilful manoeuvring; but every effort of the Confederates to drive these regiments was in vain, and they finally fell back.

At the height of this close fight Colonel Carlin had ordered his second line to the support of the first. When his aid reached Colonel Alexander, of the Twenty-first Illinois, he was surprised to see that Confederate General Polk's left regiments had made a wheel to the right as soon as Colonel Post's brigade had fallen back, and tried to pour an enfilading fire on Colonel Carlin's brigade, by falling on its right flank and in its rear. As soon as gallant Colonel Alexander observed their approach he quickly changed the front of his regiment, and repulsed the enemy in one of his dashing attacks. How splendidly the Twenty-first Illinois fought is shown by the fact that it lost in the fights of December 30th and 31st four colour-bearers in succession and two hundred and fifty in killed and wounded.

Confederate General Polk thereupon withdrew a considerable distance, and but few shots were exchanged between these forces for some time.

A short time after the first attack was made on Carlin, a new brigade, under command of Colonel Loomis, came in a north-westerly direction from the woods east of Widow Smith's house. Their left passed through the cornfields, and attacked the Twenty-fifth Illinois and Eighty-first Indiana, of Woodruff's brigade; while their right regiments, as they came closer to the Thirty-sixth Illinois and Twenty-fourth Wisconsin, executed a left half wheel, and then moved straight forward on these regiments. Woodruff's regiments, well protected by the rail-fence in their front, poured a continuous fire into the rebel ranks as they approached, while Carpenter's battery opened on them with canister.

Captain Bush's battery, the Thirty-sixth Illinois, and the Twenty-fourth Wisconsin, the right of Sill's brigade, waited till the enemy had come from the low ground on to the hill, and then commenced a vigorous fire; still the rebels moved forward to within ten rods, when the fire became terrific. The Twenty-fourth Wisconsin—a new regiment—had not only a fire from the front, but being on the extreme right, where the line of battle turned towards the west, received likewise the rebel bullets that passed over Carpenter's three guns. This cross-fire proved too much for it; the right companies fell back in disorder, carrying the left with them. As soon as Colonel Greusel saw the Twenty-fourth retreat, he quickly ordered his men to fix bayonets and charge. Jumping over their slight protection, they rushed forward with a loud cheer, and drove the rebels back to the woods, from which they had come.

Woodruff's two regiments, hearing these cheers on the left, fired with greater vigour even than before, and soon the whole of Loomis's brigade fell back. Many noble men died behind that fence. Colonel Williams, the fearless commander of the Twenty-fifth Illinois, seeing the regiment about to fall back, seized the colours and shouted to his men: "We will plant it here, boys, and rally the old Twenty-fifth around it; and here we will die." And there he stood and fought, till a bullet struck him and he sank down, dying like a gallant patriot. And there, too, brave Captain Carpenter stood like a rock, sending death from his well-served guns, and adding greatly to the repulse of the rebels at this point. He fought fearlessly till death struck him, and he fell with his face towards the foe.

After pursuing Loomis some distance orders were given to the Thirty-sixth Illinois to fall back to their former position, while the Twenty-fourth Wisconsin, which had been rallied, marched again to the right of the Thirty-sixth Illinois. In the meantime the Fifteenth Missouri and Forty-fourth Illinois of Schaefer's brigade, under command of Lieutenant- Colonel Weber, of the Fifteenth Missouri, were sent by General Sheridan to General Sill's aid, and were placed in rear of the Thirty-sixth Illinois, facing towards the south. A short time afterwards a new rebel brigade,—Preston Smith's,—under command of Colonel Vaughan, moved forward in magnificent style, from the same direction that Loomis had come; it was their second line. Woodruff held him in check for a time, and then fell back, under orders from General Davis, leaving one of Carpenter's guns on the field. The Twenty-fourth Wisconsin, seeing them give way, likewise fell back, when the Fifteenth Missouri and Forty-fourth Illinois were ordered up on the double-quick, and took the position of these regiments, both fighting gallantly.

General Sill, who was continually conspicuous by his gallantry, cheered his regiments with words of encouragement. Finally, as he was closely watching the heroic stand of the Thirty-sixth, a bullet struck him in the face, passing through the upper lip into the brain, and he fell dead to the ground. An excellent soldier, a noble man, a gentle soul, expired among those trees that morning, when General Sill breathed his last. General Sheridan thereupon ordered Colonel Greusel to take command of this brigade.

The firing again was terrific, but the Thirty-sixth Illinois stood their ground in a manner unsurpassed by any regiment on that field of battle; they lost two hundred and thirty dead and wounded in that little space. And Major Miller, its brave commander after Colonel Greusel took General Sill's place, was cursing at the men that fell back, and cheering those that stood, till his voice finally failed him; but he made them stand and fight like heroes, till at last a ball struck him down, and he, unable to be moved, fell into the enemy's hands.

As soon as Colonel Woodruff had withdrawn his two left regiments a part of Vaughan's brigade turned its attention to Carlin, and this gallant commander seeing himself attacked on three sides, finally, to avoid capture, reluctantly gave the order to "Fall back!" How splendidly these men fought is attested by the fact that they left thirty-five *per cent,* of their number either dead or wounded in that cedar glen. Proud must the men be who survived in that fight among those cedars! Napoleon would have decorated each one with a nation's cross of the Legion of Honour. Brave men, like Colonel Stem and Lieutenant-Colonel Wooster of the One-hundred-and-first Ohio; [3] Lieutenant-Colonel McKee, of the Fifteenth Wisconsin, and others who fell there, would have had their names made immortal as the heroes of a battlefield. Let us not forget Captain Mead of the Thirty-eighth Illinois, who, after his regiment had fallen back, fought with his revolver, while bleeding from three wounds, till he fell over—dead; and Lieutenant Dillon, of the same regiment, who fought with a musket till he was shot, and then drew his sword, bravely cheering his men, till death, at last, hushed his voice forever.

Colonel Carlin thereupon retired by the left flank, in a direction about two hundred yards east of Griscom's house. The Confederates tried to follow him, but as soon as they emerged from the timber General Sheridan ordered Captains Hescock and Houghtalling to

3. Colonel Stem, mortally wounded, and the body of Lieutenant Wooster, fell into the hands of the Sixteenth Alabama of Wood's brigade.

open their batteries on them, and the storm of shells that fell into their ranks soon drove them back into the cedars. Colonel Carlin again formed his troops in line near the Wilkinson pike; but the enemy being still to his right and rear, and information having reached him that General Davis desired a further withdrawal, he moved half a mile still further back; but his troops were so exhausted, and so discouraged, that it seemed useless for him to make another stand without support.

A short time after Vaughan's attack a heavy mass, Manigault's brigade, of Withers's division, moved in solid column across the cotton-field. It was a grand sight to see them approach. Captain Bush, with his battery in their immediate front, sent canister after canister; while, more to our left, Hescock and Houghtalling, under orders from General Sheridan, fired shells with incredible velocity into the midst of their ranks. Manigault says, in his report, that the artillery fire was terrible, and that no troops could have stood it. Here and there large gaps were seen as the missiles passed through them; a moment afterwards they seemed to be filled again. Closer they came, and closer still,—there was no wavering,—fifty yards only from our line, when suddenly it seemed as if an earthquake had shaken the ground, and a volley by the Eighty-eighth Illinois, reserved till then, brought the attacking column to a halt. The Twenty-first Michigan, in support of the Eighty-eighth Illinois, was ordered to advance. The men rushed forward with a cheer. The firing was fearful for a few minutes, and then a general shout arose when Manigault's men broke to the rear.

An incident occurred during Manigault's advance which nearly cost the life of a gallant officer. Houghtalling's and Hescock's batteries, being on elevated ground, were compelled to depress their guns to hit Manigault's line. One of the guns was depressed too much. When Manigault's command approached, Major Chandler, of the Eighty-eighth Illinois, was riding along the line of his regiment, encouraging the men and ordering them to hold their fire, when our batteries opened. An instant afterwards Major Chandler was brought to the ground, one of our own cannon-balls having passed through his horse.

At this time the Thirty-sixth Illinois was out of ammunition, and Colonel Greusel ordered that regiment and Bush's battery to the rear.

General Sheridan then formed his second position, along the fences and woods, on a line with Harding's house, with parts of Schaefer's and Sill's brigades, and requested General Davis to join him.

Bush took a position near Hescock, while the Thirty-sixth Illinois went further to the rear, in search of the ammunition train. As they fell back the rebels followed them, and took the Eighty-eighth Illinois on the right flank, compelling it and the Twenty-first Michigan to fall back towards the fences and out-houses near Harding's house, where they fought most gallantly, losing, respectively, seventy, and one hundred and two men.

Colonel Roberts, furious that our troops had been driven, rode to General Sheridan, who was watching the battle immediately in rear of Hescock's battery, and asked for leave to charge on the advancing rebels; and General Sheridan responded with one of his enthusiastic orders for Roberts to try the bayonet. While Sill's men had been falling back, Roberts's regiments were formed in the open field, facing south, towards Harding's house, as follows: Fifty-first Illinois on the left, Forty-second Illinois on the right, and Twenty-second Illinois in rear of Forty-second Illinois. Sending word quickly that a bayonet charge was to be made, and for no one to fire without orders, the command "Forward, march!" was given with a loud voice. The regiments moved as if on parade. A short distance in their front were the Eighty-eighth Illinois and the Twenty-first Michigan, firing from behind the fences.

Colonel Roberts thereupon ordered his adjutant to ask Colonel Sherman of the Eighty-eighth to have his regiment throw down the fence on its front, and to lie down, so that the command could march over them; but the battle raged so fiercely, and the noise was so loud, that the colonel did not understand the request, and the adjutant thereupon rode to the fence, and by motion and words got the men to level it, cease firing, and lie down. A few moments afterwards the Forty-second Illinois reached this line, the Fifty-first being impeded by obstacles in its front, and the Forty-second, after passing over the Eighty-eighth, quickly aligned itself, and the command was given, " Charge bayonets!"

Suddenly the grand form of Colonel Roberts could be seen riding in rear of the regiment, telling the officers not to let a shot be fired; then, wheeling around the left wing, he rode in front of the regiment along the whole line, with his cap in his hand, cheering the men to endless enthusiasm, and shouting to them: "Don't fire a shot! Drive them with the bayonet!"

The rebel infantry took speedy aim at the dashing officer, as he galloped along, but not one of the thousands of bullets hit him. The regiment marched forward with a quick determined step, the long bayonets glistening with fearful splendour in the sunlight, when the command of "Charge!" was heard, and with a loud hurrah the men ran for the enemy.

The Confederates did not stand till the cold steel came close to their hearts, but ran with all their might to the woods, and through it and the cornfield to their original position in the morning. During the charge a battery from Manigault's front poured canister into our men, but without doing injury as the shots struck the limbs of the trees above them. The regiment pursued as far as the rail fence, where Carpenter lost one of his guns, which was still there. Soon it was observed that a large force of Confederate infantry was moving to get to the right and rear of the regiment, whereupon General Sheridan ordered Colonel Roberts to fall back, which he did in good order, in quick step.

Chapter 4

The Battle—Continued

The second position chosen by General Sheridan proving untenable, owing to Generals Davis and Johnson falling back across the Wilkinson and towards the Nashville pike in a northerly direction, instead of falling back to the left and joining Sheridan, Colonel Greusel ordered the Eighty-eighth Illinois and the Twenty-fourth Wisconsin to take position on the left of the Eighty-first Indiana, of Woodruffs command, north of Wilkinson pike and north-west from Blanton's house; here they remained a short time and then fell back, finally taking, under orders from General McCook, a position in support of Pinney's battery, north of Overalls Creek, near the pike. The Fifteenth Missouri and Forty-fourth Illinois were likewise ordered to the rear to replenish their ammunition. General Sheridan, though annoyed that General Davis did not join on his right, determined to resist the enemy to the last. He quickly looked for another position, and chose one that in reality masked part of Negley's line.

He placed Houghtalling's splendid battery (Company C, First Illinois) at the edge of the cedars north-east of Harding's house, and south of the Wilkinson pike; to its left and rear the Twenty-second Illinois, and farther to the left the Forty-second Illinois, in the front line; the Twenty-seventh Illinois and the Fifty-first Illinois took a position north of the pike, part of these regiments facing west; the Second Missouri and part of the Seventy-third Illinois moved also north of the pike. Hescock's and Bush's batteries General Sheridan ordered to a little elevation north of the Wilkinson pike, and to the left of the Forty-second Illinois.

Shortly afterwards, when it appeared that the rebels were massing troops on the right, Lieutenant Tallioferro, of Hescock's battery, with two guns, and Lieutenant Flansberg of Bush's battery, with two guns, were sent to Houghtalling's assistance.

A few minutes afterwards Wood's brigade came in pursuit of Carlin's, and our guns, having a splendid cross-fire, opened on it with much effect. In order to escape this he made a wheel to the right, and, coming to the edge of the timber, the Twenty-seventh and Fifty-first Illinois Regiments fired on it with such precision that it fell back very rapidly.

After this there was but little firing for some time; it was the calm,—warning of the approaching storm.

The Confederate General Cheatham, a very, able and courageous officer, had seen that the troops in his front had fighting qualities in them; he had suffered already greatly, and he knew that it needed combined action to win. He ordered Manigault to bring his brigade to the right of Maney's. Turner's battery of Napoleons were placed near the brick-kiln, and orders were given to Vaughan to move to the left of Maney. Soon a magnificent column of the Confederates moved across the field west of Harding's house, making a right wheel. It was a grand sight; seldom has it been executed in a finer manner. A minute later the centre of the column struck the ground where Hescock's Battery had been placed earlier in the morning. There was no time to lose, and Houghtalling sent shells in quick succession into the advancing line. Great gaps were visible where the screeching missiles went through it; but they were soon closed up, and the column advanced over the ridge to the low grounds occupied by part of Roberts's brigade during the night. There, sheltered by an intervening ridge, they were protected from our batteries and out of our sight.

Again there was a pause. Waiting a few minutes Colonel Roberts said to his adjutant: "Let us see what they are doing"; and the two rode along the pike to within seventy-five yards of the enemy's line. There one could see that the rebels were lying flat on the ground, evidently waiting for orders. It took but a moment to swing the horses' heads around, and then they galloped back; but not a shot was fired at them. Confederate General Cheatham then ordered General Maney, who had till then remained in a parallel line to his original position, to commence his wheel to the right, and, as they advanced, Houghtalling again fired with all his energy towards Harding's house, where the rebel line had halted.

There was but little reply at first; soon an officer, Lieutenant James of the First rebel Tennessee Infantry, rode forward to our line to reconnoitre and ascertain whether we were Federal or Confederate. As he came nearer a few shots were fired, and he fell dead from his horse. Still General Maney was in doubt whether we were friends or foes. Another officer approached our lines, and when fired at he wheeled his horse and escaped. Still they were in doubt. Then the colour-bearer, Sergeant Oakley, of the Fourth rebel Tennessee, marched forward and waved his flag; and finally the colour-bearer of the regiment still further to the right, or west,—Sergeant Hooker, of the Ninth Rebel Tennessee,—climbed to the top of one of Harding's outhouses, and there began to wave the rebel flag. That was too much, and Houghtalling, Tallioferro, and Flansberg all vied with each other in striking that hated emblem down. This convinced Generals Cheatham and Maney that the guns were those of the enemy, and Turner's battery commenced to fire, with terrible effect.

To the west likewise, where Hescock's battery had been in the morning, a large number of rebel guns were planted, and an artillery duel ensued at the short range of two hundred and fifty yards that has seldom been surpassed. Tremendous branches of trees came tumbling down on our pieces; the shells burst continually among the cannons; every few seconds solid shot, missing the guns, hit the peaceful horses, quietly awaiting the guidance of their riders, and brought them to the ground wounded in the most frightful manner.

Here Colonel Roberts was again conspicuous. Being informed that the guns could not be worked, by reason of falling timber, he quickly ran over, and with his herculean strength helped to clear them of the encumbrances.

The fire slackened for a moment, and the rebels, believing the batteries silenced, commenced their attack. On they rushed, with their accustomed yell, and men from Alabama, Tennessee, and South Carolina stood face to face with well-drilled men from Illinois; but Illinois came out with colours flying. The rebels could not stand that fire, and they fell back. Cheatham was storming with rage; his own Tennesseans must take those guns. Again he led them forward, and again they fell back before that mighty brigade.

Word was sent to General Anderson, commanding Walthall's brigade of Mississippians, with a regiment from Alabama and North Carolina, to come to the rescue, and he ordered his two left regiments to help Manigault. Again the roar of battle was heard. Hescock and Bush, to the left of the brigade, now fired with all their might to their front and left, while Houghtalling, Tallioferro, and Flansberg fought like heroes towards the right. Again the same troops advanced from the south and west, while Anderson brought his Mississippians from the east.

General Sheridan had ordered Colonel Roberts to hold that point as long as he could, as the safety of the whole army depended upon it; and Roberts proposed to stay there till the last cartridge was fired and the bayonet had lost its virtue.

The yell of Maney's, Manigault's, and Vaughan's men, as they advanced the third time, was but faint; they had suffered, and knew that noise did not scare the troops in front of them; but the Mississippians had not yet been in action, and with full lungs they came on, with a tremendous yell. But it availed them little. Hescock and Bush, and the Forty-second Illinois in their front, caused fearful havoc, and in ten minutes' time the column was in foil retreat towards the breastworks in the rear.

Through all this terrible fight, in the midst of this frightful scene of death, General Sheridan could be seen riding continually, closely watching his men. Observing how splendidly these troops held their ground, and that the rebels were evidently becoming demoralized, he rode with great speed to General Thomas, and begged him to order one of his divisions to advance as quickly as possible, as he believed that the disaster might now be retrieved, and seeming defeat be turned into victory.

But General Thomas declined to comply with this request, and thus perhaps prevented the achievement of such results as General Sheridan afterwards showed at Winchester could be attained with troops eager to fight.

Again there was a temporary lull, and one had an opportunity to see what terrible havoc had been made. Death everywhere had reaped a great harvest, and our poor wounded were asking for assistance. But very little could be rendered, as every man was needed to resist the enemy. One peculiar incident occurred here, showing the pluck and nerve of some men. While Lieutenant-Colonel Walworth, of the Forty-second Illinois, was walking behind his line,—for every horse had been killed,—praising his men for their noble stand, Corporal Smith, of Company I, came up and said: "Colonel, I come to return my gun to you, for I suppose that I shall go on furlough now."

"Why, what is it?" said Walworth, as he took the gun.

"Look," he answered, and as he moved his hand from his body the intestines followed it. "To what hospital can I go?" asked the wounded man.

"Go that way," said his commander, pointing towards Blanton's house. "When the battle is over, I'll see you."

But he never saw that man again, for on the morrow he took his long furlough, to join the fallen heroes in the great beyond.

When General Anderson's regiments had been repulsed with such frightful slaughter he asked General Stewart, commanding the brigade in his rear, to send his left regiments to their assistance; but Generals Withers and Stewart believed that it was better for Stewart to take his whole brigade. Soon afterwards they came marching with quick step towards our line, while Manigault, Maney, and Vaughan renewed their assault on our right. Again the rebel artillery and infantry were burying ours under a fearful storm of branches, shells, shots, and a leaden hail; but again the gallant men responded with deadly effect, when, alas! word came that they were out of ammunition. Houghtalling had fired about the last shot—over eleven hundred that day—and Tallioferro and Flansberg in like proportion, while the regiments supporting them were likewise nearly out, and all efforts to get more had been in vain. The ammunition train of the right wing was far in the rear, and no one seemed to know where. Of Houghtalling's Battery almost every horse was disabled, and it was impossible to move the pieces by hand, owing to the volcanic formation of sink-holes in the ground.

The enemy observed very soon that the firing had ceased, and they charged upon the battery and the Twenty-second Illinois, and drove the latter towards the pike.

"Adjutant," shouted Roberts, as these brave men fell back, "rally them on the north side of the pike, and make a stand there; I'll rally the Forty-second"; and with these words he galloped towards that regiment, still south of the pike. The Twenty-second responded to the order most gallantly; they rallied and took their position along the north side of the pike, being followed by the rebels at a distance not greater than fifty feet at the most. Here again a terrible fire commenced. The all-pervading excitement; the fury displayed by some of the men; the loud commands of the officers trying to steady the troops in their firing; the general uproar,—combined to form a scene which it is impossible to describe. The excitement was so great, indeed, that many did not aim at the enemy; but, loading with greatest speed, they brought their muskets to an "aim," and fired at the top of the trees. There was but one cry: "For God's sake, get us ammunition!"

Colonel Roberts, on reaching the Forty-second, dashed in rear of the line at a furious rate, with his sword high in the air, as though he would split the head of the first man whom he should see moving to the rear. His heart, no doubt, filled with the greatest pride when he saw his beloved regiment stand like a wall of stone. But where were Walworth, Swain, and others whom he could always count upon? Not a field officer could be seen on horse. (He was not aware that every animal had been killed.) Dashing again in rear of the line he espied Lieutenant-Colonel Walworth.

As he rode towards him, his face brightened up with a smile that can never be forgotten; and when close to him he saluted with his sword, evidently as a token of his admiration for the gallant officers and men of his command. Then he galloped again towards the left, cheering his men; but, alas! it was his last effort to drive the enemy. A few minutes later three bullets penetrated that grand form. The terrible shock unnerved his arm, the reins dropped from his hands, and he fell from his horse. A few men quickly ran to his help, and he exclaimed, with husky voice, "Boys, put me on my horse again!" The effort was made, but, before it could be accomplished, a shudder passed through him, and death had vanquished the bravest of the brave.

The men in attendance carried him quickly towards the rear, on the north side of the pike, and, believing we would regain the battlefield, placed the body near a large tree, and covered it with brush, to prevent its being disturbed.

When General Stewart came closer to the Forty-second Illinois the firing again became terrific. Hescock's famous First Missouri battery and Bush's Fourth Indiana also exerted themselves as never before, while a part of Negley's division had a splendid cross-fire on Stewart's right regiments, and the rebel brigade lost many men; but the number of the Confederates was too great. Many of Roberts's men had expended the last cartridge, and, the enemy also coming in the rear, orders were given to fall back. Captain Hescock and Captain Bush, who had fought their guns with the greatest valour, and without whose accurate fire it would have been impossible for Roberts to have repelled Cheatham's repeated attacks, were likewise forced to the rear. Each of the batteries had fired nearly cloven hundred rounds up to that hour, and the firing was at such close range that two of Bush's guns fell into the enemy's hands, as almost every horse belonging to. them had been killed.

What a scene! Death and blood everywhere. Colonel Harrington, bravely leading his Twenty-seventh Illinois, was struck by a piece of a shell, which tore the jaws from his face; Lieutenant-Colonel Swanwick, of the Twenty-second Illinois, wounded and unable to be moved; nearly forty *per cent,* of the Forty-second and Twenty-second killed or wounded; gallant Captain Houghtalling carried away barely alive, the blood, as it flowed from his wound, leaving a track on the stones; and Lieutenant Tallioferro, who had never flinched, even in the hottest fire, but who seemed to grow in stature as the fire became more intense, shot dead between his cannons. Houghtalling's men, heroes every one of them, refused to leave their guns, and defended them with their revolvers, sabres, and ramrods, till they were finally overpowered and many taken prisoners.

After the Twenty-second and Forty-second Illinois regiments had fallen back north of the Wilkinson pike for some distance, they halted again, the enemy remaining nearer to the pike. General Sheridan then rode forward to Lieutenant-Colonel Walworth, and said, in a very slow and determined manner,—firmly biting a piece of a cigar meanwhile:—

"Colonel, when you cannot hold this point any longer, and are out of ammunition, move the regiment in this direction (pointing N.E.). This is about the only place for us to get out; they have nearly surrounded us."

Ascertaining that scarcely any ammunition was left, and that they stood isolated, the Twenty-second and Forty-second in a short time moved away, striking General Negley's line about thirty rods to the rear, and finally came out between the two lines of General Palmer's division. When the latter saw the regiments which had formerly been in his command, he asked Walworth:—

"Colonel, where is the balance of the Forty-second?"

"General," he answered, "this is all there is left of the Forty-second and Twenty-second."

Great tears filled the general's eyes, as he glanced along these remnants as they filed past him with their flags,—flags tattered, torn, and shot to pieces, but saved—thank God!—after all.

The Fifty-first and Twenty-seventh Illinois, posted north of the Wilkinson pike, were protected by dense cedars and rocks, behind which they found excellent shelter. They fought most gallantly, and repulsed every attack; but for these reasons, and the fact that the enemy's artillery fire was less concentrated on them, they lost not quite as many men as the other two regiments in this place. During the morning the Nineteenth Illinois took a position a few yards on the right of the Twenty-seventh Illinois, and drew the fire from the rebels for a short time. When they were ordered back, General Negley rode to Major Smith, in command of the Twenty-seventh Illinois after Herring- ton was wounded, and said, "Boys, you must get out of here; you are surrounded."

Colonel Bradley, of the Fifty-first, finding no other troops near him, and fearing, as General Negley had intimated earlier in the morning, that there was danger of being cut off, gave the command to fall back.

The Twenty-seventh and Fifty-first Illinois, passing through the cedars, came on the flank of some rebel troops, and the latter, believing that they were in danger of being captured, fell back with greatest speed. These two regiments then moved farther north to the rear, towards the Nashville pike, where they came just in time to show their discipline and courage, and cover themselves with glory. The hour was eleven o'clock when this part of the field was left to the enemy.

So conspicuous had been the bravery of Colonel Roberts that even the rebels admired him, and so splendidly had the men fought there that the Confederate General Stewart said, in his report:—

"The force which was engaged in this famous cedar brake was composed, at least in part, of regulars; the brigade was commanded by Colonel Roberts, who fell while gallantly attempting to rally his men opposite the centre of my line. He was buried Saturday evening, and the spot marked by a stone having his name scratched upon it with the point of a bayonet."

And so it was, for by that stone we found the grave that held his sacred remains.

Lieutenant-General Polk said, in his report:—

Such evidences of destructive firing as were left in the forest from which the brigade emerged have rarely, if ever, been seen. The timber was torn and crushed.

The cedars which Roberts's brigade held for so long a time were called by the men who fought there, the "Slaughter, or Bull pen,"—a term, perhaps, inelegant, but certainly very graphic, on account of the blood that stained its crevices and filtered into its soil.

So dense were the cedar bushes in front of the Forty-second Illinois that they were not aware of the approach of the enemy till they saw their glistening bayonets a few feet from them. How they received them has been narrated. In front of the other regiments the bushes were nearly as dense.

Before the fight was over, the bullets had cut them down to such an extent that but few were left standing; those that remained were stripped of their branches.

CHAPTER 5

THE BATTLE—CONTINUED

Near the Nashville pike, about three and one-half miles from Murfreesboro', were the headquarters of the commanding General. Shortly after daybreak a few rumbling sounds like the firing of distant cannons were heard coming from the extreme right, indicating that there was some activity in McCook's front. After this there was a stillness for some time; again the booming of artillery fire was heard, coming over the cedars on the west, but much nearer. What could this mean? Suddenly an aid from McCook came rushing to General Rosecrans, and informed him that General McCook was sorely pressed, and needed assistance.

"Tell him," was the response, "that he shall have help."

Then hundreds of teamsters came, panic-stricken, from the right, bringing tidings of great disaster. Soon another aid from McCook arrived with the startling report that Willich and Kirk were routed, and that Baldwin and a part of Davis's division were in retreat. What a disappointment! General McCook had agreed to hold the enemy in check at least three hours; but his extreme right had been obliged to give way almost immediately.

Instantly all the energies of General Rosecrans came at once into action. He ordered General Thomas to send General Rousseau to the right and rear of Sheridan; he also ordered General Crittenden, whose skirmishers were driving back those of Breckenridge's division, to suspend the forward movement to the east side of Stone's River, and to send Colonel Samuel Beatty's and Colonel Fyffe's brigades, of Van Cleve's division, to the right of Rousseau. A moment later he galloped at full speed to Colonel Harker and General Hascall, of Wood's division, and ordered them to move to the Nashville pike north, and form a new line. Wherever he was seen his energy and bravery filled the troops with enthusiasm, and Beatty's, Fyffe's, and Harker's men fairly ran to get into position; while Hascall's way was so blocked up with fugitives and teams that he was compelled to halt near the railway.

After Cleburne and McCown had driven Johnson's and part of Davis's divisions across the Wilkinson pike, they halted, for the purpose of re-forming their line, and to supply the men with new ammunition. After this had been done Lieut.-General Hardee ordered McCown's division, with Rains's on the right and in advance, to move on to the north-east; while Cleburne's division was ordered to move in a more northerly route, towards the Nashville pike (reversing the order of battle in the earlier morning).

In their retreat Carpenter's, Pinney's, Hotchkiss's, and other batteries tried to stem the tide of defeat, wherever the ground offered the opportunity; but, partly for the reason that the infantry supporting them were so exhausted and discouraged that they refused to stand, and partly because Generals McCook and Davis, as appears by the reports, had given orders to fall back, no strong resistance was made by these troops, and they finally reached the pike in great disorder.

Further to the rear, near Overall's Creek, there was still greater confusion. The rebel cavalry, seeing the immense wagon-trains on the Nashville pike, got a battery quickly into position, and fired on them with decided effect, causing a stampede. Colonel Fyffe, with his brigade, being the nearest at hand, was quickly ordered to the aid of our cavalry, and to save the wagon-trains from capture or destruction. He arrived at an opportune moment, for when his brigade reached the ground they saw that the rebels were leading off a part of the train, and that in front a squadron of our cavalry were being led away like sheep. It required but an instant for Captain Swallow to unlimber his battery, and to open on the enemy. The squadron, so peacefully moving off as prisoners, got new courage, and, turning round, commenced to capture their guards; and when, at the same time the Fourth Regular Cavalry, on the right, began a brilliant charge on the rebel cavalry, the latter gave way, and was soon out of sight, and our train was saved.

General Rousseau complied at once with General Thomas's order, and, at 9.30 a.m., the regular brigade (formed from right to left, *viz.*: Fifteenth, Sixteenth, Gunther's battery, First and Second battalions of Eighteenth and Nineteenth Infantry) was ordered to march into the cedars. Colonel John Beatty's brigade advanced on the left of the regulars, while Colonel Scribner's followed as a reserve. The Fifteenth and Sixteenth United States Infantry, and part of Colonel John

Beatty's brigade, moved forward into the dense timber about three or four hundred yards, and soon came face to face with the enemy. It was Rains's brigade, composed of troops from Georgia, North Carolina, and Tennessee. Driving Johnson's division in the manner hereinbefore stated, they were filled with a spirit of extraordinary enthusiasm, and they threw themselves with utter recklessness upon the troops that opposed them.

Gen. Thomas doubtless believed that the enemy on his front was advancing in largely superior numbers, as the density of the timber concealed them; and inasmuch as the artillery could not be used with advantage at that point, he ordered Gunther and Loomis to place their batteries on the elevated ground, about five hundred yards east of the cedars, and ordered the Eighteenth and Nineteenth Infantry as a support to the left of Gunther's battery. General Rousseau shortly afterwards also ordered the Second and Thirty-third Ohio from Scribner's to the support of these same batteries.

When the enemy began to drive the Fifteenth and Sixteenth Infantry the firing came continually nearer, and in the rear of Colonel Grose's brigade of Palmer's division.

Thereupon General Palmer ordered Grose to change front to his right and rear; which was done in double- quick time, Grose's line forming a V with Hazen's. Colonel Grose then sent the Sixth Ohio and Thirty-sixth Indiana forward, and they went about two hundred yards into the cedars, while batteries H and M, of the Fourth United States Artillery, under command of Lieutenants Parsons, Huntington, and Cushing, supported by the Eighty-fourth Illinois, Twenty-third Kentucky, and Twenty-fourth Ohio, were anxiously waiting for the enemy to come out of the timber. Some of Colonel John Beatty's and Scribner's regiments were also in the front; but, in the absence of proper official reports, no details can be given, except that Colonel J. B. Foreman, of the Fifteenth Kentucky, was killed, while his regiment was ordered to move to the rear.

When the Fifteenth and Sixteenth Infantry fell back, they broke through the right of the Sixth Ohio and the left of the Thirty-sixth Indiana, causing much confusion; but the latter two regiments, notwithstanding this momentary disorder, stood up manfully against the almost crushing enemy, Colonel Anderson cheering his Sixth Ohio in the thickest of the fight till he was wounded; while Major Kenley gallantly led his Thirty-sixth Indiana till a similar fate overtook him. Seeing that the remaining regiments of John Beatty's and Scribner's brigades were also ordered back to support the batteries these two regiments slowly retired before the enemy. The rebels followed, and as they came out of the cedars into the open field the hour for Parsons's, Gunther's, and Loomis's batteries had come. Their guns opened upon the enemy, and filled the air with a perfect hailstorm of bursting shells, canister, and case shots, while the infantry commenced their rattling fire. It took but a few minutes, and the victorious onward march of McCown was stemmed.

The Confederates fought with great courage. General Rains, eager to take the batteries in his front, led his men with great gallantry, when a minie-ball pierced his heart and he fell to the ground. The sudden death of their leader caused considerable confusion, and as the Union batteries kept up their excellent fire the confusion turned into a stampede, and Rains's command ran back into the timber.

(It is a singular circumstance that the same battery—Parsons's—which McCown commanded as captain before the war, and which he left to join the Rebellion, contributed so much to his first repulse in this battle.)

Early in the morning, about 8 o'clock, General Negley had sent word to General Palmer on his left that he was going to advance, and asked him to let General Cruft go forward likewise, so as to protect his left. General Palmer, after receiving permission from General Rosecrans, ordered Colonel Hazen and General Cruft to move forward, the former to observe the movements of General Wood's right, while General Cruft was ordered to keep up well with Negley. Cruft's skirmishers eagerly advanced; but as General Palmer rode to the right of his division he found that General Negley, instead of advancing, had thrown his line perpendicular to that of Graft, and to his rear. General Cruft was thereupon halted, while Colonel Hazen was ordered back to his former position. The reason for General Negley changing his line was the fact that the rebels had driven General Johnson's division already north of the Wilkinson pike, while General Davis was also retreating, and there was great danger, if General Sheridan should be forced back, that the enemy would come in the rear of Negley's line.

During the assault on Roberts's brigade by part of Anderson's brigade, Negley's artillery fired with excellent effect; and when General Stewart advanced on Roberts with his whole brigade, Colonel Stanley's artillery and infantry opened a cross-fire on it that caused Stewart to lose many men.

Scarcely twenty minutes had elapsed after General Sheridan had withdrawn his third brigade when General Withers, under orders from Lieutenant-General Polk, again advanced by commencing, with Anderson's, and on his left Stewart's, brigades, a wheel to the right against Stanley's, Miller's, and Cruft's commands; while General Cheatham moved Maney's, Manigault's, and Vaughan's brigades across the Wilkinson pike. As General Stewart wheeled to the right, Stanley, on the extreme right, felt the first shock; his command stood for a considerable time, the Eighteenth Ohio, Eleventh Michigan, and Nineteenth Illinois losing heavily.

Finally their ammunition gave out, and they fell back, partly, as is claimed by Colonel Miller, through his lines. The enemy thereupon began his attack on Colonel Miller's brigade. Colonel Miller was a daring, efficient, and courageous officer, and fought his men grandly. During the height of one of the Confederate attacks some staff-officer delivered an order to Colonel Sirwell, of the Seventy-eighth Pennsylvania, to fall back, which order was complied with by the regiment retreating about twenty rods. This action was almost disastrous to the brigade, leaving a large gap. As soon as Colonel Miller observed this he instantly galloped to the Seventy-eighth Pennsylvania and brought them back into line.

While riding at great speed to correct this error he was badly wounded in the neck, but Colonel Miller never left his men; he fought with them to the last.[1] Although the rebel Generals Anderson and Stewart made several attempts to drive him back, the brigade repelled every attack. Finally the same trouble arose that had forced Stanley's and Roberts's brigades to the rear,—want of ammunition. The Thirty-seventh Indiana was the first regiment compelled to fall back; the others, though nearly out, still kept their ground manfully. About this time one of McCown's brigades made a desperate assault on Rousseau's front, and General Negley, believing Colonel Miller's

1. When, on the following day (January 1st), Colonel Miller reported to General Rosecrans, Medical-Director Swift, being near, observed the serious nature of Colonel Miller's wound.

"Colonel," he said, "you must go to the rear; your wound looks rather ugly."

"I cannot leave the boys," replied Colonel Miller, "till the fight is over."

"No, doctor," called out General Rosecrans, "we cannot spare John Miller. I have some hard work for him to do."

"But, general," answered Dr. Swift, "the colonel's wound is dangerous."

"Will it kill me if I don't go?" asked Miller.

"I could not say that it would."

"Well, then, I'll stay with my boys," said Colonel Miller, and General Rosecrans almost shouted for joy.

brigade almost surrounded, ordered it to fall back. The dread of being made prisoners caused some of the regiments to retreat quickly, leaving five guns, of which the horses had been disabled on the field.

When General Negley retired, the Thirty-eighth Indiana and Tenth Wisconsin, from Scribner's brigade, came to their assistance, and as the enemy came on their left flank the Thirty-eighth Indiana took position to the left of Negley's right regiments, while the Tenth Wisconsin, to protect the left flank of the Thirty-eighth Indiana, changed front to the rear. A severe fight took place, the Thirty-eighth Indiana losing heavily, till finally they all fell back and took position on the right of the Second Ohio, and were ordered to support Stokes's battery. It is reported, and no doubt true, that General Rosecrans in person rallied the Twenty-first Ohio and Seventy-eighth Pennsylvania.

It is an almost impossible task to reconcile the reports of General Cruft with those of his own regiments, and that of Colonel John F. Miller.

General Cruft says, in his report:

> . . . upon giving orders to advance, my skirmishers ran rapidly forward from the wood, and engaged those of the enemy in the open field. They drove them, and my front line advanced promptly up to the rail fence in the margin of the woods. The enemy pushed towards us rapidly, and charged my line in great force, and in solid rank. The fight became very severe and obstinate about 9 o'clock a.m.
>
> My troops fought with heroism. . . . The Second Kentucky and Thirty-first Indiana nobly held their ground, and after some thirty minutes' well-directed fire drove him back again for a short distance. A respite of a few minutes in active firing enabled me to execute a passage of lines to the front, to relieve the first line, the ammunition of which was nearly exhausted. . . .
>
> The rear line (now front) (Ninetieth Ohio and First Kentucky) was soon actively engaged. . . . The First Kentucky, Colonel Enyart, on the right of the line, made a gallant charge, and drove the enemy before it, rushing forward to the crest of the hill, clear beyond, and to the right of the burnt house. The fire was so severe from the enemy's force at the burnt house that the order to move up the Ninetieth Ohio was countermanded, not, however, until many of the officers and men of this gallant regiment had pressed forward over the fence in line with the 'Old' First Kentucky.

Standart, with his gallant gunners, was throwing in grape and canister from the flanks, as my men ran forward to the charge, and thinning the enemy's ranks. He was too strong, however, and soon my gallant advance was beaten back to the point of woods. This point was still held. . .

General Negley's brigade (Miller's), on the right, first advanced with me; but, yielding to the impulsive charge of the enemy, broke up, and a portion of it drifted in disorder immediately to my rear, and left me exposed to the cross-fire of the enemy from the woods on the right. We were now completely flanked. . . . Seeing my little brigade failing rapidly, and many of its best, men carried wounded to the rear, without hope of support or further ability to hold on, I withdrew it in as good order as practicable. The enemy pressed closely, firing constantly into the retreating mass. We faced to rear, and covered the retreat of General Negley's men as well as could be done. The Second Kentucky regiment brought off three pieces, and the Nineti-eth Ohio volunteers one piece, of abandoned artillery, by hand, which the enemy was rushing upon and about to capture.

Standards battery was saved, with a loss of three men and seven horses. It had but sixteen rounds of ammunition, when the or-der to retire was given. . .

Colonel John Osborn, of the Thirty-first Indiana regiment, states, in his report:—

At this time (after they had been ordered to advance) a heavy force of the enemy appeared in our front, in an open field on a piece of rising ground, when they opened a severe fire upon our line, which was returned with a steady nerve by our men, which soon made them fall back. In a few moments they again returned to the crest of the field and attempted to charge our line; but the steady nerve of our boys, and their deadly aim, caused them to retire. Our men getting short of ammunition, the First Kentucky came to our aid, and, passing by our line, followed the enemy up into the field; but the heavy force of the enemy in front, and the regiment being exposed to a cross-fire from the enemy's battery, they were compelled to fall back with considerable loss. . . . In a short time the enemy changed their point of attack, and appeared in great force on the left of our brigade, and on the right, between our regiment and

General Negley's forces. Both our right and left falling back, I was forced to order the regiment to fall back. The men obeying the order so reluctantly, and our left being so far turned before orders to fall back were received, caused our list of missing to be so large. . . .

Colonel D. A. Enyart, of the First Kentucky, says, in his report:—

. . . . the engagement was getting warm in our front, when General Cruft ordered the First Kentucky to move forward and march over the Thirty-first Indiana into a cornfield, three hundred yards in front of them, where we were exposed to the fire of two pieces of artillery, supported by a regiment of infantry about one hundred yards distant, and directly on our left flank. Our position here was in *advance* of that held by any other regiment in the army. Being in danger of being cut off by a heavy column of the enemy, advancing on our *right*, we retired in good order to the woods, where we took a new position behind a fence. We remained here but a short time when the brigade fell back through the woods slowly, and re-formed on the road.

Colonel I. N. Ross, of the Ninetieth Ohio, says, in his report:—

About 10 o'clock the brigade moved forward in the order previously named, the Ninetieth Ohio being ordered to support the Second Kentucky, in case it needed assistance; and immediately the first line was engaged.

Firing continued to increase in rapidity and fierceness until the Second Kentucky sent back word that they needed support, when the Ninetieth Ohio was ordered forward on the double-quick.

It moved to the front, and was immediately engaged with the enemy, who appeared in great force with two batteries, planted within one hundred and fifty yards of our position, which raked us with grape and canister. In noticing the movements of the enemy I observed him massing a heavy force behind a large house in our front and left, and preparing to plant a battery in the same position; and I also observed that our support on the left had given way. . . . I determined to report the situation to General Cruft . . . and ask support. Receiving no support, I immediately returned to the regiment, and ordered it to fall back, we having maintained our position until the enemy, in overwhelming numbers, was within at least twenty-five yards of us. The regiment now fell back, with considerable disorder, through the cedar forest, in which it held position in the morning, to the railroad.

Colonel Sedgwick's report is similar to that of General Cruft, and he says in it that he discovered that General Negley's entire lines had apparently given way. He made the discovery on returning from the left, where the Ninetieth Ohio was fighting, while Miller's brigade was some distance to the right.

Colonel Sedgwick, after describing the fight, speaks of the following occurrences, which must have immediately preceded the time when the Ninetieth Ohio fell back:—

> He (General Cruft) again sent me to see the situation on our left and rear. I found the Second (Hazen's) brigade still holding their ground far in the rear, and one brigade of Negley's division formed in line, facing immediately to our rear, and firing at the enemy, who appeared to be advancing in that direction. Of these facts, and our isolated condition, I informed General Cruft, when he reluctantly gave me the order to have the brigade fall slowly back.

Colonel John F. Miller's report is as follows:—

> Soon after this (after the Seventy-eighth Pennsylvania took again its position in line) a heavy force was observed to advance on General Palmer's left, and a hard contest ensued. General Palmer's right brigade (Cruft's) held their ground for a short time, and then began to retire; just at this time I received orders from General Negley to retire slowly with my command into the woods. My troops were nearly out of ammunition; the enemy was advancing on my right flank and on my left; the fire in front was no less destructive than it had been during the engagement. . . . Five guns were lost; four were saved by the men of the batteries, assisted by the infantry.

The above statements are inserted to aid the reader in coming to his own conclusions.

It seems, however, to be true that the Confederate forces, advancing from Chalmers's front towards the Cowan House, attacked Cruft's left regiments, which sustained heavy losses; while, according to the statement of Colonel Osborn, the right regiments had a smaller force to contend with; and Colonel Sedgwick's and Colonel Osborn's statements both seem to corroborate Colonel Miller's report that Cruft was retiring just before Miller.

It may not be far out of the way to say that both fell back about the same time; but Cruft's claim, that he covered the retreat of General Negley, seems to lack proof.

When Colonel Miller and General Cruft were falling: back, the brigade of Regulars under Colonel Shepherd was resting for a short time after the repulse of Rains. Observing the critical position, General Thomas ordered them to advance at once into the cedars in the right of the pike, and hold the enemy; they moved forward on the double-quick and fought with unsurpassed bravery. They held their ground for twenty-five minutes, and the great number of dead and wounded (about 40 *per cent.*) show their discipline and courage in a manner that cannot be contradicted. Among the dead was gallant Major Carpenter, pierced by six balls. Finally they were compelled to fall back, when Parsons's, Gunther's, and other batteries opened upon the pursuing enemy such a fire that they, in return, fled to the timber in great haste, glad to be again protected by the dense screen of cedars from the destructive missiles of these splendid batteries. After this repulse there was again a lull in the battle.

In order to understand the subsequent attacks of Lieut.-General Hardee, along the Nashville pike it is necessary to keep in mind that our troops were in the following positions: General Thomas's line, along the Nashville pike, remained about the same as when Rains was repulsed. Gunther's and Loomis's batteries of Rousseau's division remained on an elevated position between railroad and pike, a short distance back of General Palmer, supported by the infantry of the division. North of General Thomas, on a small hill about three miles from Murfreesboro', General Rosecrans had placed, in the morning, Stokes's battery, supported by the three battalions of the Pioneer Corps, under Captain St. Clair Morton; to the right of Stokes stood Colonel Samuel Beatty's brigade; on his right Colonel Fyffe's brigade had been for a time, and was at this time returning from the fight with the rebel cavalry near Overall's Creek; and on the extreme right, a short distance north of the little dirt road which leads past widow Burroughs's house, was Colonel Harker's brigade, ready for action.

It was not long before the enemy approached. McNair's brigade, flushed with victory, rushed with yells out of the cedars, north of the place where Rains had been repulsed, and like mad men ran towards Gunther's and Loomis's batteries. As they advanced they fell like grass before the mower; but still they pressed on almost to the very guns, when the supporting infantry poured forth volley after volley, that left scarcely a man standing before them. A few escaped unhurt, but the ground was covered with killed and wounded; and near the batteries lay, in the midst of a host of dead rebels the colours of the Thirtieth Arkansas,—an undying evidence of the courage of the men that made the assault, and the steadiness and bravery of the troops that defended the guns.

Farther towards the north Ector's brigade came likewise out of the timber, with those unearthly Texas yells, and they rushed, like demons that knew no death, towards Stokes's battery. Bright boys from Chicago fought those guns; they had seen but little of the terrors of war before, and they seemed to hail this opportunity with delight. Some of them shouted, as the enemy came nearer: "Give it to them, boys!" while others, as the shells ploughed through the advancing column, cried out, " Great Caesar, see the Johnnies fall!" But, though they fell everywhere thick and fast, the Johnnies advanced nearer to the battery. Then came the order from the commanding officer, "Give them double canister!" and in a few seconds' time the double-shotted guns emptied their death-spreading missiles amongst Ector's men; while the Pioneers, under St. Clair Morton, throwing aside their axes and picks, aided by the regiments sent to their assistance, brought their muskets likewise on the enemy. The slaughter was great; the Texans, brave as they were, could not storm that wall of fire, and they at last fell back in the wildest confusion.[2]

General Liddell, of Cleburne's division, in pursuit of the extreme right, moved in advance of the other brigades due north, and emerged from the large timber north of the Wilkinson pike into the open field, about five hundred yards from the little Asbury church, near Overall's creek. Being without support he halted, and fired with his artillery on the trains moving towards and on the Nashville pike. Soon afterwards General Cleburne sent orders to Liddell to move by the right flank till his line would connect with (rebel) General Johnson's brigade on his right; while he ordered Johnson, with Wood on his right, and Polk on the extreme right of the division, to move forward and attack the Union line. Colonel Vaughan, commanding Preston Smith's brigade of Cheatham's division, followed in supporting distance of Wood's brigade.

---

2. Lieutenant Stevens's Pennsylvania battery also did excellent work in repelling these rebel assaults.

Colonel Sam Beatty, with the Ninth Kentucky and Nineteenth Ohio in the front line, placed by General Rosecrans in person, west of the cemetery, not far from the pike, waited till the retreating troops driven by the enemy passed through his line, and then a volley, like a sheet of flame, issued from these regiments, and brought the jubilant enemy to a stand. But he would not yield, and the rattling fire of musketry began, while Stevens's Twenty-sixth Pennsylvania battery threw shells from its position in the rear. The firing was sharp and quick, and the ammunition of the front line beginning to give out, Colonel Beatty, under direction of General Rosecrans, who was cheering the men by his presence and his words, gave the order to the second line to go to the relief of the first, and with a loud hurrah the Eleventh Kentucky and Seventy-ninth Indiana rushed to the front. The rebels gave way, and were pursued for quite a distance.

About the same time, not far from ten o'clock in the morning, Colonel Fyffe having taken position to the right of Beatty in the woods south of the cornfield (in the following lines from left to right: Fifty-ninth Ohio and Forty-fourth Indiana in the first line, Thirteenth Ohio and Eighty-sixth Indiana in the second line, while Swallow's battery remained near the pike), General Van Cleve ordered the brigade forward. They moved with some difficulty through the thicket; but as they emerged out of it, into the open field, they advanced to the woods in their front. The first line moved about twenty yards into the timber, while the second line remained at the edge, and were ordered to lie down behind the fence.

Farther to the right, Harker's brigade advanced, with the Sixty-fifth Ohio and Fifty-first Indiana in the front line, with the Seventy-third Indiana and the Sixty-fourth Ohio in the second line, while the Thirteenth Michigan moved in support of Bradley's battery; they halted about one-half mile west of the Nashville pike.

As these different brigades marched forward, the rebels likewise advanced and began their attack. Harker, observing that his line was enfiladed on the right, and threatened with being flanked, moved his brigade a little to the right. This movement had the result of exposing Colonel Fyffe's right, and the rebels were quick in taking advantage of this gap. Part of rebel General Polk's brigade attacked Colonel Samuel Beatty. Polk's left regiments and rebel General Wood's brigade stood opposite to Colonel Fyffe's; while General Johnson, who had relieved General Liddell, paid his attention to Colonel Harker.

The Fifty-ninth Ohio and Forty-fourth Indiana felt the first shock, and soon fell back on the Thirteenth Ohio and Eighty-sixth Indiana, standing behind the fence. Colonel Hawkins, of the Thirteenth Ohio, with a soul aglow with courage, cheered his men by his gallantry, and Wood's brigade fell back; but, alas! the victory was dearly bought, for it was at the expense of his life. As they were falling back Colonel Vaughan, with Preston Smith's brigade, took their place with loud yells, while General Johnson's brigade began to fire on Colonel Fyffe's right flank. Attacked in front and on the right, Fyffe's brigade fell back in some disorder, followed by the enemy.

While General Van Cleve, aided by his staff, was attempting to rally his men a bullet struck him, and the horse of his brave adjutant, Captain Otis, was killed, the latter officer narrowly escaping capture.

Fyffe's regiments having fallen back, Colonel Samuel Beatty's brigade was left in a dangerous position. The rebels advanced steadily closer towards the right of the Nineteenth Ohio, and poured upon it a destructive enfilading fire. A change of position was necessary to save it from enormous losses. Its commanding officer, Major Manderson, twice sent word to Colonel Beatty of his perilous position; but, as the latter could not be found by the messenger, Major Manderson took the responsibility upon himself. Quick action was required, for the enemy was within fifty yards. The regiment was ordered to lie flat on the ground. Taking, with the greatest dispatch, the colours and right and left general guides, he placed them in a line to the right and rear of the position then held by his regiment. As soon as this was done the men, under special instructions of Major Manderson and the company officers, quickly rose, and with all their might ran for the new position and faced about.

The rebels, seeing this movement, supposed that a new stampede had taken place, and, with loud cheers, ran after them, hoping for an easy victory. But the Nineteenth Ohio had grand material in its ranks; Quickly aligning itself, it received the yelling enemy with a murderous fire, which, together with the excellent fire of a battery to the regiment's left and rear, caused the rebels to halt and recoil. In this fight the Nineteenth lost twelve killed and sixty-seven wounded, nearly as great a loss as the other regiments in the brigade lost altogether; and that it was able to execute the above-described movement under such a fire is an evidence that it must have been well drilled and well led.

The regiment, being then entirely out of ammunition, was thereupon ordered to move by the right flank to a new position, between the Second battalion of the Pioneer Corps on the left and Fyffe's brigade on the right, where it remained till about four o'clock in the afternoon, when it was relieved by Colonel Walker's brigade.

The Seventy-ninth Indiana was likewise ordered to the support of Colonel Fyffe's brigade, while the Ninth and Eleventh Kentucky were ordered by Colonel Beatty towards the left, to the support of Stokes's and the batteries belonging to Rousseau's division, where they remained till night, without encountering any further serious attacks.

Colonel Harker, on the extreme right, had fought Confederate General Johnson's brigade successfully for about twenty minutes, when he observed that Colonel Fyffe had fallen back, and that the enemy was already to his rear on his left, and only two hundred yards from it. He thereupon quickly ordered the Sixty-fifth Ohio to take position behind a rail fence, obliquely to the first line of battle, and fire upon the enemy; then, ordering the Seventy-third Indiana to hold its position, he directed the Sixty-fourth Ohio to charge to the left, while Bradley's battery was ordered four hundred yards to the rear. But the Sixty-fourth Ohio made an error in its direction, going too far to the right, and the two left regiments of Vaughan's brigade, observing a gap, quickly sent a volley on Harker's left.

Captain Bradley's battery, being in a very dangerous position, was compelled to fall back, leaving two pieces on the field. The Confederate infantry closely followed Harker, and, finding excellent shelter behind rocks, and in the many sink-holes in the vicinity, they commenced a most destructive fire, killing a large number of Harker's men. The Thirteenth Michigan, which had not before been engaged in the battle, stood their ground well, and held the enemy in their front at bay for some minutes; but the Confederates still pressed forward, advancing on the right and left, while some few, as is claimed in their reports, reached even the Nashville pike. This was, indeed, a critical time, and everything seemed lost.

At that very moment two Illinois regiments, exhausted by hard work, and in search of ammunition, came slowly northward along the pike. They were the Twenty-seventh and Fifty-first of Roberts's brigade and Sheridan's division.

As soon as General Rosecrans saw them he galloped at full speed towards Colonel Bradley, of the Fifty-first, while General McCook rode to Major Schmidt, commanding the Twenty-seventh.

"Who commands these troops?" asked General Rosecrans.

"I do," replied Colonel Bradley.

"Send your regiments quickly into yonder thicket and stop the

171

advance of the rebels," shouted Rosecrans. "Quick! quick! lose not a moment, Colonel; this battle must be won."

"My regiments are almost out of ammunition," replied Colonel Bradley, brave, yet always careful of his men; "but we will drive them with the bayonet."

In an instant, almost, the command was halted, faced to the left, aligned, and when the order to advance was given the two regiments moved steadily forward. The enemy lay concealed in sink-holes and behind rocks. As our men came near them the rebels fired from their ambush, and, being strong, compelled them to fall back a short distance. The rebels then arose from their hiding-places and followed them.

Again General Rosecrans and General McCook rode up to them and along their line, cheered the men, and inspired them with great enthusiasm, though bullets fell almost as thick as hailstones in a summer shower.

"Colonel Bradley," shouted Rosecrans, "we must drive these rebels with the bayonet, or the day is lost"; and the gallant Colonel Bradley, full of bravery and determination, ordered the men to load their guns, which they did, in many instances using the last cartridge in the box.

The order of "Fix bayonets!" ran along the line; the men caught the spirit of their commanders. Officers, like Adjutant Rust, seized the muskets of falling men and marched in line. It was a grand moment; they were to fight under the very eyes of Generals Rosecrans and McCook, and "death or victory" was the battle-cry of all.

"Charge bayonets!" "Forward march!" and with steady quick step they moved fearlessly on. As they reached the top of a small elevation the rebels were in their immediate front. "Halt!" —"Aim!"— "Fire!"—"Double quick!"—"March!" and, with bayonets fixed, and a loud hurrah, they rushed for the enemy.

The rebels gave way. The Twenty-seventh and Fifty-first followed them far out into the open field. Many of our men wept for joy. The advance of these two regiments relieved the strong pressure on the Thirteenth Michigan; this regiment, thereupon, likewise charged forward with fixed bayonets, driving the enemy from its immediate front. When Smith's brigade gave way before Colonel Bradley's impulsive attack, Polk's, Johnson's, and Liddell's brigades became panic-stricken, the men crying out, "Our flank is turned! Our flank is turned!" A perfect rout ensued, and many did not stop in their flight till they had reached the Wilkinson pike.

The Confederate generals say, in their reports, that this retreat is perfectly incomprehensible; that there was very little firing at the time. Liddell says, that he went for a few minutes into a Federal hospital (Widow Burroughs's house), near the little dirt road, being called on for protection, and, in an incredibly short time, he found his line breaking rapidly to the rear; that he galloped quickly to head off the stragglers. On halting he found them to be Johnson's men. Riding to the right he met General Johnson looking for his men. Johnson then informed Liddell that his brigade was not far distant, in the neck of the woods. It is evident that these rebel brigades must have been utterly demoralized, and, if Col. Bradley's attack had been followed up at once, the fortunes of that day would have been changed. Finally General McCook ordered Colonel Bradley to return, and the two regiments brought back with them two hundred prisoners, and the two guns previously lost by Harker were recaptured.

General Hardee did not venture to attack again that day, and thus ended the severe battle on the right.

The importance of this success cannot be overestimated. If the Confederates had succeeded in taking and holding the Nashville pike there can be little doubt that the battle would have been lost, and a large part of the army captured. Near the Nashville pike were our ammunition trains, which would have fallen into their hands. The pike was the only road that connected us with Nashville, our base of supplies, and, in case a retreat was necessary, the only road on which the army could fall back.

But, more important still, it would have enabled the Confederates to enfilade General Thomas's Corps, and to fire on Palmer's and Wood's divisions from the rear as well as from the front.

Under the demoralizing influence of the defeat of Davis's and Johnson's divisions, but few troops could have stood a double fire like this, and they would most likely have been compelled to fall back. But in what direction? There was only one, towards the north, between river and pike; but this space was only a few yards more than one-fourth of a mile in width, and partly covered with timber. A more serious state of affairs cannot be contemplated, and only the best-disciplined troops would have succeeded in fighting their way through.

CHAPTER 6

THE BATTLE—CONTINUED

We must turn again to General Palmer's line. General Negley having, as hereinbefore stated, fallen back and formed his line at an angle to the rear of Cruft, General Palmer ordered Hazen to move back to his former position. Colonel Hazen, in complying with this order, placed his two right regiments, the Sixth Kentucky and Ninth Indiana, in the cedars on the right of the pike, protecting Cruft's left flank; while the two left regiments, the Forty-first Ohio and One-hundred-and-tenth Illinois, took positions in two lines on the east side of the pike, between it and the railway, as Colonel Wagner's brigade had moved east of the railway-track, on account of Colonel Harker being ordered north along the pike. Scarcely had their formation been made when Confederate General Chalmers began his attack. The Sixth Kentucky fought him gallantly, somewhat in advance; receiving at one time, a little later, a double fire from Chalmers on one side and from Confederate General Anderson, who, with Stewart, was driving Negley and Cruft, on the other. The Ninth Indiana was at that time endeavouring to assist Grose's brigade, engaged in repelling Rains's attack; but, being unable to do any good, they changed front to the rear, and commenced to fire on the rebels, advancing from the direction of the Cowan House.

The Forty-first Ohio, in the front line, between the pike and the railway, vigorously opened on the enemy, while Cockerell's, Estep's, and Cox's batteries poured forth a rapid cannon fire; but Chalmers's men still pressed forward with almost overwhelming power.

The Twenty-fourth Ohio was quickly sent by sturdy Colonel Grose to the left of the Sixth Kentucky, and this regiment was immediately very hotly engaged. Brave Colonel Jones and Major Terry soon fell, seriously wounded, and had to be carried off the field.

When the fight was at the highest a piece of one of our shells struck Confederate General Chalmers, and, having lost their leader, the rebel brigade fell back on Confederate General Donelson, of Cheatham's division, who had been ordered to keep his command two thousand feet in rear of Chalmers's line, ready to support him at a moment's notice.

When General Chalmers was brought . senseless from the field, and his brigade fell back in disorder, General Donelson ordered his Tennesseans forward at once. A terrible artillery fire met them, but still they advanced. The Cowan House, with its fences and out-houses, proved a serious obstruction; their line became uneven and broken, and while the Sixteenth (rebel) Tennessee and three companies of the Fifty-first went to the east of the Cowan House, the balance of the brigade, composed of seven companies of the Fifty-first, the Thirty-eighth, and the Eighth, moved forward on the west side of this historic house. There were no finer troops in the Confederate army.

Suddenly an aid, sent by General Palmer, dashed across the open space towards General Hascall, whose command was a short distance in the rear, and informed him that General Palmer's division needed help immediately. After a moment's consultation with General Wood, Hascall sent the grand old Third Kentucky, and in double-quick time this regiment rushed to the rescue, and took its position on the west side of the Nashville pike. Colonel Grose, seeing no immediate danger in his front, after Rains had been repulsed, also sent the Thirty-sixth Indiana, with Parsons's battery on the right, to Hazen's and Hascall's assistance, the Thirty-sixth forming on the right of the Third Kentucky.

A terrible fight took place; scarcely had the Third Kentucky been in its position ten minutes when a minie-ball struck its brave commander, Lieutenant-Colonel McGee, above the eye, and he fell from his horse, while the regiment lost one-fourth of its number in killed and wounded. Courageous Major Collier, though wounded in leg and breast, refused to leave the field, and stayed with his men to the end. Seeing that the Third Kentucky had suffered so severely General Hascall ordered the Fifty-eighth Indiana and Twenty-sixth Ohio to their relief as a second line; then placing Estep's battery between them, but a little to the rear, he kept the One-hundredth Illinois further back in reserve.

The slaughter was frightful. The rebel batteries on the east side of the river fired with great precision, while Donelson's men in front fought like mad men; but they had men of equal nerve opposed to them, and when Parsons's, Estep's, Cockerill's, Cox's, and other batteries farther to the rear, sent canisters, shells, and case-shots with marvellous rapidity, it seemed as if the air was filled with them, for second after second these missiles burst in the enemy's ranks. General Donelson, unable to break the line in his front, ordered his men to move into the cedars west of the Cowan House, and finally retired towards the Wilkinson pike. How hot the fire must have been here is evinced by the fact that the left regiment of Donelson's brigade, the Eighth Tennessee, lost forty-one killed and two hundred and sixty-five wounded, three hundred and six men out of four hundred and seventy-two men in action (sixty-four and one-half *per cent.*).

But the fight had been scarcely less bloody on the left of the pike;

here the splendid Forty-first Ohio had been placed with the One-hundred-and- tenth Illinois (a new regiment in reserve); the Fortieth Indiana standing to the left and a little to the rear. The Sixteenth (rebel) Tennessee and part of the Fifty-first Tennessee advanced with unquestioned courage upon the Forty-first Ohio and part of Wagner's brigade, trying to drive them from their position; but they held it nobly, losing one hundred and ten killed and wounded out of four hundred and thirteen officers and men; while the Sixteenth (rebel) Tennessee lost thirty-five killed and one hundred and fifty-five wounded out of four hundred and two men on the field, and then fell back in rear of the Cowan House, unable to retreat without certain destruction.

During the temporary lull General Hascall relieved the Third Kentucky with the Fifty-eighth Indiana, and this, being a large regiment, took up all the space between the pike and the railway; our line west of the pike was at this time drawn back a little and re-formed, to protect our men from the fire of the enemy in the cedars, where General Cruft had been fighting earlier in the day.

After General Sheridan had fallen back from the Wilkinson pike he saw General Palmer's right sorely pressed, and, without waiting for a formal invitation, quickly sent to its assistance three guns from Hescock's battery and a couple of regiments from the Second brigade, aiding in the repulse of the enemy; then ordering such of his troops of the Second and Third brigades as had not previously done so to march to the railroad for ammunition, he again was ready for action. Under direction of General Rosecrans he placed part of the Second brigade east of the railway on the left side of the track, and the Fifteenth Missouri was sent forward as skirmishers in the cornfield near the Cowan House. The firing between this regiment and the Sixteenth Tennessee and part of the Fifty-first Tennessee near this house was very sharp, and was kept up till the enemy's reinforcements came to their aid. The rebel army excelled ours greatly in organized battalions of sharpshooters. Our officers and artillery men seem to have been their favourite game, and frequently the gunners, when not engaged, were ordered to lie down flat on the ground to escape the accurate aim of these sharp-shooters.

As soon as Colonel Schaefer, commanding the brigade, saw the Fifteenth Missouri fall back, he rode forward to give the regiment some orders, when he was hit by an enemy's bullet and fell to the ground dead. Thus died the third and last brigade commander of General Sheridan's division, and an excellent and brave officer was lost to the army.

During the temporary lull in the battle, and while the front line was being relieved by regiments with ammunition, General Rosecrans ordered General Sheridan to withdraw these regiments and form the Second brigade and the Thirty-sixth Illinois in close column of attack, in rear of the Bound Forest near the railway. This column was to be used in case the enemy should succeed in breaking our lines in front; but, as every subsequent attack was repulsed, they did not come again in close contact with the enemy that day.

The Sixth Kentucky, with the Ninth Indiana on their left and the Forty-first Ohio and One-hundred-and-Tenth Illinois in the second line, took the position of Schaefer's brigade; while on the left of Colonel Hazen was the Fortieth Indiana and One-hundredth Illinois, and still farther to the left the Fifteenth and Fifty-seventh Indiana of Wagner's brigade; the Ninety-seventh Ohio having been sent, shortly after noon, to General Hascall's aid, and placed by General Rosecrans himself on the south side of the Nashville pike.

In the remote distance, where the Nashville pike crosses Stone's River, a large mass of gray troops could be seen moving from the east side of Stone's River towards the west. It was General Adams's brigade, of Breckenridge's division, which had been ordered by General Bragg to report to Lieutenant-General Polk. General Adams rode in advance of his command, and, galloping to Lieutenant-General Polk, he asked for his orders. "Look at yonder battery," he said, pointing to one stationed between the pike and the river in rear of the federal line; "take it, and the day is won."

The brigade was soon formed; the Thirteenth and Twentieth Louisiana on the right, then the Sixteenth and Twenty-fifth Louisiana, and, on the left, the Thirty-second Alabama. They advanced in excellent order. It was a magnificent brigade; here and there shells and shots would plough through their ranks, but still they moved steadily on. At the Cowan House some difficulties were again encountered; but, passing it by skilful manoeuvre, they formed again in a magnificent line and pressed forward. Suddenly one could see, by the glittering flashes of light, that they had brought their arms to a "charge bayonet," and a few moments afterwards they ran forward with a tremendous cheer.

Our artillery had poured into the enemy a well-directed and destructive fire, while our infantry had been ordered to reserve theirs; but the moment had now come when the loud commands were heard, "Commence firing!" and volley after volley burst forth from the Federal line. General Adams's men fell by the hundred; still they moved on with irresistible force. A part of our line melted away before the attack, and fell back even, for the battle raged desperately indeed. But Generals Palmer, Wood, and Hascall were closely watching their men. They strengthened the weak spots, and cheered the men by their bravery, causing them to fire with renewed steadiness, energy, and valour; then Adams's brigade was held at bay, and finally, though it fought most gallantly, compelled to yield and retreat.

When General Wagner, on the extreme left, saw the charge of the enemy, he ordered the Fifteenth Indiana, supported by the Fifty-seventh Indiana, which had advanced towards them near the river, to make a counter-charge, and well did they obey the order. Firing a few rounds they fixed their bayonets, and with a grand hurrah rushed forward, driving the enemy before them, and taking about two hundred prisoners.

But it was a dearly bought victory, for they lost one hundred and eighty in killed and wounded, out of four hundred and forty officers and men. The rebels in front of the Fifteenth Indiana retreated towards the Cowan House, and, after firing a few shots, joined their comrades that had fallen back. This assault of Adams's brigade was, without doubt, the most daring, courageous, and best-executed attack which the Confederates made on our line between pike and river; and General Adams gives great credit to our artillery, admitting that our guns were so well served that no infantry could successfully advance against them.

The loss was indeed enormous, General Adams losing thirty-three and one-third *per cent*, of his whole brigade in this historic and bloody part of the field.

General Bragg's thoughts may be easily imagined. These repeated repulses must have enraged him, and restrained every nerve and called every force into requisition to break the Federal line. He ordered General Breckenridge to leave Hanson's brigade on the east side of the river, and to cross it with Preston's and Palmer's brigades, about three thousand five hundred and thirty officers and men strong. Breckenridge was directed to rest Preston's right on the river, and to form his line at a right angle with the Nashville pike, Palmer to form on Preston's left.

His orders were to form these two brigades in one line, and, after advancing to within about two hundred yards of the Union front, to let Palmer wheel to the right and attack the Federals on the right flank.

As Preston's brigade only was under fire, it will be sufficient to state that it was formed from right to left, as follows: Twentieth Tennessee, Sixtieth North Carolina, Fourth Florida, and First and Third Florida.

It was to be the last, and perhaps decisive, attack. The gleaming bayonets of these two brigades, as they passed Stone's River toward the west, could be plainly seen by General Rosecrans, and he took at once measures to strengthen his line in front of Hazen, Hascall, and Wagner.

Parsons, with his gallant Lieutenants, Huntington and Cushing, having rested for a short time after their hard work in the morning, and replenished the ammunition of their batteries, was ordered to the railway, four guns on each side of the track.

The sun was fast sinking below the cedars on the right, and there were many anxious hearts waiting to see what the short time might bring forth ere the sun should set on that bloody day.

Finally, a waving motion in the distance gave evidence that the command of "Forward, march!" had been given to the enemy, and, as their line advanced, the whole of Palmer's and part of Preston's brigade disappeared into the cedars, where Cruft's brigade had been in the morning. They marched like veteran soldiers, and, as they approached, new batteries advanced in front of their lines (Washington and Captain Byrnes) to engage and, if possible, to silence ours.

General Rosecrans was in constant activity; he seemed omnipresent; galloping from place to place, he watched every movement, and gave his orders.

The position near the railroad seemed the post of greatest danger, and to an elevated place near it he rode, accompanied by his faithful chief, Colonel Garesché, and followed by his staff. Semple's, Cobb's, and Lumsden's cannons, in front of Hanson, sent shot and shell into our line, and the ground near the general commanding was ploughed up in many places. His staff warned him of his danger; he smiled at their anxiety. Presently a cannon-ball passed close to him; it missed him, but, striking the head of poor Garesché, severed it from the body, the latter falling heavily to the ground. His blood stained the garments of many near him, and a shudder passed through all who witnessed this awful death. But General Rosecrans remained faithfully at his post.

As Preston's regiments advanced, the Cowan House presented the same obstructions, and when they tried to form into line again our artillery and infantry in front fired on them with all their energy, Colonel Wagner's men attacking them on their right flank.

The fight did not last very long; the many repulses had demoralized the Confederate troops, and they fled as fast as they could into the cedars, from whence the rebel General Palmer intended to wheel on our right flank, but failed to do. Preston's loss was only eight and one third *per cent*, killed, wounded, and missing, while the rebel General Palmer lost only twenty-three men in all.

Soon after this last assault by Preston and Palmer, and their repulse, night began to throw her dark mantle over the battlefield; burying parties from both sides moved in front of their lines, and Federal and Confederate soldiers frequently mingled together in momentary concord to place the gallant dead gently in their last resting-places. Many wounded, too weak to walk alone, found willing help to carry them to the hospitals in the rear, until at last there was perfect silence where the fiercest battle had raged but a few hours before.

Between Generals Bragg and Breckenridge a serious quarrel had broken out concerning the support which the latter ought to, and failed to, render. As early as 10 o'clock a.m. General Bragg had sent an order to General Breckenridge for one brigade, and soon after for another to be sent to Lieutenant-General Hardee; but General Breckenridge replied to the first order that the Federal troops were crossing the river in his immediate front; and, to the second, that they had already crossed, and were advancing on him in two lines.

General Breckenridge was then ordered by General Bragg to advance and meet them. The orders for these two brigades were therefore countermanded, and measures taken to reinforce him; but, before they were carried out, it was ascertained that there were but a few skirmishers on Breckenridge's front, and it was then too late to send these brigades to Hardee's assistance on the rebel left.

It was certainly of great importance to the Union army that Breckinridge's men did not come earlier into action. If Cleburne's attack on the Nashville pike had been renewed with reinforcements, or if Chalmers's and Donelson's attacks had been quickly followed by Adams's, Preston's, and Palmer's, or made at the same time, the fight near the pike and railway would have been far more serious; but as , these assaults followed each other, with the exception of Donelson's, quite slowly, Generals Rosecrans, Palmer, and Wood had sufficient time to re-form their lines and relieve such regiments as had exhausted their ammunition, or suffered severely.

The abandoned attack of Van Cleve and Wood thus bore some good fruit, after all.

CHAPTER 7

THE BATTLE OF JANUARY 2ND, 1863, AND THE CONFEDERATES' RETREAT

In the evening General Rosecrans called the several corps commanders to report in regard to the condition of their commands and their supply of ammunition. They assembled in a little old log-cabin, occupied by General Negley, and opposite the headquarters of the commanding general.

The first order given by General Rosecrans was to the effect that all spare ammunition be issued forthwith. Then, turning to General Crittenden, General Rosecrans asked this question, "General, do you deem it advisable to fight out this battle on the ground we now occupy?"

General Crittenden replied, "General, this question is too grave and vital to be decided by me; whatever you decide, we will stand by."

General Rosecrans then turned to General McCook, and asked the same question. The latter replied, "I think that we are substantially the only barrier Between the rebel army and the Ohio River. If we fall back to Nashville we can hold them in check south of the Cumberland river until we can get sufficient reinforcements to resume offensive operations. I think, therefore, that it would be the most prudent course to fall back to Nashville."

General Rosecrans then turned to General Thomas and asked the same question. He replied, "General, the exigencies are so grave, and the consequences so serious, that I think no one can decide this except the general commanding. Whatever you decide upon, we will stand by."

General Rosecrans then turned to General Stanley, and said, "General, what do you think?"

General Stanley replied, "I concur in the views expressed by General McCook."

General Rosecrans then rose and said, "Gentlemen, as I have not had time so far to examine the ground in our rear towards Overall's Creek, having arrived here during the night of the 29th, please remain here until I make this examination. General Stanley, you will accompany me." General Rosecrans then rode to Overall's Creek, and, after examining the ground, returned quickly.

On entering the log-cabin he exclaimed, "Gentlemen, we will fight it out here. Go to your commands, and get ready for battle."

Grand old General Thomas's face glowed with delight, while Generals McCook and Crittenden were equally pleased. Then, as each one of the corps commanders took the hand of the general commanding in bidding him good-night, they gave him a soldier's warm grasp, and said, "We will stand by you, General, to the last."

There was, however, a report current at the time of the battle, and generally believed, that in this consultation of generals it was considered best to fall back, and that General Rosecrans started to the rear to select the best place. After he had passed Overall's Creek, strange lights, like torches, were seen in the distance moving northerly, and a report was brought in that the enemy was moving to our rear.

This, of course, made the retreat of the army during the night an impossibility. This report being believed, although the lights were in fact those of our own cavalry, who were making fires against orders, the general commanding returned, and orders were issued to re-form our lines.

Neither general nor private soldier had much sleep that night, and the task of getting ready to fight another battle began. In forming the line, General McCook's Corps, with Colonel Walker's brigade, which had come from the rear, were ordered to remain in the position held by them in the early evening. This line of battle commenced on the Nashville pike, about three and a quarter miles from Murfreesboro', and, making a curved line towards the west, struck the pike again about half a mile beyond, extending towards the east as far as the railway. To McCook's left was Captain Stokes's battery, supported by the Pioneers, and to their left General Thomas's Corps, including Colonel Starkweather's brigade, which had arrived from Jefferson late December 31st.

About 3 o'clock in the morning, orders were sent to Generals Palmer and Hascall[1] to retire, their line varying in distance from three Hundred to seven hundred yards.

Colonel Harker, who had reported back to General Hascall about 11 o'clock the previous evening, was placed east of the pike, his right resting near it; to his left Colonel Wagner's brigade, with Colonel

---

1. The latter having assumed command of Wood's division. General Wood had been wounded in the heel early on December 31st, but remained in the saddle till 7 o'clock p.m.

Buelll, commanding General Hascall's brigade, in reserve, in rear of the interval between Barker and Wagner.

General Palmer's division moved in to the interval between Wagner's brigade and the river.

About the same hour orders were sent to Colonel Beatty, commanding Van Cleve's division after the latter was wounded, to cross Stone's River at the upper ford. Colonel Beatty, in compliance with this order, crossed it at daybreak, and placed Price's and Fyffe's brigades about half a mile above the ford, their right resting near the river, and their line running perpendicular to it. His own brigade, now commanded by Colonel Grider, occupied a position in support of Price.

During the night a large number of wagons, with wounded men, were sent back to Nashville, which fact, being reported to General Bragg by his cavalry, gave him and other Confederate generals the impression that the Union troops were in full retreat. Great was their surprise, therefore, when in the morning they saw a large force, with the stars and stripes in their front, near the railway and pike, though somewhat in rear of the line of battle of the previous day.

As soon as General Bragg observed this he ordered his troops to advance into the Round Forest, near the railway, and took about the same position that Hazen, Hascall, and Wagner held the day before.

Throughout January 1st, 1863, there were skirmishes in various places, to ascertain the position of the Union troops. In the afternoon Lieutenant-General Hardee ordered General Cleburne to make a reconnoissance without bringing on an engagement. General Liddell's brigade was directed to make it, and advanced from the woods, not far from Overall's Creek and Asbury church, in a northerly direction, crossing the little dirt road, and passing the white house used as a hospital on the right. None of our troops being very near, there was very little firing in consequence. Hardee sent word to Cleburne that he could not hear any of his guns, and the latter sent Wood's brigade to advance on

Liddell's right. They had moved but a short distance when they appeared in Sheridan's front, and orders were given to the artillery to open on them. They fell back almost immediately, and our infantry, being sent out, captured a number of prisoners. On other parts of the field various attempts were also made to feel our lines, none of which can be called more than a little skirmish or artillery duel. General Rosecrans expected General Bragg to attack him, while General Bragg anxiously waited for General Rosecrans to withdraw.

Colonel Grose's brigade was also ordered across the river as a support to Van Cleve's division; but, as the enemy made no attack, it returned to its previous position at night.

The cold and bad weather, the scarcity of food, and the want of sleep, had a somewhat demoralizing effect on many men. The great majority were hopeful that a victory might still be gained; others grew feint-hearted, and were inclined to retreat to Nashville. A conspicuous example of the latter feeling was shown by a general commanding a division, although no one would suspect it by reading his report of the battle. In the evening of the first day of January he came to one of his brigade commanders, who may be called Colonel X., a very brave man, and said to him, "This army is whipped; the rebels are between us and Nashville, and the only thing to do now is to cut our way through. Someone has to take the lead, and I want you to do it tomorrow; otherwise we shall all be captured."

Colonel X. answered, "General, this army is not beaten, by a good deal; it is in a better position than ever before, and we will whip them yet." Then, thinking a moment, he added, "Have you consulted General Rosecrans about your proposed action?"

"No," replied the division commander; "but be ready tomorrow to cut your way through to Nashville."

After the latter had left, Colonel X., considering the matter for a few minutes, went to another brigade commander in the same division, who may be called Colonel Q., to ascertain whether anything of similar import had been said to him.

"Has our division commander told you that he wants us to cut our way through to Nashville tomorrow?" asked Colonel X. of Colonel Q.

"Yes," answered the latter.

"What are you going to do about it?"

"My God!" responded Colonel X., full of indignation and anger, "if he orders me to desert the balance of this army, and run away to Nashville, I'll arrest him as a traitor, and march him under guard to General Rosecrans's headquarters."

It is very probable that this reply was communicated to the division commander, for the order to retreat to Nashville never came.

On the morning of January 2nd Colonel Grose's command was again ordered to take the same position as on the day before, and the Union line, on the east side of the river, stood, previous to Breckenridge's attack, in the following manner:—

Van Cleve's division, Colonel Beatty commanding, remained in the same position as on the previous day, and the regiments were in the following lines from right to left, commencing at the river: Fifty-first Ohio, Eighth Kentucky, Drury's, designated in the reports as Livingston's battery, Thirty-fifth Indiana (of Price's brigade), Seventy-ninth Indiana (of Grider's brigade), Forty-fourth Indiana, and Thirteenth Ohio. In the second line, Twenty-first Kentucky, Ninety-ninth Ohio, Eighty-eighth Indiana and Fifty-ninth Indiana. In the third line, Nineteenth Ohio, Ninth Kentucky and Eleventh Kentucky; three hundred yards in rear of this last regiment the Twenty-fourth Ohio; one hundred and fifty yards north-east of the left of Twenty-fourth Ohio the right of the Thirty-sixth Indiana, facing south-east; and about one hundred and fifty yards north of the Thirty-sixth Indiana the Sixth Ohio, with the Eighty-fourth Illinois on its right, the latter touching the river; the last five regiments constituting Colonel Grose's brigade.

Immediately after Grose's regiments got into position they made breastworks from rails, logs, and stones.

Wood's division, commanded by General Hascall, was the first to feel the enemy's fire. The rebels, having placed Robertson's battery west of the pike, Scott's between the pike and the railway, and Stanford's, Carnes's, and Turner's batteries between the railway and the river, commenced about 8 o'clock a rapid fire on Wood's line. Estep's battery, on the right, being much exposed, suffered so severely that it was compelled to withdraw to the rear; and two of his guns, on account of disabled horses, had to be drawn off the field by the infantry.

Captain Bradley, whose guns had a better position, handled them with marked precision, and was doing excellent work, when Stokes's battery, about two hundred and fifty yards in the rear, fired into them, wounding five men and several horses, and demoralizing the men to a considerable extent.

It is claimed by Captain Bradley that Captain Stokes fired canister; but, in all probability, the injuries were caused by the leaden bands around some of their shot.

After a duel, lasting about half an hour, the firing ceased.

The Union troops still remaining on General Bragg's front, he ordered Colonel Brent, his adjutant-general, and Captain Robertson, a very able artillery officer, to go in front of Breckenridge, and find the best position on the east side of Stone's River for enfilading the Union line with artillery.

After looking over the ground carefully the two officers came to the conclusion that the elevated ground held by Van Cleve's division was best suited for that purpose, and reported this fact to General Bragg.

It was, indeed, an important point, for it was an eminence from which Lieutenant-General Polk's line was both commanded and enfiladed, and compelled General Bragg either to change General Polk's position or drive out Van Cleve.

General Bragg thereupon ordered General Breckenridge to concentrate his command, and ordered Captain Robertson to report to the latter, with his own battery of six twelve-pound Napoleon guns, and four twelve-pound Napoleons from Semple's battery; while Wharton's and Pegram's cavalry, amounting to two thousand men, were likewise ordered to report to Breckenridge.

General Bragg thereupon ordered him to make the attack in the following manner:

"The infantry were to clear the hill, and as soon as this was accomplished two twelve-pound howitzers were to take position and rake down the slopes to the river; Robertson's battery was to occupy the highest ground, and Semple's Napoleons, under Lieutenant Fitzpatrick, were to occupy the ridge running to the right (east) from the hill-top."

The distance between Breckenridge's line and Van Cleve's was about sixteen hundred yards, Van Cleve's being nearly perpendicular to Hanson's line.

General Breckenridge formed his command in two lines, as follows, from left to right: first line, Hanson's and Pillow's brigades; second line, one hundred and fifty to two hundred yards in rear of first, Adams's and Preston's brigades followed by Moses's, Wright's, and Vaughan's, and still farther in the rear by Robertson's and Semple's batteries; the whole command, excluding cavalry, amounting to over six thousand officers and men.

General Breckenridge informed his commanding general that he would make the attack at 4 o'clock in the afternoon, and Lieutenant-General Polk was ordered to commence firing at that hour with three batteries from the Confederate centre, to distract the attention of the Federal forces from Breckenridge's attack.

But the movements of the rebel troops were observed, and the skirmishers in our front reported great activity early in the day.

General Rosecrans, ever watchful, was also frequently on the left, examining the position of the troops across the river; and, expecting an attack, ordered Negley's division, about 1 o'clock p.m., and, later, the Pioneer brigade, to the east side of the railway, near the fords across Stone's river.

Every movement of the enemy was eagerly watched by the skirmishers of Van Cleve's command.

At noon the rebel artillery fired a few rounds, and then ceased. About 2.30 p.m. it was reported to General Crittenden that more guns were being placed in the rebel front; and finally, at 3 o'clock, the report came that the enemy's skirmishers were throwing down the fences in their front.

This, of course, meant fight.

About 2 o'clock in the afternoon General Bragg sent for General Breckenridge to come to his headquarters for final orders, and the two officers met near a large sycamore tree close to the banks of the Stone's River, not far from where the Nashville pike crosses it.

General Breckenridge was opposed to the attack as ordered by General Bragg, and tried to persuade him that it would result in disaster, as the ground occupied by the Federal troops was so much higher than the ridge which he was ordered to take that they could mass their artillery and sweep the whole field. In urging his opinions he drew, with a stick, on the ground, the positions of the opposing commands. Considerable time was occupied in their discussion, but General Bragg remained firm, and ordered Breckenridge to proceed. The hour for the contemplated attack drawing near, the latter galloped quickly to the extreme right of his command, and sought to encourage his men by appealing to their pride and gallantry.

As General Breckenridge rode past General Preston, he beckoned the latter aside, and said:

General Preston, this attack is made against my judgment, and by the special orders of General Bragg. Of course we all must try to do our duty, and fight the best we can. If it should result in disaster, and I be among the slain, I want you to do justice to my memory, and tell the people that I believed this attack to be very unwise, and tried to prevent it.

With a few words, in which each expressed the wish that the other might survive, the two generals parted, and rode to their respective positions in the line of battle.

Promptly at 4 o'clock the artillery in Polk's front gave the signal for the attack. Scott's, Stanford's, and Carnes's batteries commenced their fire from Chalmers's position in the direction of the woods lining the river, for the purpose of driving out our skirmishers; while Breckenridge's division, with guns loaded and bayonets fixed, marched with steady step to the assault.

But the ground was so peculiar that, as they advanced, the lines of the two front brigades were crowded together at the centre, and when they reached the ground near where Price's brigade was posted in line, the rebel Sixth Kentucky and part of the Second Kentucky, on the extreme left of Hanson's brigade, were entirely crowded out by the river; these troops thereupon waded through it, and commenced to ascend its west bank.

As the massed column's of Breckenridge's division came nearer to Van Cleve's line, the Thirty-fifth and Seventy-ninth Indiana were ordered to lie down and remain concealed. Hanson's regiments, which had not been in action on December 31st, were anxious to show their courage, and the men pushed with great vigour towards the Fifty-first Ohio, Eighth Kentucky, and Drury's battery. Lieutenant Livingston, in command of the latter, gave them shell and canister as rapidly as his men could work their pieces; but when he saw that there was great danger that his guns, would be captured, he quickly withdrew them across the river.

As the guns moved to the rear, Hanson's men ran with loud cheers towards the Fifty-first Ohio and Eighth Kentucky, and sought to drive them back; but these two regiments stood their ground well for a short time, and their fire was so hot and so accurate that Colonel Gibson, in command of Adams's brigade, [2] deemed it best to ride forward and consult with General Hanson as to when the second line should move to his support. As he approached General Hanson he saw this general fall from his horse, mortally wounded, and part of his brigade give way. Instantly the command was given by him to Adams's brigade to advance, and with loud cheers they ran forward to the assistance of Hanson's line, except the Sixteenth Louisiana, which followed the Sixth Kentucky across the river.

General Pillow, in command of the brigade on Hanson's right, had also moved steadily forward. Suddenly a mass of blue-coated men arose on his front, as though they had risen from the ground, and the Thirty-fifth and Seventy-ninth Indiana poured into his men a fearful

2. General Adams was wounded December 31st.

fire. General Pillow ordered his men to drive the Federals out of the timber on his right; but these two regiments would not yield an inch. He thereupon ordered Lieutenant Anderson, in command of Moses's Georgia battery, to come forward and assist in driving them back. A decidedly bloody fight ensued. Both sides fought with the utmost valour; but two regiments were no match for a rebel brigade supported by artillery. Colonel Mullen, in command of the Thirty-fifth Indiana, says that he twice appealed to the Ninety-ninth Ohio to, come to his assistance, but in vain.

Preston's brigade had in the meantime also been ordered to advance, and, with tremendous shouts and yells, the whole division of Breckenridge rushed in a solid mass, without much order, close to these four regiments. They gave way, and fell back towards the second line, the Ninety-ninth Ohio and Twenty-first Kentucky; but neither of these regiments held their ground, and both fell back.

The firing along the front had lasted perhaps ten minutes when Colonel Samuel Beatty felt convinced that his line could not be held, and he sent Lieutenant Murdock, his *aide-de-camp*, to ask Major Manderson to come with the Nineteenth Ohio to the rescue. Although this order should have come through Colonel Grider, the brigade commander, Major Manderson, deeming the occasion one of extreme emergency, immediately ordered the Nineteenth to advance at the double quick. It was indeed a moment of great peril. The regiments of Price's brigade came pouring in the greatest confusion through the ranks, and a regiment less well drilled would have become panic-stricken at this sight. But the Ohio men acted like Germany's veterans, and steadily advanced on the enemy; then firing their muskets upon the nearest foe, they did not wait to reload, but with fearful oaths, justified by the terrible occasion, they rushed with unconquerable fury forward, and brought the butt-ends of their muskets with all the power they could muster on the heads of the opposing rebels, crushing their skulls or fracturing their shoulders.

The enemy was checked for some minutes, disorder being visible in many places, when a new force of rebels came pouring over the steep bank of Stone's River, and began their attack on the right and rear of this regiment. The right being thus forced back, Major Manderson was compelled, in order to prevent his line being broken into pieces, to order the left of his regiment to fall back likewise. While this movement was being executed, gallant Colonel Grider rode up, and, seeing the dangerous position, ordered Major Manderson to fall back to the foot of the hill. Twice did this excellent regiment form into line and resist the enemy before it was driven across Stone's River.

About the same time, when the Nineteenth Ohio advanced, orders were given by Colonel Grider to the Ninth and Eleventh Kentucky to move to the relief of the lines in front of them. Moving as quickly as possible through the thick undergrowth of wild briers, their lines became somewhat broken, and here also the panic-stricken men of the front line came rushing through the ranks of these regiments. Though the sight of such confusion is indeed demoralizing, these two regiments steadily advanced, holding them in check. But as soon as the Nineteenth Ohio fell back, the rebels also opened a flank fire on the Ninth Kentucky, and this excellent regiment was thereupon ordered by its commanding officer, Lieutenant-Colonel Cram, to fall back. Major Motley, of the Eleventh Kentucky, observing the Ninth move towards the rear, gave orders to his regiment to retreat likewise.

Breckenridge's division was almost wholly concentrated on these few regiments, and they were finally driven in confusion across the river, Price's brigade losing seventy-nine in killed and three hundred and sixty-five in wounded; while Grider's lost forty-nine in killed and two hundred and four in wounded men.

On the west side of the river the greatest activity had prevailed in the meantime.

Captain Mendenhall, Chief of Artillery of the left wing, as he was riding with General Crittenden on the Nashville pike, had observed the advance of Breckenridge. Immediately he galloped from battery to battery belonging to Crittenden's corps, and in an incredibly short time forty-three pieces of artillery, including Drury's, were massed on the elevated ground north-west of the position where Price was fighting; soon afterwards Captain Stokes's battery came also into line, with six guns, while General Negley sent nine more.

Imagine the eagerness of the cannoneers of these fifty-eight guns for the moment to arrive when Price's and Grider's brigades should be out of the way, and they could open on the enemy's massed columns.

To the left of these batteries was General Negley's division, lying flat on the ground, also awaiting the approach of the enemy with the greatest intensity.

What a yell burst forth from these six thousand rebel throats when Price and Grider gave way! What a scene of disordered retreat and pursuit followed! What a scene of confusion, of bloodshed, of war, was revealed to the eyes! Standing near one of the batteries one could see blue-coated men running with all their might, closely followed by a dense mob of butternut-clothed troops, who were cheering and yelling, and crazy almost with delight. A few shells shot over our men fell into their ranks; but they rushed wildly forward, caring nothing for the few that fell. A few moments later Price's and Grider's men had found shelter behind the Federal lines, and the rebels had reached the river, and stood face to face with our artillery.

What a carnival of death followed! What a deafening noise all around! Cheers here; yells there. Suddenly the ground shook as if rocked by a fearful earthquake, and the fifty-eight cannons emptied their double-shotted contents on this living human mass in front of them; but a few seconds intervened, and again and again the fifty-eight cannons spread death into Breckenridge's men; while Negley's regiments quickly rose up when the enemy readied the opposite bank of the river, and from the crest of the hill poured forth a terrific fire. Then the enemy halted. The yells, the cheers of the pursuing rebels grew fainter and fainter, and at last ceased. Look at them! See how many throw up their arms; see how they fall over; see the large gaps in this mass of men where the shells and canister plough through it; look at the quivering bodies, at the streams of life's blood flowing from a thousand wounds! It was a scene that made the heart sick, and touched a spring of sympathy in the souls of all, though the men that were suffering and dying were enemies, and would gladly welcome us to bloody graves.

Colonel Miller, in command of one brigade, then ordered his men forward to a rail fence nearer to the river, and fired at a range where every shot told. To the rebels' right and rear gallant Colonel Grose, aided by Colonel Fyffe, who had fallen back on the former when Price had given way, [3] also commenced a rattling fire on the enemy.

This fight could not last long. Every effort of Breckenridge's men to take these batteries or cross the river was in vain, though the Confederate officers after reaching the river bank, tried with great gallantry to form their men into line, preparatory to a charge on Negley's men.

Colonel John F. Miller, observing their action, quickly rode to Colonel Scott, of the 19th Illinois, not far from him, and said: "Colo-

---

3. It seems a pity that Colonel Fyffe did not seize the opportunity of changing front, and attacking the rebels on their flank. He had the rare chance of pouring upon them, as they moved in a solid mass, a most destructive enfilading fire.

nel, if we don't charge the rebels, they will charge us. Will you join me if I do?"

"Certainly," responded brave Colonel Scott; "I'll get my command ready."

It took but a short time, and Colonel Miller, without waiting for orders from General Negley, quickly ordered his men to cross the river. Seeing this advance, Colonel Stanley's brigade, the Nineteenth Illinois, with gallant Colonel Scott leading, likewise rushed down the river bank, the colours of the Nineteenth Illinois and Seventy-Eighth Pennsylvania being the first to cross.

When the Confederates saw this attack, consternation took the place of their enthusiasm of a few minutes ago, and this same great rebel mass, that came on yelling like madmen at their supposed victory, suddenly turned, and, terror-stricken, sought safety in flight. Once across, Negley's men ran with greatest speed up the opposite bank and after the fleeing rebels, followed by many men of Grider's brigade.

In so doing all these regiments got mixed, and the honour of taking three guns (two of Wright's battery and one of Semple's) is claimed by the Nineteenth Illinois, Seventy-eighth Pennsylvania, and other regiments; though this much is certain, that the Nineteenth Illinois brought one of the guns off the field and delivered it to Parsons's battery, where it was used in place of a piece of the same calibre that had been disabled. [4]

General Negley, in the meantime, did not cross the river; seeing troops a little farther north from his command, he galloped towards them and shouted, "Whose command is this?"

"Mine," says St. Clair Morton; "these are the Pioneers."

"For God's sake," called out Negley, "help my division and the left." Instantly the order was given, and the Pioneers came on a run towards the river. But the day had already been gained, and the rebels were in full retreat; still Captain Morton led his men on to help, if possible, in completing the victory.

As soon as the rebel line began to give way Colonels Grose and Fyffe likewise advanced on Breckenridge's division from the (rebel) right, aided by Colonel Hazen, whose brigade had been ordered to Grose's assistance as soon as General Palmer observed the overwhelm-

---

4. A part of Miller's brigade was detained by General Palmer, and used by him in connection with the Thirty-first and Thirty-second Indiana and Ninetieth Ohio, to drive the Second and Sixth rebel Kentucky and the Sixteenth Louisiana from the position held by them.

ing mass that Bragg was sending against Van Cleve's division.

The enthusiasm of the Union troops was unbounded. All the regiments became intermingled, and a great deal of irregular straggling, or running towards the front, was the result. Colonel Hazen sought to check this with the aid of Colonel Grider, of the Ninth Kentucky. Finally darkness overtook our men in the pursuit of the enemy, and the troops were halted; but still a battery, about four hundred yards distant, fired a few rounds upon our line, when the Forty-first Ohio and other regiments were ordered to fire one volley. It was done, and the battery withdrew.

When Breckenridge made his attack on Van Cleve's division, General Rosecrans, accompanied by Generals Thomas and McCook, was near the Nashville pike, it being the belief of the former, that the assault on the extreme left was merely a feint, and that the Confederates intended to develop their full strength either on our centre or right. When, however, it became apparent that the offensive movement of the Confederates was confined to the east side of Stone's river, and that Price's and Grider's brigades were driven back by overwhelming numbers, General Rosecrans quickly ordered General Davis who was on the extreme right, to go to the assistance of the left.

Woodruff, held in reserve, led the other brigades, and, as soon as they heard the order to march against the enemy they responded with loud cheers; but they also came too late to share in the glory. Davis's and Wood's divisions both crossed the river, and formed in line of battle near Van Cleve's earlier position; Hascall formed on Davis's left, while Colonels Hazen and Grose took positions farther to the left and rear.

Thus ended the battle on January 2nd; only an hour and twenty minutes elapsing from the time of the advance of the rebels till they reached their line again in a perfect rout, leaving one thousand three hundred and thirty-eight killed and wounded on the field.

Captain Robertson, the rebel officer before referred to, and Lieutenant-General Polk's acting Chief of Artillery, says, in his report, that their infantry was so demoralized that there was nothing in the way to prevent the Federals from marching into Murfreesboro' that night. He tried to prevent pursuit by firing with his artillery, but with this exception there was utter demoralization." [5]

---

5. I was recently informed by a near relative of General Breckenridge that Captain Robertson had afterwards admitted that this part of his report was not correct. It is said that this incorrect statement was made at General Bragg's suggestion.

As soon as the disastrous result to Breckenridge was seen, General Bragg ordered the splendid brigade of J. Patten Anderson across the river, which took position near where Hanson had been in the morning.

During the night, Davis's, Hascall's, Hazen's, and Grose's commands constructed breastworks to protect themselves.

General Davis's division having been sent across Stone's River, the extreme right became rather weak, and General Rosecrans deemed it, therefore, wise to give the enemy the impression that he was receiving large reinforcements. In order to deceive General Bragg, he organized a large number of men endowed with stentorian voices, who were to represent the commanding officers of companies, regiments, and brigades, composing a division.

As soon as these men were properly stationed a loud voice could be heard calling out: "Fourteenth Division, halt!" Immediately afterwards other voices could be heard commanding brigades and regiments to halt, followed by a number of company commands. A few minutes intervened and again these loud voices could be heard, in the stillness of the night, giving the necessary orders by which the imaginary regiments were to take their respective camping-grounds, and companies to stack arms and break ranks.

A short time after this had taken place General Rosecrans ordered men to build camp-fires in front of these supposititious new reinforcements.

Whether this ruse had the effect of preventing an attack is perhaps doubtful, though General Bragg states, in his report, that the Federal army had been largely reinforced.

On January 3rd rain began to fall again in torrents, and continued all night, and as Stone's river began to swell in volume, General Rosecrans deemed it best to withdraw the troops from the east side; and the boys cheerfully waded waist-deep through the water in the cold night of winter, though many lost either life or health in consequence of this severe exposure.

In the meantime several of the Confederate generals had come together for consultation. It was found that their troops had suffered enormously; that they had lost over nine thousand men in killed and wounded.

Generals Cheatham and Withers, as able commanders as any in that army, and whose troops had fought splendidly, addressed a letter, soon after midnight on January 2nd, to General Bragg, stating that only three divisions were at all reliable; that even some of these were more or less demoralized, and that they believed it to be their duty to say that the army should promptly be put in retreat.

Lieutenant-General Polk, to whom this letter was presented at 1.30 a.m. of January 3rd, made this endorsement:

Seeing the effect of the operations today (January 2nd), added to that produced on the troops by the battle of December 31st, I very greatly fear the consequences of another engagement at this place on the ensuing day. Should we fail in the meditated attack the consequences might be very disastrous.

At 2 o'clock that morning this letter was handed to General Bragg by Lieutenant-General Polk's *aide-de-ca*mp. On reading only one-half of it he replied, "Say to the General we shall maintain our position at every hazard."

Lieutenant-General Polk, however, considered the situation so grave that at 3 o'clock he sent the note signed by Generals Cheatham and Withers, with his own endorsement, to Lieutenant-General Hardee, to inform him of the opinion of himself and his two division commanders.

Owing to the incessant rains on January 3rd no general attack was made by either army; but General Polk, observing that during the previous evening the Federal troops had again taken possession of the "Round Forest" (it was the Forty-second Indiana, under Lieutenant-Colonel Shanklin, of John Beatty's brigade), he ordered a heavy artillery fire from several batteries to open upon it, and ordered Colonel White, of Chalmers's, and Colonel Coltart, of Loomis's, brigades, to take part of their commands and charge upon the Federals at this small forest.

The Forty-second Indiana was driven back, and their Lieutenant-Colonel and thirteen men were taken prisoners.

The "Round Forest" was, however, equally important as a position to the Federals, and General Rousseau asked and received permission from General Thomas to retake it.

Just before night Loomis's and Gunther's batteries were ordered to shell this position, firing as rapidly as possible six rounds from each gun; then the Third Ohio and Eighty-eighth Indiana, under command of Colonel John Beatty, and the First and Second East Tennessee regiments, from Speer's brigade, on their left, marched forward. They met with some resistance; but the enemy yielded, though the skirmish fire lasted till about 8 o'clock in the evening.

Still later the pickets of the Confederate line immediately in front of our centre were relieved by Colonel Carter's cavalry.

At 11 o'clock that night the rebel army commenced its retreat, and long before daybreak its infantry was miles away on the road towards Tullahoma and Shelbyville, while their cavalry withdrew slowly at daybreak, burning bridges as they moved south.

While this retrograde movement of General Bragg's army was going on, and each hour of this Saturday night was widening the distances between the contending forces, our men lay in the muddy and rain-drenched ground, ready at the earliest dawn to repel the enemy's attacks. Soon, however, a report came, incredible at first, that the enemy had evacuated Murfreesboro'.

Can it be true? was in everybody's mouth, but few believed it; others argued that some hired spy had probably brought the news, to draw us out of our position, that the battle might be continued a few miles south of Murfreesboro'.

A short time after the first news had reached our line our cavalry pickets reported no enemy in sight, and parties sent to the town confirmed the report that General Bragg had retreated.

What shouts arose on every side! The news seemed to travel with the speed of lightning, and regiment after regiment caught the cheering inspiration, and the men began to shout and hurrah with all the power of their lungs. Some hugged each other and danced, while others wept for joy.

All the sleepless nights, the wet beds in the mud, the fatigues and privations, the want of food and of water fit to drink, the absence of fire and of dry clothing, seemed to be forgotten in a moment; and the joy over the tidings that the battle was over, that the victory had been won, that the enemy was in foil retreat, burst forth throughout the day in frequent and renewed cheers and evidences of intense delight.

But the victory had been dearly bought. How many had fallen! How many friends and companions were missing from our ranks!

Where are the brave Generals Sill and Kirk? Where the impetuous and fearless Roberts? Where the gallant Colonels Schaefer, Stem, Harrington, Williams, Bead, and Foreman? And where are Lieutenant-Colonels Garesché, Houssum, Wooster, Samuel McKee, David McKee, Drake, Major Carpenter, Askew, and the hundred other officers in minor commands, who bravely led their men and helped to gain the battle? All gone! Gone from our sight to fill soldiers' graves!

Side by side with them lay over one thousand six hundred of our private soldiers, many of them unsurpassed by any officer in personal patriotism and acts of daring and courage during this battle. Some of them fill graves not even marked by a stone, to indicate the brave man's name, and thus keep his memory green, be it even for a few years only! How pitiful that this bravery is so little remembered, and so soon forgotten!

From seven thousand eight hundred wounds blood flowed on this historic ground, while three thousand seven hundred captured prisoners were dragged towards those pens of infamy at Andersonville and Libbey,—prisons which have caused more feelings of revenge and bitterness towards the South than the fearful losses which were sustained in legitimate warfare.

Our losses can be considered to have been as follows: total force engaged December 31st, 1862, 42,000 officers and men. Losses, 1,730 killed, 7,800 wounded, and 3,700 missing,—a total of 13,230, or about 31½ *per cent*. Starkweather's and Walker's brigades were in reality not in the battle at all, as they arrived too late on the field December 31st, and were not in action January 2nd.

On the Confederate side the losses were nearly as severe. They had in action 37,800 officers and men, and lost 1,270 in killed, 7,964 in wounded, and 1,070 in missing,—a total of 10,306, or about 28 *per cent*, of their effective force. In killed and wounded men their relative loss was even larger.

That the Confederates fought gallantly, and with a great deal of *esprit*, every one ought to concede cheerfully. They were well drilled and well led, and the beautiful and skilful movements which they executed while under our fire were a convincing proof to those who were opposed to them in this battle that they were brave foes, and worthy of our admiration as good soldiers.

The importance of gaining this victory cannot be overestimated. When it is remembered that after President Lincoln's proclamation, in September, 1862, in regard to the emancipation of slaves on January 1st, 1863, New York, Pennsylvania, Illinois, Indiana, and other States, had gone Democratic, electing Democratic Legislatures and a Democratic Congress, and that this party at that time was opposed to the continuation of war, and believed in making an early peace; when it is remembered that threats had been made that the States should order the recall of their troops, and that Congress should refuse to vote supplies.

It is well to pause and reflect for one moment what the result might have been if the Army of the Cumberland had been less gallant, and if, instead of gaining this hard-fought battle, it had been compelled to fall back in full retreat towards Nashville, and, owing to the enemy's superiority in cavalry, perhaps even as far as the Ohio River.

In thanking Almighty God for the success of our arms, General Rosecrans, in closing his official report of this battle, appropriately used the beautiful words of the Psalmist: "*Non nobis, Domine, non nobis, sed nomine tuo da gloria.*" "Not unto us, O Lord, not unto us, but unto thy name give the glory."

CHAPTER 8

STATEMENTS:

Taken from Federal and Confederate reports of the number of the forces engaged in the battles of December 31st, 1862, and January 2nd,

Union forces at the Battle of Stone's River, commanded by General W. S. Rosecrans.

	KILLED.		WOUNDED.		MISSING.		
	Officers.	Men.	Officers.	Men.	Officers.	Men.	TOTAL.
Gen. Rosecrans, staff and escort.........	1	3	2	3	..	..	9
RIGHT WING. Maj.-Gen. A. McD. McCook com'nd'g. **FIRST DIVISION.** Brig.-Gen. Jeff. C. Davis commanding. Staff and escort, 36th Ills. Cav., Co. B, Capt. T. B. Sherer; 2d Ky. Cav., Co. G, Capt. M. R. McCulloch..........	1	..	..	4	..	6	11

	KILLED.		WOUNDED.		MISSING.		
	Officers.	Men.	Officers.	Men.	Officers.	Men.	TOTAL.
First Brigade.							
Col. P. S. Post commanding.							
59th Ills., Capt. H. E. Paine	0	7	..	43	..	30	80
22d Ind., Col. M. Gooding	0	7	5	34	..	18	64
74th Ills., Col. J. Marsh..............	0	8	1	34	..	42	85
75th Ills., Lt.-Col. J. E. Bennett......	0	2	2	19	..	59	82
5th Wis. Batt'y, Capt. O. F. Pinney....	0	1	1	5	..	6	13
Total	0	25	9	135	..	155	324
Second Brigade.							
Col. W. P. Carlin commanding.							
21st Ills., Col. John W. S. Alexander..	2	55	7	180	..	59	303
38th Ills., Lt.-Col. D. H. Gilmer.......	2	32	5	104	..	34	177
15th Wis., Col. Hans C. Heg..........	2	13	5	65	1	33	119
101st Ohio, Col. L. Stem..............	1	19	5	121	..	66	212
2d Minn. Batt'y, Capt. W. A. Hotchkiss.	0	3	1	5	..	1	10
Total	7	122	23	475	1	193	821
Third Brigade.							
Col. W. E. Woodruff commanding.							
Staff	..	..	1	..	..	..	1

	KILLED.		WOUNDED.		MISSING.		
	Officers.	Men.	Officers.	Men.	Officers.	Men.	TOTAL.
25th Ills., Col. T. D. Williams	1	15	3	72	..	5	96
35th Ills., Lt.-Col. W. P. Chandler	..	10	2	49	..	25	86
81st Ind., Lt.-Col. John Timberlake ...	1	4	2	46	1	15	69
8th Wis., Capt. S. J. Carpenter........	1	..	..	4	..	1	6
Total	3	29	8	171	1	46	258
Total, First Division	11	176	40	785	2	400	1414
SECOND DIVISION.							
Brig.-Gen. R. W. Johnson commanding.							
3d Ind. Cav., Cos. G, H, I, and K, Maj. R. Klein, escort....................	0	4	..	6	..	15	25
First Brigade.							
Brig.-Gen. A. Willich commanding..	..	..	..	..	1	..	1
49th Ohio, Col. W. H. Gibson	2	18	6	88	..	108	222
15th Ohio, Col. Wm. Wallace	0	17	2	68	1	127	215
39th Ind., Lt.-Col. F. A. Jones........	0	30	3	116	2	229	380
32d Ind., Lt.-Col. F. Erdelmeyer	0	12	..	40	..	115	167
89th Ills., Lt.-Col. C. T. Hotchkiss.....	1	9	1	45	..	94	150
Batt'y "A," 1st Ohio, Capt. W. F. Goodspeed,[1] Lieut. E. B. Belding	0	1	..	4	..	24	29
Total	3	87	12	361	4	697	1164

[1] Capt. Goodspeed acted as Gen. Johnson's Chief of Artillery.

	KILLED.		WOUNDED.		MISSING.		TOTAL.
	Officers.	Men.	Officers.	Men.	Officers.	Men.	
Second Brigade.							
Brig.-Gen. E. N. Kirk commanding	..	..	1	..	..	..	1
77th Penn., Lt.-Col. P. B. Housum. In action, 19 officers, 288 men.......	1	4	1	28	2	28	64
29th Ind., Lt.-Col. D. M. Dunn. In action, 24 officers, 313 men...........	1	14	2	66	1	51	135
30th Ind., Col. J. B. Dodge. In action, 25 officers, 463 men	1	30	2	108	2	70	213
79th Ills., Col. Sheridan P. Read. In action, 21 officers, 416 men..........	1	23	3	68	3	121	219
34th Ills., Maj. Alex. P. Dysart. In action, 24 officers, 330 men..........	2	19	2	98	2	72	195
1st Ohio, Batt'y E, Capt. W. P. Edgarton.	0	3	..	5	2	22	32
Total	6	93	11	273	12	364	859
Third Brigade.							
Col. P. P. Baldwin commanding.							
6th Ind., Lt.-Col. H. Tripp	0	17	..	50	1	36	104
1st Ohio, Maj. J. A. Stafford	0	8	1	46	..	81	136
93d Ohio, Col. Charles Anderson	0	12	3	45	..	64	124
5th Kentucky, Lt.-Col. Wm. W. Berry. In action, 320 men	1	18	7	73	..	26	125
5th Ind. Battery, Capt. P. Simonson commanding	0	3	1	18	..	1	23
Total	1	58	12	232	1	208	512
Total, Second Division............	10	242	35	972	17	1284	2560

	KILLED.		WOUNDED.		MISSING.		TOTAL.
	Officers.	Men.	Officers.	Men.	Officers.	Men.	
THIRD DIVISION.							
Brig.-Gen. P. H. Sheridan com'nd'g.							
2d Ky. Cav., Co. I, Lt. Forman, escort.							
First Brigade.							
Brig.-Gen. J. W. Sill commanding.							
Staff and escort	1	..	1	..	..	..	2
36th Ills., Col. N. Greusel	1	45	7	144	2	13	212
88th Ills., Col. F. T. Sherman.........	1	13	2	48	..	48	112
24th Wis., Maj. E. C. Hibbard.........	0	19	2	55	..	98	174
21st Mich., Lt.-Col. W. B. McCreary ..	0	18	7	82	..	36	143
4th Ind. Battery, Capt. A. K. Bush	0	6	..	17		3	26
Total	3	101	19	346	2	198	669
Second Brigade.							
Col. F. Schaefer commanding.........	1	..	..	..	..	..	1
2d Mo., Lt.-Col. B. Laiboldt	0	7	..	40	1	14	62
15th Mo., Lt.-Col. John Weber	3	9	4	51	..	5	72
44th Ills., Capt. W. W. Barrett [1].......	1	28	5	104	..	17	155
73d Ills., Maj. W. A. Presson..........	1	15	3	61	1	7	88

[1] This differs from Gen. Sheridan's report, which makes the loss very much less; Gen. Sheridan permitted only those to be counted as wounded who were unfitted for duty.

	KILLED.		WOUNDED.		MISSING.		
	Officers.	Men.	Officers.	Men.	Officers.	Men.	TOTAL.
Battery "G," 1st Mo., Capt. H. Hescock,	1	5	..	13	..	1	20
Total	7	64	12	269	2	44	398
Third Brigade.							
Col. G. W. Roberts commanding	1	..	..	..	..	..	1
22d Ills., Lt.-Col. F. Swanvick	0	21	7	109	2	54	193
27th Ills., Col. F. A. Harrington	1	8	2	67	..	25	103
42d Ills., Lt.-Col. N. H. Walworth	1	18	..	96	1	45	161
51st Ills., Col. L. P. Bradley..........	1	6	4	37	..	9	57
Battery "C," 1st Ills., Capt. C. Hough-talling	0	5	2	19	..	25	51
Total	4	58	15	328	3	158	566
Total, Third Division.............	14	223	46	943	7	400	1,633
Total, Right Wing	35	641	121	2700	26	2084	5607
CENTRE.							
Maj.-Gen. George H. Thomas com'nd'g.							
Escort	0	1	..	..	..	..	1
9th Mich., Col. John G. Parkhurst .. ⎫ Head-quarters and Provost Guard.... ⎭	0	....	..	..	..	..	.....

	KILLED		WOUNDED		MISSING		TOTAL.
	Officers.	Men.	Officers.	Men.	Officers.	Men.	
FIRST DIVISION.							
Maj.-Gen. L. H. Rousseau com'nd'g.							
Staff and escort (2d Ky. Cav., 6 companies, Major T. P. Nicholas)	0	..	1	4	..	..	5
First Brigade.							
Col. B. F. Scribner commanding	..	..	1	..	1	..	2
38th Ind., Lt.-Col. D. F. Griffin........	1	13	3	91	..	4	112
94th Ohio, Col. J. W. Frizell..........	0	3	2	21	..	28	54
2d Ohio, Lt.-Col. John Kell............	2	9	3	31	..	7	52
33d Ohio, Capt. E. J. Ellis	0	2	..	21	..	11	34
10th Wis., Col. A. R. Chapin commanding. In action, 11 officers, 250 men..	0	3	1	15	..	6	25
Total	3	30	10	179	1	56	279
Second Brigade.							
Col. John Beatty commanding.							
15th Ky., Col. J. B. Foreman..........	2	8	1	31	1	17	60
3d Ohio, Lt.-Col. O. A. Lawson........	0	17	1	65	..	23	106
10th Ohio, Lt.-Col. J. W. Burke [1]......	0	..	..	..	..	..	..
42d Ind., Lt.-Col. J. M. Shanklin	0	17	6	75	2	32	132

[1] This regiment acted as head-quarters guard; was not in action.

	KILLED.		WOUNDED.		MISSING.		
	Officers.	Men.	Officers.	Men.	Officers.	Men.	TOTAL.
88th Ind., Col. George Humphrey......	0	8	4	47	..	19	78
1st Mich. Battery, Lt. G. W. Van Pelt,[1]	0	1	..	10	..	2	13
Total............................	2	51	12	228	3	93	389
Third Brigade.[2]							
Col. J. C. Starkweather commanding.							
79th Penn., Col. H. A. Hambright	0	1	..	9	..	6	16
1st Wis., Lt.-Col. G. B. Bingham	0	..	1	11	..	16	28
21st Wis., Lt.-Col. H. C. Hobart	0	1	1	4	..	37	43
24th Ills., Col. G. Mihalotzy	0	..	..	4	..	52	56
1st Ky. Light Artillery (2 sections), Capt. Stone......................	0	..	..	1	..	2	3
Total	0	2	2	29	..	113	146
Fourth Brigade.							
Lt.-Col. O. L. Shepherd commanding.							
Staff in action, 4 officers, 1 man.							
1st Bat. 15th U.S. Infantry, Maj. J. H. King. In action, 16 officers, 304 men..	1	10	4	74	..	17	106
1st Bat. 16th U.S. Infantry, Maj. A. J. Slemmer. In action, 15 officers, 293 men	0	16	7	126	..	16	165

[1] Capt. C. O. Loomis of this battery acted as Gen. Rousseau's Chief of Artillery.
[2] This brigade was not in battle, but sustained its losses in guarding wagon-trains against rebel cavalry near Lavergne.

	KILLED.		WOUNDED.		MISSING.		TOTAL.
	Officers.	Men.	Officers.	Men.	Officers.	Men.	
1st Bat. 18th U.S. Infantry, Maj. J. N. Caldwell. In action, 16 officers, 272 men	1	28	6	115	..	2	152
2d Bat. 18th U.S. Infantry, Maj. Fred. Townsend. In action, 16 officers, 298 men	1	30	5	98	..	5	139
1st Bat. 19th U.S. Infantry, Maj. S. D. Carpenter. In action, 10 officers, 198 men	1	6	..	57	..	10	74
Battery " H," 5th U.S. Artillery, Lt. F. L. Guenther. In action, 3 officers, 120 men	0	..	..	5	..	..	5
Total in action, 80 officers, 1,486 men	4	90	22	475	..	50	641
Total, First Division	9	173	47	915	4	312	1460
SECOND DIVISION.							
Brig.-Gen. J. S. Negley commanding.							
First Brigade.[1]							
Brig.-Gen. J. G. Spears commanding.							
1st East Tenn., Col. R. K. Byrd	0	3	..	16	..	..	19
2d East Tenn., Lt.-Col. J. A. Melton	0	..	1	6	..	..	7
85th Ills., Col. R. S. Moore	0	..	..	..	..	..	..

[1] The 85th Ills., 14th Mich., and two sections of the 10th Wis. Battery were ordered by Gen. Mitchell, at Nashville, to report temporarily to Gen. Spears.

	KILLED.		WOUNDED.		MISSING.		TOTAL.
	Officers.	Men.	Officers.	Men.	Officers.	Men.	
14th Mich., Major M. W. Quackenbush.	0	2	..	5	..	..	7
10th Wis. (2 sections), Capt. Y. V. Beebe commanding...................	0	..	..	..	..	..	..
Total	0	5	1	27	..	..	33

Second Brigade.

Col. T. R. Stanley commanding.

Staff, in action, 7 officers.

	KILLED.		WOUNDED.		MISSING.		TOTAL.
	Officers.	Men.	Officers.	Men.	Officers.	Men.	
18th Ohio, Lt.-Col. J. Given. In action, 23 officers, 423 men	1	25	8	107	..	26	167
69th Ohio, Col. W. B. Cassily, Maj. E. J. Hickox. In action, 23 officers, 523 men	1	4	6	47	..	38	96
19th Ills., Col. J. R. Scott. In action, 23 officers, 350 men	1	13	8	75	..	11	108
11th Mich., Col. W. L. Stoughton. In action, 17 officers, 423 men..........	2	28	6	78	..	25	139
Battery " M," 1st Ohio, Capt. F. Schultz. In action, 2 officers, 75 men.	0	1	1	..	..	1	3
Total in action, 95 officers, 1,794 men	5	71	29	307	..	101	513

Third Brigade.

Col. J. F. Miller commanding.

	KILLED.		WOUNDED.		MISSING.		TOTAL.
	Officers.	Men.	Officers.	Men.	Officers.	Men.	
Staff and escort......................	0	..	1	3	..	..	4
78th Penn., Col. W. Sirwell. In action, 15 officers, 540 men	1	15	3	130	..	39	188

	KILLED.		WOUNDED.		MISSING.		
	Officers.	Men.	Officers.	Men.	Officers.	Men.	TOTAL.
21st Ohio, Lt.-Col. J. M. Neibling. In action, 21 officers, 590 men..........	0	24	5	104	..	26	159
74th Ohio, Col. G. Moody. In action, 18 officers, 381 men	0	8	6	92	..	19	125
37th Ind., Col. J. S. Hull. In action, 17 officers, 437 men	2	25	5	110	..	8	150
1st Ky. Battery, Lt. A. A. Ellsworth. In action, 2 officers, 47 men.........	0	1	1	2	..	2	6
Battery " G," 1st Ohio, Lt. A. Marshall. In action, 3 officers, 110 men........	0	4	..	9	..	3	16
Total in action, 76 officers, 2,105 men	3	77	21	450	..	97	648
Total, Second Division	8	153	51	784	..	198	1194

THIRD DIVISION.

Brig.-Gen. S. S. Fry commanding (not present).

First Brigade.

Col. M. B. Walker commanding.

17th Ohio, Col. J. M. Connell	0	..	1	4	..	..	5
31st Ohio, Lt.-Col. F. W. Lister.......	0	..	..	6	..	..	6
38th Ohio, Col. E. H. Phelps	0	..	1	5	..	..	6

	KILLED.		WOUNDED.		MISSING.		TOTAL.
	Officers.	Men.	Officers.	Men.	Officers.	Men.	
82d Ind., Col. M. C. Hunter...........	0	..	..	5	..	..	5
4th Mich. Battery, Capt. J. W. Church..	0	..	..	..	..	..	..
Total	0	..	2	20	..	..	22
Total, Centre....................	17	327	101	1719	4	510	2678
LEFT WING.							
Maj.-Gen. T. L. Crittenden com'nd'g ..	..	..	1	..	..	..	1
FIRST DIVISION.							
Brig.-Gen. Th. J. Wood commanding ..	..	..	1	..	..	..	1
First Brigade.							
Brig.-Gen. Milo S. Hascall com'nd'g.							
26th Ohio, Capt. W. H. Squires. In action, 12 officers, 374 men..........	1	11	2	85	..	..	99
58th Ind., Col. George P. Buell. In action, 19 officers, 386 men..........	1	16	4	93	..	..	114
100th Ills., Col. F. A. Bartleson. In action, 27 officers, 394 men..........	1	6	6	33	..	..	46
3d Ky., Lt.-Col. Samuel McKee. In action, 13 officers, 300 men..........	2	12	8	77	..	34	133
8th Ind. Battery, Lt. George Estep.....	0	..	..	8	..	..	8
Total in action, 71 officers, 1,454 men	5	45	20	296	..	34	400

	KILLED.		WOUNDED.		MISSING.		
	Officers.	Men.	Officers.	Men.	Officers.	Men.	TOTAL.
Second Brigade.							
Col. G. D. Wagner commanding.							
15th Ind., Lt. Col. G. S. Wood········	2	36	7	136	..	7	188
57th Ind., Col. C. C. Hines. In action, 19 officers, 312 men ···············	0	11	6	55	..	6	78
40th Ind., Col. J. W. Blake···········	0	4	5	63	..	13	85
97th Ohio, Col. John Q. Lane ·········	0	3	..	15	..	6	24
10th Ind. Battery, Capt. J. B. Cox ·····	0	1	..	4	..	..	5
Total ···························	2	55	18	273	..	32	380
Third Brigade.							
Col. C. G. Harker commanding.							
51st Ind., Col. A. D. Streight ·········	0	7	2	32	..	9	50
13th Mich., Col. M. Shoemaker········	0	17	2	70	..	..	89
73d Ind., Col. G. Hathaway. In action, 22 officers, 309 men··········	2	22	3	48	..	36	111
64th Ohio, Lt.-Col. A. McIlvaine ······	1	23	3	61	..	17	105
65th Ohio, Lt.-Col. A. Cassil. In action, 382 men ····················	2	33	8	92	..	38	173
6th Ohio Battery, Capt. C. Bradley ····	0	1	1	8	..	1	11
Total ···························	5	103	19	311	..	101	539
Total, First Division·············	12	203	58	880	..	167	1320

	KILLED.		WOUNDED.		MISSING.		TOTAL.
	Officers.	Men.	Officers.	Men.	Officers.	Men.	
SECOND DIVISION.							
Brig.-Gen. J. M. Palmer commanding ..	..	..	1	..	..	..	1
First Brigade.							
Brig.-Gen. Charles Cruft commanding.							
1st Ky., Col. D. A. Enyart	0	13	1	51	1	30	96
2d Ky., Col. T. G. Sedgwick..........	0	9	2	56	..	10	77
31st Ind., Col. J. Osborne	0	5	1	44	3	34	87
90th Ohio, Col. I. N. Ross. In action, 300 men...........................	0	17	5	67	2	46	137
Battery "B," 1st Ohio, Capt. W. E. Standart...........................	0	5	..	12	..	3	20
Total	0	49	9	230	6	123	417
Second Brigade.							
Col. W. B. Hazen commanding.	..	..	4	1	..	..	5
41st Ohio, Lt.-Col. A. Wiley. In action, 19 officers, 394 men..........	1	13	2	102	..	6	124
6th Ky., Col. W. C. Whitaker.........	2	11	5	85	..	10	113
9th Ind., Col. W. H. Blake. In action, 27 officers, 345 men	1	10	5	82	..	11	109
110th Ills., Col. T. S. Casey	1	6	3	46	..	2	58
Battery "F," 1st Ohio, Capt. D. T. Cockerill	0	2	1	13	..	2	18
Total	5	42	20	329	..	31	427

	KILLED.		WOUNDED.		MISSING.		
	Officers.	Men.	Officers.	Men.	Officers.	Men.	TOTAL.
Third Brigade.							
Col. W. Grose commanding.							
36th Ind., Maj. Isaac Kinley. In action, 430 officers and men.........	2	23	6	85	..	18	134
6th Ohio, Col. N. L. Anderson	2	23	4	134	..	14	177
24th Ohio, Col. F. C. Jones. In action, 14 officers, 314 men..........	4	10	4	68	..	12	98
84th Ills., Col. L. H. Waters. In action, 24 officers, 336 men.....	2	33	5	119	..	8	167
23d Ky., Maj. T. H. Hamrick. In action, 282 men	0	8	3	50	..	22	83
Batteries " H " and " M," 4th U.S. Art'y, forming battalion; Lts. H. C. Cushing and H. A. Huntington commanding batteries; Lt. C. C. Parsons commanding battalion	0	2	..	14	..	6	22
Total	10	99	22	470	..	80	681
Total, Second Division	15	190	52	1029	6	234	1526
THIRD DIVISION.							
Brig.-Gen. H. P. Van Cleve com'nd'g.	..	..	1	..	..	..	1
First Brigade.							
Col. Samuel Beatty commanding.							
19th Ohio, Maj. C. F. Manderson......	3	24	3	122	..	34	186
9th Ky., Col. B. C. Grider	4	18	7	80	..	3	112

	KILLED.		WOUNDED.		MISSING.		
	Officers.	Men.	Officers.	Men.	Officers.	Men.	TOTAL.
11th Ky., Maj. E. L. Mottley..........	0	7	4	81	..	10	102
79th Ind., Col. Fred. Knefler. In action, 341 officers and men...........	1	10	6	68	..	36	121
26th Pa. Battery, Lt. A. J. Stevens	0	2	..	7	..	..	9
Total	8	61	20	358	..	83	530
Second Brigade.							
Col. J. P. Fyffe commanding...........	..	..	1	..	..	..	1
44th Ind., Col. W. C. Williams. In action, 316 men	0	10	2	54	..	25	91
86th Ind., Lt.-Col. George F. Dick. In action, 368 officers and men	1	33	5	55	2	99	195
13th Ohio, Col. J. G. Hawkins.........	2	29	6	79	..	69	185
59th Ohio, Lt.-Col. Wm. Howard. In action, 291 officers and men	0	3	2	35	2	43	85
7th Ind. Battery, Capt. G. R. Swallow..	0	4	1	7	..	..	12
Total	3	79	17	230	4	236	569
Third Brigade.							
Col. S. W. Price commanding.							
51st Ohio, Lt.-Col. R. W. McClain.....	0	24	4	118	..	44	190
99th Ohio, Col. Peter T. Swaine. In action, 369 officers and men	0	12	5	41	1	29	88

	KILLED.		WOUNDED.		MISSING.		TOTAL.
	Officers.	Men.	Officers.	Men.	Officers.	Men.	
35th Ind., Col. B. F. Mullen. In action, 272 men...........................	0	22	5	77	..	33	137
8th Ky., Lt.-Col. R. May and Maj. G. B. Broddus...........................	2	7	6	69	..	27	111
21st Ky., Lt.-Col. J. C. Evans.........	2	10	2	34	..	9	57
3d Wis. Battery,[1] Lt. C. Livingston. In action, 3 officers, 111 men........	0	..	..	4	..	..	4
Total	4	75	22	343	1	142	587
Total, Third Division	15	215	60	931	5	461	1687
Total, Left Wing	42	608	171	2840	11	862	4543
CAVALRY.[2]							
Brig. Gen. D. S. Stanley commanding.							
FIRST DIVISION.							
Col. Jno. Kennett commanding.							
First Brigade.							
Col. R. H. G. Minty commanding.							
3d Ky., Col. E. H. Murray............	0	1	1	7	0	1	10
4th Mich., Lt.-Col. W. H. Dickinsen...	0	1	1	6	0	12	20

[1] Capt. Drury acted as Gen. Van Cleve's Chief of Artillery.
[2] Losses from Dec. 26th, 1862, to Jan. 5th, 1863.

	KILLED.		WOUNDED.		MISSING.		TOTAL.
	Officers.	Men.	Officers.	Men.	Officers.	Men.	
7th Pa., Maj. Jno. E. Wynkoop	0	2	0	9	0	50	61
2d Ind., Co. M, Capt. J. A. S. Mitchell.	0	1	0	0	1	13	15
Total, 1st Brigade................	0	5	2	22	1	76	101
Second Brigade.							
Col. Lewis Zahm commanding.							
1st Ohio, Col. Minor Milliken	3	2	1	10	1	14	31
3d Ohio, Lt.-Col. D. A. Murray	0	6	0	15	0	13	34
4th Ohio, Maj. J. L. Pugh	0	7	0	18	0	31	56
Total, 2d Brigade	3	15	1	43	1	58	121
The Reserve.							
Gen. Stanley commanding in person.							
15th Pa. Anderson Troop, Maj. Frank B. Ward	1	0	1	5	0	0	7
1st Middle Tenn., Col. W. B. Stokes...	0	0	1	5	1	8	15
2d East Tenn., Col. Daniel M. Ray	1	2	0	10	0	5	18
Bat. " D," 1st Ohio Artillery, Lt. N. W. Newell	..	1	..	..	..	..	1
4th U.S. Cav., Capt. Elmer Otis. Body-guard to the General commanding the army.....................	0	3	1	9	0	12	25
Total, Reserve...................	2	6	3	29	1	25	66
Total, Cavalry...................	5	26	6	94	3	159	293

	KILLED.		WOUNDED.		MISSING.		TOTAL.
	Officers.	Men.	Officers.	Men.	Officers.	Men.	
Pioneer Brigade.							
Capt. Jas. St. Claire Morton com'nd'g. In action, 1,600 men.							
1st Battalion, Capt. Lyman Bridges....	..	2	3	6	..	..	11
2d Battalion, Capt. R. Clements.......	..	1	..	5	..	..	6
3d Battalion, Capt. Calvin Hood.......	..	4	..	8	..	1	13
Board of Trade Battery, Capt. James H. Stokes	..	3	1	5	..	..	9
1st Mich., Engineers and Mechanics,[1] Col. Wm. P. Innes commanding. Men in line, 391; not in battle	..	2	..	9	..	5	..

[1] Loss at Lavergne in defending wagon-train.

Confederate forces engaged in the Battle of Stone's River, commanded by General Braxton Bragg:—

	KILLED.		WOUNDED.		MISSING.		TOTAL.
	Officers.	Men.	Officers.	Men.	Officers.	Men.	
POLK'S (FIRST) CORPS.							
Lt.-Gen. L. Polk commanding.							
FIRST DIVISION.							
Maj.-Gen. B. F. Cheatham.							
First Brigade.							
Brig.-Gen. D. S. Donelson.[1]							
8th Tenn., Col. W. L. Moore. In action, 472 men	..	41	..	265	..	..	306
16th Tenn., Col. John H. Savage. In action, 402 men	..	36	..	155	..	16	207
38th Tenn., Col. John C. Carter	..	12	..	73	..	..	85
51st Tenn., Col. John Chester. In action, 290 men	..	11	..	72	..	3	86
84th Tenn., Col. S. S. Stanton. Not in action; guarded Carnes' Battery; not counted by Confederates	..	..	..	..	..	..	..
W. W. Carnes' Battery (Steuben Art.), Lt. J. G. Marshall	..	2	..	5	..	..	7
Total	..	102	..	570	..	19	691

[1] The returns of Donelson's, Stewart's, and Maney's Brigades give total of officers and men.

	KILLED.		WOUNDED.		MISSING.		
	Officers.	Men.	Officers.	Men.	Officers.	Men.	TOTAL.
Second Brigade.							
Brig.-Gen. A. P. Stewart.[1]							
4th and 5th Tenn. Vols. (cons.), Col. O. F. Strahl	..	8	..	68	..	..	76
19th Tenn., Col. F. M. Walker. In action, 382 men	..	16	..	111	..	..	127
24th Tenn., Col. H. L. W. Bratton	..	9	..	44	..	..	53
31st and 33d Tenn. (cons.), Col. E. E. Tansil	..	14	..	71	..	2	87
Stanford's Miss. Battery, Capt. T. J. Stanford..........................	..	3	..	7	..	..	10
Total	..	50	..	301	..	2	353
Third Brigade.							
Brig.-Gen. George Maney.[1]							
1st and 27th Tenn. (cons.), Col. H. R. Field	..	8	..	75	..	..	83
4th Tenn. (Conf.), Col. J. A. McMurry.	..	5	..	49	..	..	54
6th and 9th Tenn. (cons.), Col. C. S. Hurt................................	..	5	..	32	..	5	42
Frank Maney's Comp. Sharp-shooters..	..	1	..	4	..	..	5
M. Smith's Battery, Lt. W. B. Turner commanding	..	1	..	4	..	1	6
Total	..	20	..	164	..	6	190

[1] The returns of Donelson's, Stewart's, and Maney's brigades give total of officers and men.

	KILLED.		WOUNDED.		MISSING.		TOTAL.
	Officers.	Men.	Officers.	Men.	Officers.	Men.	
Fourth Brigade.							
Brig.-Gen. Preston Smith.							
Col. A. J. Vaughan, Jr., commanding.							
12th Tenn., Maj. J. N. Wyatt..........	1	17	12	125	..	9	164
13th Tenn., Capt. R. F. Lanier and Lt.-Col. W. E. Morgan..................	1	12	6	82	1	8	110
29th Tenn., Major J. B. Johnson. In action, 220 men	0	27	8	74	..	..	109
47th Tenn., Capt. W. M. Watkins	1	10	7	56	1	11	86
154th Tenn. (senior), Lt.-Col. M. Magenney, Jr. In action, 245 men	1	13	6	78	..	3	101
9th Texas, Col. W. H. Young	2	16	8	94	1	1	122
Sharp-shooters (P. T. Allen's), Lt. J. R. J. Creighton and Lt. T. T. Pattison ..	1	2	1	5	..	3	12
Scott's Battery, Capt. W. L. Scott, and Lieut. W. M. Polk	0	1	..	..	..	..	1
Total	7	98	48	514	3	35	705
Total, First Division..............	..	277	..	1597	..	651	1939
SECOND DIVISION.							
Major-General J. M. Withers.							
First Brigade.							
Brig.-Gen. Z. C. Deas (Cols. J. Q. Loomis and J. G. Coltart commanding).							

	KILLED.		WOUNDED.		MISSING.		TOTAL.
	Officers.	Men.	Officers.	Men.	Officers.	Men.	
1st La. Inf., Lt.-Col. F. H. Farran, Jr...	2	6	7	64	..	23	102
19th Alabama........................	1	7	13	130	..	3	154
22d Alabama	2	9	6	77	..	..	94
25th Alabama, Col. J. Q. Loomis	3	13	10	79	..	4	109
26th Alabama, Col. J. G. Coltart	0	4	6	70	..	..	80
39th Alabama........................	0	3	9	83	..	..	95
Battalion of sharp-shooters............	0	3	1	14	..	..	18
Robertson's Battery (temporarily assigned on Jan. 2d to Gen. Breckenbridge), Capt. F. H. Robertson......	0	..	..	19	..	1	20
Total	8	45	52	536	..	31	672
Second Brigade.							
Brig.-Gen. J. R. Chalmers and Col. T. W. White, staff....................	..	..	1	..	..	..	1
7th Mississippi	3	9	9	88	..	4	113
9th Mississippi, Col. T. W. White	0	8	5	66	..	5	84
10th Mississippi.....................	2	6	8	62	..	6	84
41st Mississippi	3	22	8	115	..	8	156
44th Mississippi	0	4	1	30	1	16	52
Blyth's Battalion of sharp-shooters, Capt. O. F. West..................	0	7	..	22		..	29

	KILLED.		WOUNDED.		MISSING.		
	Officers.	Men.	Officers.	Men.	Officers.	Men.	TOTAL.
Garrity's (late Ketchum's) Battery, Co. "A," Alabama State Artillery, Capt. James Garrity	0	3	2	18	..	..	23
Total	8	59	34	401	1	39	542
Third Brigade.							
Brig.-Gen. E. C. Walthall (Brig.-Gen. J. Patton Anderson commanding).							
45th Alabama, Col. James Gilchrist....	0	13	5	66	..	7	91
24th Miss., Lt.-Col. R. P. McKelvaine .	0	8	5	103	..	..	116
27th Miss., Lt.-Col. James L. Autry....	2	9	5	66	..	1	83
29th Miss., Col. W. F. Brantley and Lt.-Col. J. B. Morgan	4	30	14	188	..	..	236
30th Miss., Lt.-Col. J. J. Scales.......	6	57	10	136	..	..	209
39th North Carolina (temporarily attached on the field), Capt. A. W. Bell.	1	1	3	33	..	6	44
Barret's Mo. Batt'y, Capt. O. W. Barret.	0	..	..	4	..	..	4
Total	13	118	42	596	..	14	783
Fourth Brigade.							
Brig.-Gen. J. Patton Anderson (Col. A. M. Manigault commanding).							
24th Alabama........................	1	19	3	92	..	3	118

	KILLED.		WOUNDED.		MISSING.		
	Officers.	Men.	Officers.	Men.	Officers.	Men.	TOTAL.
28th Alabama........................	1	16	11	77	..	11	116
84th Alabama........................	0	11	6	71	..	..	88
10th S. Carolina.....................	0	16	6	85	..	2	109
19th S. Carolina, Col. A. J. Lythgoe ...	1	7	8	64		..	80
Waters's Battery, Capt. D. D. Waters..	0	1	..	5	..	..	6
Total	3	70	34	394	..	16	517
Total, Second Division...........	32	292	162	1927	1	100	2514

HARDEE'S (SECOND) CORPS.

Lieut.-Gen. W. J. Hardee commanding.

FIRST DIVISION.

Maj.-Gen. J. C. Breckenridge.

First Brigade.

Brig.-Gen. D. W. Adams (Col. R. L. Gibson com'nd'g Jan. 1 to 3, 1863).

82d La., Col. Alexander McKinstry and Lt.-Col. H. Maury..................	2	19	4	82	..	21	128
13th and 20th La. (cons.), Col. R. L. Gibson and Maj. Chas. Guillet	3	43	15	153	1	101	316

	KILLED.		WOUNDED.		MISSING.		
	Officers.	Men.	Officers.	Men.	Officers.	Men.	TOTAL.
16th and 25th La. (cons.), Col. S. W. Fisk and Maj. F. C. Zacharie. In action, 475 men	3	37	4	173	..	21	238
Battalion sharp-shooters, Maj. J. E. Austin	0	4	1	8	..	2	15
5th Company of Washington Artillery, of Louisiana, Lt. W. C. D. Vaught..	0	1	..	5	..	..	6
Total	8	104	24	421	1	145	703
Second Brigade.							
Col. J. B. Palmer (Brig. Gen. G. J. Pillow, com'nd'g part of, Jan. 2, 1863).							
18th Tenn., Col. J. B. Palmer. In action, 430 men	2	15	16	104	..	8	145
26th Tenn., Col. John M. Lillard	2	8	7	73	1	17	108
28th Tenn., Col. P. D. Cummings......	3	8	7	49	..	9	76
45th Tenn., Col. A. Leary	0	13	2	80	1	16	112
S. A. Moses' Georgia Battery, Lt. R. W. Anderson	0	..	..	4	..	..	4
Total	7	44	32	310	2	50	445
Third Brigade.							
Brig.-Gen. William Preston.[1]							
1st and 3d Fla. (cons.), Col. William Miller. In action, 531 men.........	..	7	..	88	..	43	138

[1] This return includes officers and enlisted men.

	KILLED.		WOUNDED.		MISSING.		
	Officers.	Men.	Officers.	Men.	Officers.	Men.	TOTAL.
4th Fla., Col. W. L. L. Bowen and Maj. John T. Lesley. In action, 468 men....................................	..	34	..	129	..	31	194
60th N. Carolina, Col. J. A. McDowell,	..	3	..	58	..	14	75
20th Tenn., Col. T. B. Smith..........	..	10	..	101	..	7	118
Wright's Tennessee Battery, Capt. E. E. Wright and Lt. John W. Mebane,	..	4	..	8	..	2	14
Total	..	58	..	384	..	97	539
Fourth Brigade.							
Brig.-Gen. R. W. Hanson (Col. R. P. Trabue com'nd'g on Jan. 2, 1863).							
41st Ala., Col. H. Talbird and Lt.-Col. M. L. Stansel.....................	2	14	4	90	..	38	148
2d Ky., Maj. James W. Hewitt	0	13	9	61	..	21	104
4th Ky., Col. R. P. Trabue............	6	6	6	43	..	8	69
6th Ky., Col. Joseph H. Lewis. In action, 269 men [1]....................	1	1	8	21	..	14	45
9th Ky., Col. Thomas H. Hunt.[2]							
Cobb's Battery, Capt. R. Cobb	0	3	..	3	..	..	6
Total	9	37	27	218	..	81	372
Total, First Division [3]............	..	267	..	1412	..	376	2055

[1] This differs from other returns.

[2] Its loss was 1 officer killed, and 5 officers and 23 men wounded. The regiment was left to guard Cobb's Battery, and is probably not counted as being engaged, though it held an advanced position.

[3] This return includes officers and enlisted men.

	KILLED.		WOUNDED.		MISSING.		TOTAL.
	Officers.	Men.	Officers.	Men.	Officers.	Men.	
SECOND DIVISION.							
Maj.-Gen. P. R. Cleburne, staff.........	..	..	..	2	..	..	2
First Brigade.[1]							
Brig.-Gen. L. E. Polk.							
1st Ark., Col. John W. Colquitt	..	11	..	90	..	1	102
13th Ark., Maj. C. H. Carlton ⎫ .... 15th Ark., Maj. R. A. Duncan ⎭	..	4	..	59	..	5	68
5th Confederate, Col. J. A. Smith......	..	7	..	64	..	12	83
2d Tenn., Col. W. D. Robinson.......	..	4	..	59	..	..	63
5th Tenn., Col. B. J. Hill.............	..	1	..	24	..	..	25
Helena Battery (J. H. Calvert's), Lt. T. J. Key	..	3	..	2	..	1	6
Total	..	30	..	298	..	19	347
Second Brigade.[1]							
Brig.-Gen. St. John R. Liddell, and staff,	..	..	..	3	..	..	3
2d Ark., Col. D. C. Govan	..	15	..	94	..	9	118
5th Ark., Lt.-Col. John B. Murray. In action, 336 men	..	12	..	135	..	1	148
6th and 7th Ark. (cons.), Col. S. G. Smith.............................	..	29	..	140	..	8	177

[1] This return includes officers and enlisted men.

	KILLED.		WOUNDED.		MISSING.		TOTAL.
	Officers.	Men.	Officers.	Men.	Officers.	Men.	
8th Ark., Col. John H. Kelly	..	29	..	124	..	..	153
Charles Swett's Battery (Warren Lt. Art., Miss.), Lt. H. Shannon.........	..	1	..	7	..	..	8
Total	..	86	..	503	..	18	607
Third Brigade.[1]							
Brig.-Gen. B. R. Johnson, and staff. In action, 6 officers....................	..	..	2	..	..	..	2
17th Tenn., Col. A. S. Marks. In action, 598 men	..	17	..	164	..	26	207
33d Tenn., Lt.-Col. R. H. Keeble. In action, 272 men....................	..	3	..	40	..	8	51
25th Tenn., Col. J. M. Hughs. In action, 336 men	..	16	..	89	..	15	120
37th Tenn., Col. M. White. In action, 225 men	..	11	..	51	..	6	68
44th Tenn., Col. John S. Fulton. In action, 509 men	..	14	..	136	..	2	152
Jefferson Artillery, Capt. Put. Darden. In action, 70 men	..	..	..	6	..	..	6
Total	..	61	..	488	..	57	606
Fourth Brigade.[1]							
Brig.-Gen. S. A. M. Wood, staff.......	..	..	1	..	..	..	1
16th Ala., Col. W. B. Wood	..	24	..	142	..	..	166
23d Ala., Col. Samuel Adams..........	..	14	..	86	..	1	101

[1] This return includes officers and enlisted men.

	KILLED.		WOUNDED.		MISSING.		
	Officers.	Men.	Officers.	Men.	Officers.	Men.	TOTAL.
3d Confederate, Maj. J. F. Cameron ···	··	5	··	27	··	37	69
45th Miss., Lt.-Col. R. Charlton. In action, 217 men ···················	··	5	··	39	··	70	114
2 companies sharp-shooters, Capt. A. T. Hawkins ····················	··	3	··	25	··	5	33
Semple's Bat. (detached to Hanson's brigade, Breckinridge's division, up to January 1, 1863, when it returned), Henry C. Semple···················	··	1	··	19	··	···	20
Total ··················	··	52	··	339	··	113	504
Total, Second Division[1]···········	··	229	··	1630	··	207	2066

SMITH'S (THIRD) CORPS.

Lt.-Gen. E. K. Smith commanding (not present).

Jackson's Brigade.

	KILLED.		WOUNDED.		MISSING.		
5th Georgia, Col. W. T. Black. In action, 173 men ···················	2	10	··	48	··	··	60
2d Ga. Battalion (sharp-shooters), Maj. J. J. Cox. In action, 152 men········	0	3	3	26	··	··	32
5th Miss., Lt.-Col. W. L. Sykes. In action, 170 men ·················	1	5	3	66	··	··	80
8th Miss., Col. John C. Wilkinson. In action, 282 men···················	1	19	12	101	··	··	133

[1] This return includes officers and enlisted men.

	KILLED.		WOUNDED.		MISSING.		TOTAL.
	Officers.	Men.	Officers.	Men.	Officers.	Men.	
E. E. Pritchard's Battery, at Murfrees-boro'..........................	..	..	..	..	..	..	..
C. L. Lumden's Battery (2 pieces). In action, 97 men. Lt. H. H. Cribbs...	..	..	..	..	..	..	..
Total	4	37	23	241	..	..	305
SECOND DIVISION.							
Maj.-Gen. J. P. McCown, and escort...	0	2	..	2	..	1	5
First Brigade.							
(Dismounted Cavalry.)							
Brig.-Gen. M. D. Ector, staff..........	0	..	2	2	..	..	4
10th Tex. Cav., Col. M. F. Locke. In action, 350 men	0	10	12	82	1	13	118
11th Tex. Cav., Col. J. C. Burks	0	7	8	79	3	17	114
14th Tex. Cav., Col. J. L. Camp	2	3	11	42	1	9	68
15th Tex. Cav., Col. J. A. Andrews. In action, 313 men	0	5	7	29	..	3	44
Douglas Battery, Capt. J. P. Douglas..	0	..	..	2	..	..	2
Total	2	25	40	236	5	42	350
Second Brigade.							
Brig.-Gen. James E. Rains (Col. R. B. Vance commanding after fall of Gen. Rains).							
3d Ga., Lt.-Col. M. A. Stovall. In action, 300 men....................	0	6	5	28	..	..	39

	KILLED.		WOUNDED.		MISSING.		TOTAL.
	Officers.	Men.	Officers.	Men.	Officers.	Men.	
9th Ga., Maj. Jos. T. Smith	0	1	2	9	..	..	12
29th North Carolina, Col. R. B. Vance. In action, 300 men................	0	5	3	47	..	5	60
11th Tenn., Col. G. W. Gordan and Lt.-Col. William Thedford..............	0	8	10	54	..	11	83
Eufaula Light Art., Lieut. W. A. McDuffie..........................	0	..	..	3	..	2	5
Total	0	20	20	141	..	18	199

Third Brigade.

Brig.-Gen. E. McNair and Col. R. W. Harper commanding.

	KILLED.		WOUNDED.		MISSING.		TOTAL.
1st Arkansas Mounted Rifles (dismounted), Col. R. W. Harper........	0	9	13	69	..	4	95
2d Ark. Mounted Rifles, Lt.-Col. J. A. Williamson	1	9	17	82	4	7	120
4th Ark., Col. H. G. Bunn	0	8	9	52	1	9	79
30th Ark., Capt. W. A. Cotter.........	4	6	11	52	..	22	95
4th Arkansas Battalion, Maj. J. A. Ross,	1	4	..	19	..	5	29
Humphreys' Battery, Capt. J. T. Humphreys	0	..	1	5	..	..	6
Total	6	36	51	279	5	47	424
Total, Second Division............	8	83	111	658	10	108	978

	KILLED.		WOUNDED.		MISSING.		TOTAL.
	Officers.	Men.	Officers.	Men.	Officers.	Men.	
CAVALRY.							
Brig.-Gen. Joseph Wheeler.							
Wheeler's Brigade (attached to Hardee), Brig.-Gen. Joseph Wheeler.							
1st Ala., Col. W. W. Allen (wounded)	..	..	..	..	..	..	..
3d Ala., Capt. T. H. Mauldin..........	..	..	..	..	..	..	..
51st Ala., Lt.-Col. Jas. D. Webb	..	..	..	..	..	..	..
8th Confederate......................	..	..	..	..	..	..	..
1st Tenn., James E. Carter's (attached)	..	..	..	..	..	..	..
Douglass's (Tennessee) Battalion......	..	..	..	..	..	..	..
Holman's (Tennessee) Battalion	..	..	..	..	..	..	..
Wiggins's (Arkansas) Battery..........	..	..	..	..	..	..	..
Wharton's Brigade.							
Brig.-Gen. J. A. Wharton.							
14th Ala. Batt., Lt.-Col. Jas. Malone...	..	..	..	..	..	..	..
1st Confederate, Col. John T. Cox	..	..	..	..	..	..	..
3d Confed., Lt.-Col. William N. Estes...	..	..	..	..	..	..	..
2d Ga., Lt.-Col. J. E. Dunlop	..	..	..	..	..	..	..
3d Ga. (detachment), Maj. R. Thompson	..	..	..	..	..	..	..
2d Tenn., Col. H. M. Ashby	..	..	..	..	..	..	..
4th Tenn., Col. Baxter Smith..........	..	..	..	..	..	..	..

	KILLED.		WOUNDED.		MISSING.		TOTAL.
	Officers.	Men.	Officers.	Men.	Officers.	Men.	
8th Texas, Col. Thomas Harrison · · · · · ·	· ·	· ·	· ·	· ·	· ·	· ·	· ·
Davis's (Tenn.) Batt., Maj. John R. Davis	· ·	· ·	· ·	· ·	· ·	· ·	· ·
Murray's reg., Maj. W. S. Bledsoe · · · · ·	· ·	· ·	· ·	· ·	· ·	· ·	· ·
White's (Ga.) Battery, Capt. B. F. White ·	· ·	· ·	· ·	· ·	· ·	· ·	· ·
Buford's Brigade.							
Brig.-Gen. A. Buford.							
3d Ky., Col. J. R. Butler	· ·	· ·	· ·	· ·	· ·	· ·	· ·
5th Ky., Col. D. H. Smith · · · · · · · · · · · ·	· ·	· ·	· ·	· ·	· ·	· ·	· ·
6th Ky., Col. J. Warren Grigsby · · · · · · ·	· ·	· ·	· ·	· ·	· ·	· ·	· ·
Pegram's Brigade.							
Brig.-Gen. John Pegram.							
1st Georgia	· ·	· ·	· ·	· ·	· ·	· ·	· ·
1st Louisiana	· ·	· ·	· ·	· ·	· ·	· ·	· ·
Artillery.							
Baxter's (Tennessee) Battery · · · · · · · · ·	· ·	· ·	· ·	· ·	· ·	· ·	· ·
Burtwell's (Alabama) Battery · · · · · · · · ·	· ·	· ·	· ·	· ·	· ·	· ·	· ·
Byrne's (Kentucky) Battery · · · · · · · · · ·	· ·	· ·	· ·	· ·	· ·	· ·	· ·
Gibson's (Georgia) Battery · · · · · · · · · · ·	· ·	· ·	· ·	· ·	· ·	· ·	· ·

Effective force of the Army of the Cumberland, Gen. W. S. Rosecrans commanding, at the battle of Stone's River, December 31st, 1862, to January 3d, 1863, and its losses from December 26th, 1862, to January 5th, 1863:—

	Force engaged.	KILLED.		WOUNDED.		MISSING.		TOTAL.
		Officers.	Men.	Officers.	Men.	Officers.	Men.	
Gen. Rosecrans, staff and escort.	..	1	3	2	3	..	..	9
RIGHT WING.								
Gen. A. McD. McCook.								
FIRST DIVISION.								
Gen. J. C. Davis.								
Staff and escort	..	1	..	..	4	..	6	11
1st Brigade, Col. Post	1418	..	25	9	135	..	155	324
2d " Col. Carlin	1781	7	122	23	475	1	193	821
3d " Col. Woodruff	1200	3	29	8	171	1	46	258
Total	4399	11	176	40	785	2	400	1414
SECOND DIVISION.								
Gen. R. W. Johnson.								
Staff and escort	..	..	4	..	6	..	15	25
1st Brigade, Gen. Willich	2571	3	87	12	361	4	697	1164

	Force engaged.	KILLED.		WOUNDED.		MISSING.		TOTAL.
		Officers.	Men.	Officers.	Men.	Officers.	Men.	
2d Brigade, Gen. Kirk	2030	6	93	11	373	12	364	859
3d " Col. Baldwin	1470	1	58	12	232	1	208	512
Total	6071	10	242	35	972	17	1284	2560
THIRD DIVISION.								
Gen. Sheridan.								
1st Brigade, Gen. Sill	1665	3	101	19	346	2	198	669
2d " Col. Schaefer......	1496	7	64	12	269	2	44	398
3d " Col. Roberts	1542	4	58	15	328	3	158	566
Total	4703	14	223	46	943	7	400	1633
Grand total	15173	35	641	121	2700	26	2084	5607
CENTRE.								
Gen. G. H. Thomas.								
Escort	..	..	1	..	..	..	..	1
FIRST DIVISION.								
Gen. Rousseau.[1]								
Staff and escort	..	..	..	1	4	..	..	5
1st Brigade, Col. Scribner	1588	3	20	10	179	1	56	279
2d " Col. J. Beatty	1534	2	51	12	228	3	93	389

[1] See Remarks.

	Force engaged.	KILLED.		WOUNDED.		MISSING.		TOTAL.
		Officers.	Men.	Officers.	Men.	Officers.	Men.	
4th Brigade, Col. Sheppard	1566	4	90	22	475	..	50	641
	4688							
8d Brig., Col. Starkweather. .. (Not in action Dec. 31, '62.)	1548	..	2	2	29	..	113	146
Total	6236	9	173	47	915	4	312	1460
SECOND DIVISION.								
Gen. Negley.								
2d Brigade, Col. Stanley	1889	5	71	29	307	..	101	513
8d " Col. Miller	2181	3	77	21	450	..	97	648
	4070							
1st Brigade, Gen. Spear's ...... (Not in action Dec. 31, '62.)	800	..	5	1	27	..	..	33
Total	4870	8	153	51	784		198	1194
THIRD DIVISION.								
Gen. Fry.								
1st Brigade, Col. Walker ...... (Not in action Dec. 31, '62.)	1875	..	..	2	20		..	22
Grand total	12981	17	327	101	1719	4	510	2678
Total in action Dec. 31, '62 ..	8758							

	Force engaged.	KILLED.		WOUNDED.		MISSING.		TOTAL.
		Officers.	Men.	Officers.	Men.	Officers.	Men.	
LEFT WING.								
Gen. Crittenden.[1]								
Staff and escort	..	..	..	1	..	..	..	1
FIRST DIVISION.								
Gen. Wood..........	..	..	..	1	..	..	..	1
1st Brigade, Gen. Hascall	1525	5	45	20	296	..	34	400
2d " Col. Wagner	1487	2	55	16	273	..	32	380
3d " Col. Harker	1887	5	103	19	311	..	101	539
Total	4887	12	203	58	880		167	1320
SECOND DIVISION.								
Gen. Palmer	..	..	..	1	..	..	..	1
1st Brigade, Gen. Cruft	1207	..	49	9	230	6	123	417
2d " Col. Hazen	1391	5	42	20	329	..	31	427
3d " Col. Grose	1788	10	99	22	470	..	80	681
Total	4386	15	190	52	1029	6	234	1526
THIRD DIVISION.								
Gen. Van Cleve	..	..	..	1	..	..	..	1
1st Brigade, Col. S. Beatty	1395	8	63	21	358	..	88	538

[1] See Remarks.

	Force engaged.	KILLED.		WOUNDED.		MISSING.		TOTAL.
		Officers.	Men.	Officers.	Men.	Officers.	Men.	
2d Brigade, Col. Fyffe	1380	3	77	16	230	4	236	566
3d " Col. Price	1750	4	75	22	343	1	142	587
Total	4535	15	215	60	931	5	461	1687
Grand total	13808	42	608	171	2840	11	862	4534
Cavalry Corps, Gen. Stanley ...	3000	5	26	6	94	3	159	293
Pioneer Brigade, } Capt. St. Clair Stokes's Battery, } Morton.	1600	..	10	4	24	..	1	39
Engineers not in battle	391	..	2	..	9	..	5	16
Grand total in Army	46953	100	1617	405	7389	44	3621	13176
Total of Army present on field of battle, Dec. 31, '62...	42339							

1863, and the respective losses of each army.

Remarks.—At the time when these reports were made, there were no columns giving number of men "Present for duty equipped," nor the actual number taken into battle; it is, therefore, an almost impossible task to give the actual number of men taken into action, except in a few cases. From a consolidated return in the War Record Office, it appears that the above-mentioned number, stated as having been taken into action by the right wing, is entirely too large. It is probable that in some returns the number given as present on December 20th, 1862, were taken at a date previous to the time when the army commenced the march from near Nashville, and that the number included all those that report themselves sick on the eve of every battle and who were left in the rear.

The following is the return of the right wing on December 31st, 1862, above referred to:—

	Officers	Enlisted Men	Total
Gen. McCook and staff	4	—	4
1st Division, Gen. Davis	201	3,563	3,764
2nd " Gen. Johnson	275	4,584	4,859
3rd " Gen. Sheridan	204	3,950	4,154
Cavalry	9	276	285
Artillery	23	690	713
Total	716	13,063	13,779

It must be remembered that a large detail from each brigade was sent to guard the wagon and ammunition train on its circuitous route to Nolensville, Triune, and thence to Murfreesboro'; a force not required by the other wing and centre, their trains going the direct route, under guard of Starkweather's brigade, the Michigan Engineers, the 9th Michigan Regiment, aided by a part of the Cavalry command and Colonel Walker's brigade.

In Rousseau's division it seems that the artillery, except in the regular brigade, has not been counted. In Fyffe's brigade, of Van Cleve's division, there is an error of some kind. In the tri-monthly report, December 20th, 1862, this brigade has 50 men less than Colonel Samuel Beatty's brigade. In the official report of General Rosecrans the number of Colonel S. Beatty's brigade is given as 1,216, and Colonel Fyffe's at only 798, while the official reports of the officers commanding regiments is as follows: Forty-fourth Indiana, 316 men; Eighty-sixth Indiana, 368, rank and file; Fifty-ninth Ohio, 291 officers and men.

The Thirteenth Ohio reports no number, but its losses in killed, wounded, and missing are 185. It must have had, at least, 350, which would make the number of the brigade 1,325. Add to this the battery of artillery, averaging about 95 men, and the true number of officers and men were probably 1,420. In my estimate I have given the number at 1,380.

In the left wing, commanded by General Crittenden, the reports of brigade commanders *do not include* the effective *force* of their *artillery*, which seems to have acted especially under the orders of the Chief of Artillery. In the monthly report of December 31st, 1862, the artillery for the left wing is given as follows:—

	Officers	Men	Total
Wood's Division	12	279	291
Palmer's Division	9	438	447
Van Cleve's Division	8	301	309
Total in Left Wing	29	1,018	1,047

If I am correct, that the artillery is not counted in the left wing, the force engaged was as follows:—

Infantry	13,808
Artillery	1,047
Total effective force in the left Wing	14,885

In the Confederate reports the number of muskets taken into battle are counted only. If the Union forces are calculated on the same basis, I believe that the number in battle Dec. 31st, 1862, were as follows, leaving out, of course, all wagon and headquarters guards:—

Right Wing	13,779,	including officers.
Left Wing	14,500	" "
Centre, less provost guards	8,500	" "
Cavalry	2,300	" "
Total force engaged, Dec. 31st, 1862	39,709	

*Effective force of the Army of the Tennessee, com-
manded by Gen. Braxton Bragg, in the Battle of
Stone's River, near Murfreesboro', Tenn., Dec. 31st,
1862, to Jan. 3d, 1863:* —

| | IN ACTION. | | | | |
	Officers.	Men.	Killed.	Wounded.	Missing.
LT.-GEN. L. POLK'S (FIRST) CORPS.					
FIRST DIVISION.					
Maj.-Gen. Cheatham.					
1st Brigade, Gen. Donelson	..	1400	102	570	19
2d " Gen. Stewart............	..	..	50	301	2
3d " Gen. Maney.............	..	..	20	164	6
4th " Gen. Preston Smith	..	1813	105	562	38
Total	496	5863	277	1597	65
SECOND DIVISION.					
Maj.-Gen. Withers.					
1st Brigade, Gen. Deas and Col. Loomis.	..	..	53	588	31
2d " Gen. Chalmers	..	..	67	435	40
3d " Gen. J. P. Anderson......	..	..	131	638	14
4th " Col. Manigault	..	..	73	428	16
Total	537	7237	324	2089	101
Grand total, officers and men	..	14133	601	3686	166

	In Action.				
	Officers.	Men.	Killed.	Wounded.	Missing.
LT.-GEN. J. W. HARDEE'S (SECOND) CORPS.					
FIRST DIVISION.					
Maj.-Gen. Breckenridge.					
1st Brigade, Gen. Adams.............	100	1584	112	445	146
2d " Gens. Palmer and Pillow..	129	1446	51	332	52
3d " Gen. Preston.............	143	1808	58	384	97
4th " Gen. Hanson	141	1752	46	245	81
Total	513	6540	267	1412	376
SECOND DIVISION.					
Gen. Cleburne.					
1st Brigade, Gen. Polk.............	..	1343	30	298	19
2d " Gen. Liddell..............	..	1709	86	503	18
3d " Gen. Johnson	..	2016	61	488	57
4th " Gen. Wood	..	1100	52	339	113
Total	840	6168	229	1630	207
Grand total, officers and men		14061	496	3042	583
LT.-GEN. SMITH'S CORPS.					
SECOND DIVISION.					
Gen. McCown, escort	..	..	2	2	1
1st Brigade, Gen. Ector..............	..	..	27	276	47

	In Action.		Killed.	Wounded.	Missing.
	Officers.	Men.			
2d Brigade, Gen. Rains..............	..	..	20	161	18
3d " Gen. McNair	..	..	42	330	52
Total.........................	319	4095	91	769	118
Jackson Brigade (attached to Breckenridge)..........................	89	785	41	264	
Grand total.....................	408	4880	132	1035	118
Cavalry.					
Wheeler's Command	124	1045	22	61	84
Wharton's "	158	1792	20	131	113
Pegram's "	30	450		No ret'n	
Buford's "	52	586	1	11	6
Total	364	3873	43	203	203
Grand total of Army.............		37719	1272	7964	1070
Total loss		10306			

LEONAUR

ALSO FROM LEONAUR
AVAILABLE IN SOFTCOVER OR HARDCOVER WITH DUST JACKET

THE RELUCTANT REBEL *by William G. Stevenson*—A young Kentuckian's experiences in the Confederate Infantry & Cavalry during the American Civil War..

BOOTS AND SADDLES *by Elizabeth B. Custer*—The experiences of General Custer's Wife on the Western Plains.

FANNIE BEERS' CIVIL WAR *by Fannie A. Beers*—A Confederate Lady's Experiences of Nursing During the Campaigns & Battles of the American Civil War.

LADY SALE'S AFGHANISTAN *by Florentia Sale*—An Indomitable Victorian Lady's Account of the Retreat from Kabul During the First Afghan War.

THE TWO WARS OF MRS DUBERLY *by Frances Isabella Duberly*—An Intrepid Victorian Lady's Experience of the Crimea and Indian Mutiny.

THE REBELLIOUS DUCHESS *by Paul F. S. Dermoncourt*—The Adventures of the Duchess of Berri and Her Attempt to Overthrow French Monarchy.

LADIES OF WATERLOO *by Charlotte A. Eaton, Magdalene de Lancey & Juana Smith*—The Experiences of Three Women During the Campaign of 1815: Waterloo Days by Charlotte A. Eaton, A Week at Waterloo by Magdalene de Lancey & Juana's Story by Juana Smith.

TWO YEARS BEFORE THE MAST *by Richard Henry Dana. Jr.*—The account of one young man's experiences serving on board a sailing brig—the Penelope—bound for California, between the years 1834-36.

A SAILOR OF KING GEORGE *by Frederick Hoffman*—From Midshipman to Captain—Recollections of War at Sea in the Napoleonic Age 1793-1815.

LORDS OF THE SEA *by A. T. Mahan*—Great Captains of the Royal Navy During the Age of Sail.

COGGESHALL'S VOYAGES: VOLUME 1 *by George Coggeshall*—The Recollections of an American Schooner Captain.

COGGESHALL'S VOYAGES: VOLUME 2 *by George Coggeshall*—The Recollections of an American Schooner Captain.

TWILIGHT OF EMPIRE *by Sir Thomas Ussher & Sir George Cockburn*—Two accounts of Napoleon's Journeys in Exile to Elba and St. Helena: Narrative of Events by Sir Thomas Ussher & Napoleon's Last Voyage: Extract of a diary by Sir George Cockburn.

LEONAUR

ALSO FROM LEONAUR

AVAILABLE IN SOFTCOVER OR HARDCOVER WITH DUST JACKET

ESCAPE FROM THE FRENCH *by Edward Boys*—A Young Royal Navy Midshipman's Adventures During the Napoleonic War.

THE VOYAGE OF H.M.S. PANDORA *by Edward Edwards R. N. & George Hamilton, edited by Basil Thomson*—In Pursuit of the Mutineers of the Bounty in the South Seas—1790-1791.

MEDUSA *by J. B. Henry Savigny and Alexander Correard and Charlotte-Adélaïde Dard* —Narrative of a Voyage to Senegal in 1816 & The Sufferings of the Picard Family After the Shipwreck of the Medusa.

THE SEA WAR OF 1812 VOLUME 1 *by A. T. Mahan*—A History of the Maritime Conflict.

THE SEA WAR OF 1812 VOLUME 2 *by A. T. Mahan*—A History of the Maritime Conflict.

WETHERELL OF H. M. S. HUSSAR *by John Wetherell*—The Recollections of an Ordinary Seaman of the Royal Navy During the Napoleonic Wars.

THE NAVAL BRIGADE IN NATAL *by C. R. N. Burne*—With the Guns of H. M. S. Terrible & H. M. S. Tartar during the Boer War 1899-1900.

THE VOYAGE OF H. M. S. BOUNTY *by William Bligh*—The True Story of an 18th Century Voyage of Exploration and Mutiny.

SHIPWRECK! *by William Gilly*—The Royal Navy's Disasters at Sea 1793-1849.

KING'S CUTTERS AND SMUGGLERS: 1700-1855 *by E. Keble Chatterton*—A unique period of maritime history-from the beginning of the eighteenth to the middle of the nineteenth century when British seamen risked all to smuggle valuable goods from wool to tea and spirits from and to the Continent.

CONFEDERATE BLOCKADE RUNNER *by John Wilkinson*—The Personal Recollections of an Officer of the Confederate Navy.

NAVAL BATTLES OF THE NAPOLEONIC WARS *by W. H. Fitchett*—Cape St. Vincent, the Nile, Cadiz, Copenhagen, Trafalgar & Others.

PRISONERS OF THE RED DESERT *by R. S. Gwatkin-Williams*—The Adventures of the Crew of the Tara During the First World War.

U-BOAT WAR 1914-1918 *by James B. Connolly/Karl von Schenk*—Two Contrasting Accounts from Both Sides of the Conflict at Sea D uring the Great War.

LEONAUR

ALSO FROM LEONAUR

AVAILABLE IN SOFTCOVER OR HARDCOVER WITH DUST JACKET

IRON TIMES WITH THE GUARDS *by An O. E. (G. P. A. Fildes)*—The Experiences of an Officer of the Coldstream Guards on the Western Front During the First World War.

THE GREAT WAR IN THE MIDDLE EAST: 1 *by W. T. Massey*—The Desert Campaigns & How Jerusalem Was Won---two classic accounts in one volume.

THE GREAT WAR IN THE MIDDLE EAST: 2 *by W. T. Massey*—Allenby's Final Triumph.

SMITH-DORRIEN *by Horace Smith-Dorrien*—Isandlwhana to the Great War.

1914 *by Sir John French*—The Early Campaigns of the Great War by the British Commander.

GRENADIER *by E. R. M. Fryer*—The Recollections of an Officer of the Grenadier Guards throughout the Great War on the Western Front.

BATTLE, CAPTURE & ESCAPE *by George Pearson*—The Experiences of a Canadian Light Infantryman During the Great War.

DIGGERS AT WAR *by R. Hugh Knyvett & G. P. Cuttriss*—"Over There" With the Australians by R. Hugh Knyvett and Over the Top With the Third Australian Division by G. P. Cuttriss. Accounts of Australians During the Great War in the Middle East, at Gallipoli and on the Western Front.

HEAVY FIGHTING BEFORE US *by George Brenton Laurie*—The Letters of an Officer of the Royal Irish Rifles on the Western Front During the Great War.

THE CAMELIERS *by Oliver Hogue*—A Classic Account of the Australians of the Imperial Camel Corps During the First World War in the Middle East.

RED DUST *by Donald Black*—A Classic Account of Australian Light Horsemen in Palestine During the First World War.

THE LEAN, BROWN MEN *by Angus Buchanan*—Experiences in East Africa During the Great War with the 25th Royal Fusiliers—the Legion of Frontiersmen.

THE NIGERIAN REGIMENT IN EAST AFRICA *by W. D. Downes*—On Campaign During the Great War 1916-1918.

THE 'DIE-HARDS' IN SIBERIA *by John Ward*—With the Middlesex Regiment Against the Bolsheviks 1918-19.

LEONAUR

ALSO FROM LEONAUR
AVAILABLE IN SOFTCOVER OR HARDCOVER WITH DUST JACKET

THE 9TH—THE KING'S (LIVERPOOL REGIMENT) IN THE GREAT WAR 1914 - 1918 *by Enos H. G. Roberts*—Mersey to mud—war and Liverpool men.

THE GAMBARDIER *by Mark Severn*—The experiences of a battery of Heavy artillery on the Western Front during the First World War.

FROM MESSINES TO THIRD YPRES *by Thomas Floyd*—A personal account of the First World War on the Western front by a 2/5th Lancashire Fusilier.

THE IRISH GUARDS IN THE GREAT WAR - VOLUME 1 *by Rudyard Kipling*—Edited and Compiled from Their Diaries and Papers—The First Battalion.

THE IRISH GUARDS IN THE GREAT WAR - VOLUME 1 *by Rudyard Kipling*—Edited and Compiled from Their Diaries and Papers—The Second Battalion.

ARMOURED CARS IN EDEN *by K. Roosevelt*—An American President's son serving in Rolls Royce armoured cars with the British in Mesopatamia & with the American Artillery in France during the First World War.

CHASSEUR OF 1914 *by Marcel Dupont*—Experiences of the twilight of the French Light Cavalry by a young officer during the early battles of the great war in Europe.

TROOP HORSE & TRENCH *by R.A. Lloyd*—The experiences of a British Lifeguardsman of the household cavalry fighting on the western front during the First World War 1914-18.

THE EAST AFRICAN MOUNTED RIFLES *by C.J. Wilson*—Experiences of the campaign in the East African bush during the First World War.

THE LONG PATROL *by George Berrie*—A Novel of Light Horsemen from Gallipoli to the Palestine campaign of the First World War.

THE FIGHTING CAMELIERS *by Frank Reid*—The exploits of the Imperial Camel Corps in the desert and Palestine campaigns of the First World War.

STEEL CHARIOTS IN THE DESERT *by S. C. Rolls*—The first world war experiences of a Rolls Royce armoured car driver with the Duke of Westminster in Libya and in Arabia with T.E. Lawrence.

WITH THE IMPERIAL CAMEL CORPS IN THE GREAT WAR *by Geoffrey Inchbald*—The story of a serving officer with the British 2nd battalion against the Senussi and during the Palestine campaign.